PRAISE FOR *TEN GREAT IDEAS FROM FIRST CORINTHIANS*

"The message of the apostle Paul to the young church in Corinth two thousand years ago is not out of date. The human condition has not changed, even though the expressions of it has. Thus, this very readable book is startlingly relevant to churches around the world, inescapably applied, and very challenging."
—BILL HOUSTON, Regional Director for Africa, retired, Overseas Council International

"Shaw and Renner make the teachings of 1 Corinthians fresh in an amazing manner. Ten truths are each founded on well-informed historical context and well-expressed, sound exegesis. Positive response to the challenge . . . would go a long way in changing God's worldwide church."
—SAMUEL NGEWA, Professor of Biblical Studies, Africa International University Seminary

"Can a letter written two thousand years old revitalize the church in 2021? *Yes,* when that letter is 1 Corinthians and the scholars digging into it are George Renner and Mark Shaw. This is a change-agent book that should be on every pastor's reading list."
—ALICE MATHEWS, Academic Dean, retired, Gordon-Conwell Theological

"*Ten Great Ideas from First Corinthians* is a fascinating read. This fresh take on 1 Corinthians opened my eyes to how incredibly relevant Paul's letter is for church renewal and revitalization today. You may not agree with every conclusion they come to, but you will be challenged and edified by Shaw and Renner's detailed explanation of the text, their unquenchable hope in where redemptive history is headed, and their rubber-meets-the-road practical applications for ministry leaders."
—GARRETT SPITZ, Lead Pastor, Peninsula Community Chapel

"This book is about the healing of the church, the bride of Jesus Christ—a must-read for those who wish to see the power of the life and cross of Jesus impact lives, neighborhoods, nations, and the world. I am thrilled to recommend this book to fellow biblical scholars, church worker, and Christians whose passion is the renewal of the church of Jesus Christ in the twenty-first century."

—DAVID M. KASALI, President, Congo Initiative-Christian Bilingual University of Congo (CI-UCBC)

Ten Great Ideas
from First Corinthians

Ten Great Ideas
from First Corinthians

A Leader's Guide to Renewing Your Church

GEORGE RENNER and MARK SHAW

WIPF & STOCK · Eugene, Oregon

TEN GREAT IDEAS FROM FIRST CORINTHIANS
A Leader's Guide to Renewing Your Church

Wipf & Stock
An Imprint of Wipf and Stock Publishers
199 W. 8th Ave., Suite 3
Eugene, OR 97401

www.wipfandstock.com

PAPERBACK ISBN: 978-1-7252-8684-9
HARDCOVER ISBN: 978-1-7252-8683-2
EBOOK ISBN: 978-1-7252-8685-6

10/05/21

Contents

Preface   ix

Chapter 1   The Church: Monument or Movement?   1

Chapter 2   The Message That Renews: How the Cross Changes
             Everything (Ch. 1:10-2:5)   11

Chapter 3   The Light That Renews: The Spirit as God's
             Enlightening Presence (Ch. 2:6-16)   30

Chapter 4   Leaders Who Renew (Chapters 3 and 4)   45

Chapter 5   A Renewed Community: Practicing Our Citizenship
             in the New Creation (Ch. 5:1-6:11)   60

Chapter 6   Sexual Renewal: Transforming Marriage and Morality
             in Light of the New Creation (Ch. 6:12-7:40)   82

Chapter 7   A Renewed Humanity: Holiness and Human
             Flourishing in New-Creation Perspective
             (Chapters 8, 9, and 10)   106

Chapter 8   Renewing the Role of Women: Gender and
             New Creation (Ch. 11)   132

Chapter 9   Renewing Worship: Celebrating the New Creation
             (Ch. 11:17–34)   160

Chapter 10 Gifts That Renew: Body Life in the New Creation
             (Chapters 12 and 14)   183

Chapter 11 Renewing Love: The Currency of the New Creation
             (Ch. 13)   206

Chapter 12   An Open Letter to the Leaders of Christ's Church
Everywhere   229

Bibliography   235

Preface

Paul's first letter to the Corinthian congregation is a love letter. That description might surprise you if you are familiar with the epistle because you no doubt remember all the struggles and disturbing immorality swirling around in that young gathering of Christ-followers. I am not referring to it as a love letter only because it contains the treasured hymn to love in chapter 13. Paul loves the church. Even when he rebukes the believers and speaks with biting sarcasm in his admonition, Paul is loving them. Remember that love is not sentimentality or mushy, warm feelings. Love is giving everything you've got to see that the one you love will experience God's presence and grace to the fullest extent possible. In a later letter that he wrote to the believers in Asia Minor, Paul would describe the church as Jesus' "bride" (Eph 5:25–27). Christ loves the church and he gave up his life as a life-giving sacrifice on behalf of this chosen bride. Paul loves the church because Jesus, his Master, loves the church.

I also have been affected by love and passion for Jesus' church. I think the flame was ignited years ago in a New Testament theology course taught by Professor Glenn Barker at Gordon Conwell Seminary. This eye-opening, deep dive into the New Testament texts was the catalyst for me to a lifelong pursuit. I have been afflicted with a passion to see the church recover and live out the dream of its founder and Lord. My journey has led me into house churches, megachurches, liturgical churches, urban-slum churches, churches in rural African villages, charismatic churches, and an extraordinary New England Baptist congregation. Love drives a person to do everything possible to see the church "shine like stars in the sky as we hold firmly to the word of life" (Phil 2:15–16).

In recent decades, the white evangelical church in USA (my church) has lost its "shine." Jesus' metaphor for this disastrous treachery speaks of salt that has lost its saltiness. Like it or not, the reputation of Jesus and the lifestyle of those of us who claim to be Christians are tied together. Today, as I write, we in America are bringing shame and ridicule to Jesus' reputation as a result of unholy political alliances. This study of Paul's love letter will of necessity zero in on some of the contemporary church's failures. My discernment of deficiencies is not spoken with a desire to hurt, but to heal.

Years ago, Canadian pastor George Mallone wrote a book[1] that was a huge inspiration to me as I began my pastoral journey. Mallone said that he had the "gift of discontentment." I get what he means and I suffer with a similar affliction. George said what is in my heart when he wrote:

> I am now a critical lover, rather than just a critic. I have chosen to move into the glass house and live there with others. . .I love the local expressions of Christ's body, and I would do nothing to see them destroyed. The church and the gospel are intricately related to one another . . . At the same time, I feel no constraint of insincerity in pointing out some of the deficiencies I see in the church today.[2]

My reflections on the teachings found in First Corinthians are rooted in a vision of what church has the Spirit-endowed grace to become. Doing life together, we are supposed to think like, speak like, act like, and love like Jesus. It's an ongoing process and I know we'll never arrive at perfection until the bridegroom returns to be with us, face to face. But I remain captivated by Paul's vision statement found in his letter to the Ephesians: "This will continue until we all come to such unity in our faith and knowledge of God's Son that we will be mature in the Lord, measuring up to the full and complete standard of Christ" (Eph 4:15–16).

I still have so much to learn about love. But God has been inexpressibly generous to me by grounding me in a master class on love. I am slowly being shaped by a master teacher. Her name is Linda. She thinks, feels, discerns, acts, and speaks in ways that are the flowering of a heart shaped by God's love. God gave us to each other fifty years ago in marriage. My gratitude can never be fully expressed. I am not her best student. Yet for fifty years she has been my faithful mentor. This work is dedicated to her. Without her companionship, I would not have completed these chapters or grasped, to the limited extent that I do, Jesus' excellent way of love.

A friend and fellow pastor, Normund Strautin, employed his exceptional gifts to provide me with a generous service. Thank you, Normund, for examining these chapters with such great care.

My fellow pilgrim and kindred spirit, Dr. Bill Houston, was kind enough to read the chapters and serve as a creative dialogue partner and wise counselor. Bill has served Africa for a generation in theological education and so his South African wisdom is particularly valuable to me.

I must also express my gratitude to my coauthor, Mark Shaw. He has been a Barnabas—"son of encouragement"—to me. God has woven our lives together and I am richer as a result. Mark was the friend who first enticed me to explore Africa. He opened many African doors and waited patiently for me to enter. The privilege of serving God's people on that sublime and yet confounding continent has been one of God's most cherished gifts to me. Living among fellow Christ-followers in Africa has revitalized and enriched my experience of Jesus and his church.

Mark and I have been privileged to serve together on the faculty of NEGST for a couple of decades. Mark is the consummate historian. His thinking about the Christian movement is spacious and deeply grounded in the communion of the saints. I am the assiduous exegete, always scratching around in the nitty-gritty of the New Testament documents like a chicken scratching for insects in the yard. We exegetes seem to have a particular contribution/affliction in that we are always questioning traditions and current practices based on what we claim to be fresh, disciplined readings of the biblical text. Mark and I have engaged in decades' worth of friendly arguments —church historian vs. exegete. Without a doubt, the Spirit used Mark to prevent me from going off the rails. Mark Shaw believed I could, and should, write, and so he patiently paved the way for this present work. I owe Mark a deep debt of gratitude for his enriching friendship, as a result of which I have been to some degree liberated from my narrowness and self-absorption.

Mark and I share a longing for revival. Understanding the Spirit-empowered dynamics of church revitalization movements around the world has been Mark's scholarly focus. But for Mark this is much more than an arcane academic reporting. Mark has given his life and sacrificed greatly to serve Jesus and his bride, and to entice the church to grasp and become obsessed with God's vision for the church: "His intent was that now, through the church, the manifold wisdom of God should be made known to the rulers and authorities in the heavenly realms, according to his eternal purpose that he accomplished in Christ Jesus our Lord. In him and through faith in him we may approach God with freedom and confidence" (Eph 3:10–12).

As we've studied First Corinthians together, we've come to understand more clearly what "revitalization" might involve. We've come to embrace the dream articulated by another contemporary church leader who wrote: "I dream of a 'missionary option,' that is, a missionary impulse capable of transforming everything, so that the church's customs, ways of doing things, times and schedules, language and structures can be suitably channeled for the evangelization of today's world rather than for her self-preservation." This pastor continues and explains the cost of such revival:

> The Church must look with penetrating eyes within herself, ponder the mystery of her own being. . . . This vivid and lively self-awareness inevitably leads to a comparison between the ideal image of the church as Christ envisaged her and loved her as his holy and spotless bride (cf. Eph 5:27), and the actual image which the Church presents to the world today. . . .This is the source of the Church's heroic and impatient struggle for renewal: the struggle to correct those flaws introduced by her members which her own self-examination, mirroring her exemplar, Christ, points out to her and condemns."[3]

It is my prayer that these short reflections on God's timeless word will be a spark that ignites fresh, Spirit-empowered expressions of resurrection living throughout Jesus' church.

GEORGE RENNER
Lent 2021

ENDNOTES

1. Mallone, *Furnace of Renewal.*
2. Mallone, *Furnace of Renewal,* 12.
3. Pope Francis, *"Evangelii Gaudium,"* 1.1.26

Chapter 1

The Church

Monument or Movement?

"All that is not eternal is eternally out of date."[1]
—C. S. Lewis

In 2000, Simon Jenkins, former editor of the *Times* of London, published his book, *England's Thousand Best Churches*. Reviewers loved it. Readers loved it too. It sold well, and in 2002, Jenkins published a revised edition. The casual reader of Jenkins's book may have been surprised, however, by what was not included in his highly regarded study of England's churches. One finds, for example, nothing about church leadership, mission, and theology. There is no mention of healthy congregational life. He gives no advice on church growth, emerging churches, the missional church, or how to reach millennials. Jenkins's book avoided each of these topics because his book was not about people at all—tt was about architecture. Gothic arches, not growing congregations, was his chosen topic. For Jenkins and his audience of travelers looking for new tourist destinations, the emptier the church, the better. Judged by the title alone, England's best churches are the ones that are dead.

1. Lewis, *Four Loves*, 176.

Some may find it unusual that writers and readers in the West would so readily identify the church of Jesus Christ as a building with stained glass, slate roofs, and rood screens. Old habits die hard. For a thousand years, churches of place (where I have to go) dotted the landscape of Christian Europe. They were visible reminders of a fantastic political experiment composed of a rough alliance between popes and emperors. The experiment was called Christendom, or the Holy Roman Empire, or even the kingdom of God on earth. Like a brooding T-Rex, this mighty creature dominated its environment for a millennium. Even in Napoleon's day Christendom still had enough kick in it for "the Little Corporal" to let the pope crown him Holy Roman Emperor. That day is gone. In post-Christian Europe, at least in the eyes of some, all that is left of the church is an ecclesiastical Jurassic Park dotted with the bones of its now-extinct dinosaurs. Hence Simon Jenkins's book.

GOD IS BACK

But something new is happening in the world. The ancient amber of early Christianity and its vitally preserved DNA has been discovered once again, producing new kinds of movements, ones that will never find their way into any of Jenkins's guidebooks. All over the world, churches of choice (where I want to go), rather than churches of place, are flooding new landscapes, new languages, and new lives.

In 2010, another respected British editor, John Micklethwaite, formerly of *The Economist*, wrote a vastly different guidebook to the same British public addressed by Jenkins. Like Jenkins's book it was about the church, but this time the church was not seen as a building but rather as a movement. This was the church of the living people variety, exploding in new movements, structures, mission, and worship by the hundreds of millions all over the world. Written with Micklethwaite's co-author, Adrian Wooldridge, *God Is Back: How the Global Rise of Faith Is Changing the World* added their evidence to a large and growing literature documenting the new resurgence of Christianity as a global movement.[2]

Putting these two books side by side is not a bad way to capture the paradoxical trends of twenty-first-century religious life. The church is

---

2. Some of the most useful studies of the new world Christianity include: Jenkins, *Next Christendom*; Sanneh, *Disciples of All Nations*; Sanneh, *Whose Religion Is Christianity?*; Noll, *New Shape of World Christianity*; Kim & Kim, *Christianity as a World Religion*; Burrows and Gornik, *Understanding World Christianity*; and Farhadian, *Introducing World Christianity*.

growing in the so-called Global South while dying in the Global North. As missiologist and historian Andrew Walls frames the phenomenon: we are witnessing a world made up of a post-Christian West and a post-Western Christianity. If you are a pastor or an interested layperson in a Western congregation or even a non-Western one, you may have heard this paradox frequently in the last ten years. "I don't need another book describing the paradox," I hear you saying. "I need a book that helps me do something about it."

This book is more than just a reflection of the contradictions of Christianity in the modern world. It seeks to move beyond Jenkins's architectural definition (the church as monument to the past) and more towards Micklethwaite's (the church as a movement changing the world). It addresses both the post-Christian West, as well as the post-Western Christian Global South, and makes what might be an obvious but outrageous suggestion: the church around the world is coming back to life and your church can be part of this new phenomenon. In brief, I believe that what God is doing in the church around the world, he can do in the church around the corner.

How can this happen? How can that stately white congregational church that graced Main Street in the little New England town catch fire once again? How can that Texas Methodist chapel, the First Baptist Church of Anywhere, the Mosaic church downtown, or the Deliverance Church in many African cities, roll back time and become the kind of movements that once shaped their nations? Can those historic churches of Africa, Asia, and Latin America that feel left behind by the renewal around them come alive once again? I believe they can. Acts may seem the obvious choice of sourcebook for this kind of renewal, but perhaps the most useful biblical guidebook to the revitalization of the Christian church today is Paul's First Letter to the Corinthians. To turn one's church into a movement requires recovering this ancient roadmap found in the New Testament and seeing its relevance in our world today.

So what makes a church come alive again? Whatever answer we give to this question must begin with the admission that church revitalization is a work of God and not something that results from sociology or the latest marketing gimmicks. Why not yours? What do they know that the rest of us need to know? How does one turn the church into a movement?

HOW DO YOU RAISE THE DEAD?

There is a large and growing literature on revival and revitalization. Some of it is concerned with biblical foundations of these critical questions. However,

what is often missing is what the Bible says about the renewal of specific local congregations. Acts looks at the expansion of the Christian movement
across the Roman empire but doesn't focus on a single church. Paul's Pastoral Epistles do a great job of showing how to order a local congregation, but
do not specifically deal with helping a local church get unstuck. Romans is
not a manual of local church renewal but written to the Church of Rome for
missionary reasons, to validate Paul's missionary message of the gospel to
the gentiles. Many of the other Epistles are written to groups of churches or
to local churches of which we know little. The grand exceptions in the New
Testament are Paul's letters to the church in Corinth. He writes very specifically about the practical problems in Corinth, a local church that, while
young in its faith, seemed to be stuck trying to navigate its way through a
very aggressive pagan culture.

This book is about connecting what Paul has to say regarding the renewal of the local congregation in Corinth to the local church today. The
conviction we bring to this study is that Paul presents a timeless roadmap
to help a church lost in the present find its way into the future. Let me say a
few things about the church in Corinth and then give an overview of what
the rest of the book will look like.

WHY FIRST CORINTHIANS?

Most of what we know about the founding of the church comes from Acts 18.
Paul arrived in Corinth from Athens (probably walking the entire fifty-mile
journey). After arriving, he met and stayed with Aquila and Priscilla, fellow tentmakers and Jews who had recently relocated to Corinth from Rome,
from which they, along with much of the rest of the Jewish population, had
been expelled by the emperor Claudius. They eagerly embraced Paul's message and listened in rapt attention as he preached to groups of Jews and gentiles around the city. His message produced both friends and enemies. Paul
was taken to court by angry Jewish leaders. Gallio was the brother of the
famous stoic philosopher Seneca, mentor to the young emperor-in-waiting,
Nero. His two-year appointment as proconsul or governor of the province
of Achaea from AD 51–52 helps fix the date of Paul's Corinthian mission.
Gallio dismissed all charges and issued the crucial judgment that the new
Christian movement enjoyed the religious exemptions that Rome had given
to Judaism. Corinthian Jesus-followers would be exempt from the legal re-
quirement to worship the emperor and make ritual offerings at his temple.
Paul nonetheless felt that this brush with the law was his sign to move on.
Shortly after his trial, he wrapped up his eighteen-month mission and left for

Ephesus. Corinth would be the most extended single mission in his career, apart from Ephesus. When he left, there were an estimated 100 believers, clustered in a handful of local house churches, full of new faith and vibrant testimonies.[3]

THE CITY OF CORINTH

What kind of world did these new believers have to navigate? The first Christians in Corinth lived in a large city with an estimated population of 100,000.[4] It was also a city with a controversial past. The original Corinth, so infamous for its sexual license (Strabo) was also politically radical. It had rebelled against Roman rule in 146 BC and paid the price for this action. The city was demolished brick by brick. For a century it lay silent and desolate. Then it came back to life. A new Corinth rose from the ashes. The new city was designed and constructed by Julius Caesar in 44 BC. Caesar was looking for a place to pension off his faithful legionaries, as well as to relieve Rome of its excess population. The new city that Paul would visit a century later was in many ways a junior version of Rome itself. It was a city of classical architecture, economic vitality, religious plurality (twenty-six different temples), and ethnic diversity. Jews, Romans, Greeks, slaves, and free all jostled for position in Corinth's bustling marketplace and social structure. Corinth was a city on the move. Garland writes about "a building boom [that] occurred between the reigns of Augustus and Nero, making Corinth 'arguably the most dazzling and modern of Greek cities.'"[5] Corinth's strategic position along the sea trade routes flowing out of and into Rome made it a city of wealth and decadence. Fee captures the character of the city when he comments that "Paul's Corinth was at once the New York, Los Angeles, and Las Vegas of the ancient world."[6]

Cities can be intimidating, overwhelming places to live. They represent an enormous social pyramid with a few elite at the top, a small middle class in the center, and the struggling majority at the bottom. To live in a city is to live with the constant pressure not only to survive but to thrive, to move up the pyramid. Cities not only cast a long social shadow but also offer a stairway to the stars for the bright, the talented, and the ambitious. The small Christian movement soaked in this urban culture and mirrored some

3. See Garland, *1 Corinthians*, 2003.
4. Winter, *After Paul Left Corinth*, loc. 2449 of 4840.
5. Garland, *1 Corinthians*, loc. 525 of 28028.
6. Fee, *First Epistle to the Corinthians*, 2.

of its strengths and weaknesses. Garland describes how the young movement absorbed the culture around it:

> Values that were antithetical to the message of the cross—
> particularly those related to honor and status so basic to the
> Greco-Roman social system, in which power manifesting itself
> in ruthlessness and self-advancement is thought to be the only
> sensible course—percolated into the church, destroying its fel-
> lowship and its Christian witness as some members sought to
> balance civic norms with Christian norms. Secular wisdom—
> which reflected the code of conduct of the social elites, who
> jostled one another for power, prestige, and popularity—had
> its hold on members of the church. Its values played havoc on
> Paul's attempt to build a community based on love, selflessness,
> and the equal worth of every member. Corinthian society was
> riddled by competitive individualism, and this ethos spilled
> over into the relationships in the church.[7]

Put another way, the Christians in Corinth reflected the constant and contemporary dilemma of Christians in the world in every culture and generation: How can we be in the world without being of it? Gordon Fee makes
clear the connections between Christians then and now:

> The cosmopolitan character of the city and church, the strident
> individualism that emerges in so many of their behavioral aber-
> rations, the arrogance that attends their understanding of spiri-
> tuality, the accommodation of the gospel to the surrounding
> culture in so many ways—these and many other features of the
> Corinthian church are but mirrors held up before the church of
> today.[8]

THE CHURCH IN CORINTH

The house churches in Corinth were not perfect, but were composed of enthusiastic followers of Jesus when Paul left town. Then something happened.
In the years between Paul's departure and his writing of First Corinthians
from Ephesus in AD 54, the Corinthian church took three hits that shook
it to its core.

The first hit was a revival of the federal imperial cult. Octavius, aka
Augustus Caesar, had gotten the deification ball rolling in AD 14 when the

7. Garland, *1 Corinthians*, loc. 554 of .

8. Fee, *First Epistle to the Corinthians*, 19.

Senate (under imperial pressure) decided that Octavius's amazing achievements (ending a civil war) revealed him to be more than a man, and therefore a god. This new status required new devotion on behalf of the Roman Empire's citizens. In a somewhat twisted burst of modesty, Augustus constructed temples around his empire, not only in his name but in the name of his favorite family members. Annual offerings were required. New temples began to dot the Corinthian landscape. Most impressive was the imperial temple of Octavia, Caesar's beloved sister, which dominated the Corinthian skyline. But the imperial revival was not just about temples. The Senate and the emperor (Claudius, until AD 54 when he was murdered by his wife and succeeded by her divine son, Nero) turned up the political heat all over the empire in the early 50s by elaborate public shows of patriotism and imperial piety on pain of exile or even death. Though Paul's trial before Gallio had meant that Christians were exempt from the demand to worship the emperor, the intensification of the federal imperial cult would have turned up the cultural and social heat on the young Christian community. Paul would find himself warning the church later in his letter about the severe spiritual compromises that could come with participating in these imperial temple rituals. This imperial cult embodied what the ancient world called "Romanitas," a style of architecture and art, but also a way of thinking and living described below.

The second hit was the pagan revival inspired by the Isthmus Games. These famous games had returned to Corinth, probably in AD 52 after a long absence. Next to the Olympic Games, the Isthmus Games were the most popular sporting event in the eastern empire. They were also steeped in pagan ritual and symbolism. Events were dedicated to the Olympian gods, and pagan oaths, practices, ethics, and social pressure came with these games. Paul will tackle this issue of an aggressive paganism in his letter.

The third hit was economic. Extensive evidence points to an empire-wide famine in AD 52–53. The Egyptian grain harvest, so crucial to feeding much of the empire, failed, with widespread economic fallout and mass riots in some cities. Corinth was hit hard. Paul, when he refers to the "current distress" (1 Cor 7:26) as a reason to consider remaining single, may well have had in mind this devastating economic crisis.

These challenges help explain both some of the visible problems and underlying causes that Paul writes about. These hits were hits on the gospel. The gospel seemed to be shrinking in direct proportion to the growing influence of Roman religious imperialism, Greek paganism, and economic desperation. What did the cross have to do with restoring the economic, social, and political life of the Corinthians? The gospel may have many inward spiritual benefits, but it didn't seem to support the bold gospel of the apostles, that Jesus was Lord and Caesar was not. The world became bigger and more real in the eyes of the church even as Christ and his cross became smaller.[9]

RELATIVIZING ROMANITAS

We need to keep the underlying ideology of Romanitas in mind when we ask the question why Paul wrote the letter. The list of problems addressed in the letter is the most obvious reason for writing. Disunity topped that list. Paul sought to expose and overcome the power struggles behind rival house churches and their powerful patrons.[10]

On a deeper level, however, Paul was writing against a worldview that was rocking the young church of Corinth. Romanitas was the kingdom of God on earth. The gospel of Romanitas proclaimed that Rome was an all-powerful empire, defended by an invincible army, and ruled by the wisest laws known to man and the most significant leaders known to history. Rome represented the highest level of progress and achievement in human history. Romanitas was the underlying message behind every building lining the streets of Corinth, every imperial eagle flapping in the breeze. The message ground into the marble that lined every city street was that Rome was the real power that controlled life. Roman military, political, religious, and economic power—these were the forces that defined reality. You could live in your head and imagine alternative realities to help you cope with life; there was not much Caesar could do about that. However, the real world, the world everybody had to live in most of the time, was a Roman world, ruled by Roman ideals, and by a single Roman lord. Rational thinking demanded the acknowledgment of the supremacy of Romanitas.[11]

As Paul writes on each practical matter brought to his attention, he never loses sight of the underlying reasons behind power struggles among the leaders, and moral confusion among the members. Roman realities were too big. Gospel realities were too small. Corinthian Christianity would get moving again only if it relativized Romanitas. Paul had to find a way to deal with this reality distortion field.

9. See the extensive scholarly discussion of these three hits in Winter, *After Paul Left Corinth*, especially ch. 1.

10. Gordon Fee supports this view as the most helpful sketch of the underlying problem. See the introduction to Fee, *First Epistle to the Corinthians*.

11. Bruce Winter takes the underlying problem one step further when he points to the common culture of the Corinthian house church leaders, the culture of Romanitas. This was, on one level, a style of architecture and material culture that planted its signature all over the city in the new construction that took place in the 50s.

WHAT IS CROSS POWER?

Paul's answer to the problem of Roman power is *cross* power. The cross was a place of pardon and cleansing that justified us before a holy God. It was all this, but it was also more. Paul's cross is explosive. It is to history what the Big Bang was to the cosmos. It creates a new world. Cross power produces a new creation begun now, unfolding in and through the people of God and to be completed at the end of the age. The great idea behind all the great ideas: *The cross has created a new creation into which Jesus followers are invited to live and work beginning now.* As Fee writes, "Thus for Paul, believers are thoroughly eschatological people, determined and conditioned by the reality of the future that has already begun, but still awaiting the final glory. We are therefore living in the new creation 'already' and 'not yet.'"[12] For Paul this new creation eschatology is not just theological. It is comprehensively practical. Fee elaborates:

> If Romans and Galatians make it plain that one is not saved by obedience to the law, 1 Corinthians makes it equally plain that the saved are expected to live out their lives in obedience to the "commandments of God" (7:19) and the "law of Christ" (9:21). If such obedience is not required for entry into faith, it is nonetheless required as the outflow of faith. Paul understands Christian ethics in terms of "becoming what you are," a perspective that emerges in 1 Corinthians in a number of ways.[13]

To put it another way, Paul seeks to restore confidence in the power of the cross by showing that through the cross the Triune God has been unleashed in time and history. The Father, through Christ and by his Spirit, is making all things new. The new creation has begun. To be a Christian is not just to believe a specific set of doctrines and keep a few rules; to be a Christian is to live in this new world created by the cross. The purpose of the church is to make the new creation real to a present-day pagan world which is still stuck in the old order of things. The church gets moving again when it breaks the tyranny of the now and brings the future eternal into the broken present. As Paul addresses specific problems in the Corinthian church, he will weave the message of cross power and the new creation it inaugurates into his discussions of marriage, sexuality, culture, unity, worship, and men and women in ministry.

This book seeks to focus on several of Paul's key ideas to unleash cross power and new-creation thinking and living into the church. It identifies

12. Fee, *First Epistle to the Corinthians*, 16.
13. Fee, *First Epistle to the Corinthians*, 16.

ten great ideas that can help our churches get moving. However, each idea is connected to cross power. The overall message of this book, and of First Corinthians, is that *cross power produces resurrection living.* Every theological, ecclesial, moral, and cultural challenge they faced and that we face become fresh opportunities to drink more deeply of this new wine of cross power and the resurrection life that it creates. Though each of the key ideas presented here are distinct, they are but so many branches off the main stem of cross power.

How can we get our churches moving again? How can we change our world in the twenty-first century just as powerfully as the early church did in the first century? Paul's answer in this Letter to the Corinthians is that renewal of our purpose and mission comes through *believing, preaching, and practicing the cross power that generates resurrection living.* The future is now here, not entirely, but in powerful ways through the presence of the conquest of death at the cross, the forgiveness of sins, the resurrection of Jesus, and life in the Spirit. The active Father, the active Son, and the active Spirit, as we will see in the next chapter, have been unleashed in our world, and won't stop until the new creation defeats death and evil and brings about the renewal of all things.

I have no real objection with Simon Jenkins writing a book about *England's Thousand Best Churches.* Good for him. However, I think Paul would have something to say. If, when we use the word "church," we are not talking about people on the move, then we should not be talking about buildings on the edge of town. First Corinthians would probably be his response to Jenkins's book. It would also be his response to us and what we should be talking about. But to talk about the church as liberated people and not just gothic arches means that we need to talk about what we believe, what kind of gospel we preach. This liberation begins in the saving acts of Jesus in history as presented by the apostles. However, it also becomes a liberating message when it frees me internally in heart and mind, bristling as it is with the high-voltage charge of messianic truth and capable of jolting the world into new life. To that first and foundational great idea we now turn.

Chapter 2

The Message That Renews

How the Cross Changes Everything

"The Cross is our whole Theology."[1]

—Luther

READ: 1 COR 1:1—2:4 AND CHAPTER 15

Nairobi Chapel is a resurrection story. It began its life as a Brethren Assembly for English soldiers stationed in Nairobi during World War II. By 1980, the chapel's glory days seemed to be over. Though located strategically on the edge of the University of Nairobi, the chapel's membership had dwindled down to a handful of people. The turning point came with the arrival of a new pastor. A young seminary graduate, Oscar Muriu was invited to come and either save the church or bury it. Oscar's gift of dynamic biblical preaching changed the direction of the chapel. Soon thousands of university students began attending. In 2005, the chapel had grown so much that it split into five different church plants around the city. Each is now a thriving urban congregation of its own. The Nairobi Chapel network today is an international movement planting new churches in Africa and Europe.

---

1. Luther, *Luther's Commentary on the First Twenty-Two Psalms*, 1:289.

What was the key to turning the church around? One might point to the dynamic worship that was introduced shortly after Oscar came. More fundamental, however, was the new kind of preaching. Oscar's style was not new, continuing the expository teaching the chapel had enjoyed in its healthier days. Nor was there any real change in content. Oscar was thoroughly biblical in his preaching. He preached the cross. He preached through Bible books.

What changed was the emphasis. The message of the cross turned from one that was mostly negative and escapist to one that was mostly positive and empowering. The old emphasis was about personal salvation through the cross from the sinking ship of the world. The new emphasis declared that through the cross everything was being made new. The new music, the new people, the new sense of mission and vision—all of these reinforced this message. When new hearers grasped the message that the power of the cross changes everything, they wanted more. As the gospel became bigger, the movement grew larger.

There are different ways to preach the gospel of eternal life through faith in the death and resurrection of Christ. Whether this is heard as a positive message that empowers us for life or a negative message disengaged from life makes all of the difference. I don't know if Pastor Oscar got his new emphasis from Paul's first chapter to the Corinthians. He could have. The first great idea that Paul teaches in his letter is about the message we preach. For Paul, there are two ways to preach the cross. Consider verse 17: "For Christ did not send me to baptize but to preach the gospel, and not with words of eloquent wisdom, lest the cross of Christ be emptied of its power." One way empties the gospel of its power and the other way unleashes its power. Paul's first great idea is about how to avoid the one and ensure the other. *The gospel changes everything when we show that, through the cross, all of the Father, all of the Son, and all of the Spirit have been unleashed into all of our world, for all of time, to make all things new.* Let's take a closer look.

THE SHAKEN CONFIDENCE OF A YOUNG CHURCH

Corinthian Christianity, for all of its youthful vigor, was a movement in trouble. We pointed out in the previous chapter that the movement was under pressure from the surrounding culture. Romanitas was everywhere one looked. Its persistent message was that Caesar was Lord, and God was not. Roman military might and punishment by crucifixion backed up this message. Romanitas was a blazing cultural and political sun that threatened to wilt the faith of the church in Corinth. A resurgent polytheism, stimulated by the athletic games with their vows to the gods, made exclusive loyalty to Christ trickier than ever. Famine produced economic hardships. If the gospel was so great, why was life so hard?

These local pressures shook the young church's confidence in the gospel. In turn this shaken confidence produced a host of new tensions in the local house churches. They had a unity, morality, marriage, theology, lawsuit, and worship problem. They also had a missions problem: they were not effectively engaging the unreached, they were not changing their world. Rather, the world was changing the church. Where should Paul begin?

Paul starts with the unity problem. These divisions seem to be part of a popularity contest between the house churches over who was the best Christian teacher. The problem was not with Cephas or Apollos. The problem was with the followers. Groups were forming around specific preachers and leaders informally. Followers were searching for a kind of rhetoric that would renew their confidence in the gospel.

There may have been other factors behind this disunity. One recent study suggests that there may have been ethnic tensions percolating just below the surface:

> It is possible, though, that the divisions among the churches in Corinth were not theological. We may be failing to note ethnic markers that Paul sprinkled all over the text. Apollos was noted as an Alexandrian (Egyptian Jew) (Acts 18:24). They had their own reputation. Paul notes that Peter is called by his Aramaic name, Cephas, suggesting the group that followed him spoke Aramaic and were thus Palestinian Jews. Paul's church had Diaspora Jews but also many ethnic Corinthians, who were quite proud of their status as residents of a Roman colony and who enjoyed using Latin.[2]

It would be easy to exaggerate the ethnic factor. Don't miss the point, however: identity differences are never far away when a group is under pressure. The differences were piling up. Personality differences, varied teaching styles, pagan culture, and ethnic rivalries may all help account for the disunity in Corinth. For Paul, though, they all pointed to a single, root problem. When our differences become big, it means the gospel has become small. Reducing the good news of Jesus to just another bit of religious self-help taught by a teacher of choice emptied the gospel of its power (1 Cor 1:17).

Paul sought to fix the problem of a small gospel by showing how big the message is. The gospel is big, not because it is all about us, but because it is all about the biggest reality imaginable: the Triune God and his work

---

2. Richards and O'Brian, *Misreading Scripture with Western Eyes,* loc. 666 of 2703.

in history. Paul's message is that because of the power of the cross, God is at work all around us, making us and all things new. Paul develops this "cross power" in four ways. First, cross power means all of the Father is at work in all of the world, making all things new (1:18–26). Second, cross power means all of the Son is at work in all of the world, making all things new (1:27–30). Third, cross power means that all of the Spirit is at work in all of the world, making all things new(2:1–16). Fourth, in chapter 15, cross power means that the future is at work all around until all things are made new.

CROSS POWER ONE: THE FATHER IS AT WORK ALL AROUND US, MAKING ALL THINGS NEW

In 1 Cor 1:18–25, Paul contrasts the power of the cross with conventional power. Conventional power depends on strength. It wins by being bigger, stronger, smarter than its rivals. Whoever has more muscle, money, or science on their side wins. This is how Rome worked then, this how modern nations work now. This is how Judaism worked then, this is how many religions, churches, and denominations work now. Power produces power. Success can only come through money, science, and/or domination. God the Father, because of the cross, is rejecting this path to change. He is bringing about the salvation of the whole world, the new creation, not through conventional power, but through cross power. Cross power contradicts conventional brain power or brawn power. God is so powerful that he can produce the radical transformation of all things through what the world regards as weakness and folly. Here's how he puts it in verses 18–25:

> For the word of the cross is folly to those who are perishing, but to us who are being saved it is the power of God. For it is written, "I will destroy the wisdom of the wise, and the discernment of the discerning I will thwart." Where is the one who is wise? Where is the scribe? Where is the debater of this age? Has not God made foolish the wisdom of the world? For since, in the wisdom of God, the world did not know God through wisdom, it pleased God through the folly of what we preach to save those who believe. For Jews demand signs and Greeks seek wisdom, but we preach Christ crucified, a stumbling block to Jews and folly to gentiles, but to those who are called, both Jews and Greeks, Christ the power of God and the wisdom of God. For the foolishness of God is wiser than men, and the weakness of God is stronger than men. (ESV)

Cross power (v. 18) is the salvation of the world. Its method of saving was carefully chosen by the Almighty Father, to relativize the power and intimidation of two of the most impressive systems of the ancient world—Roman militarism and Jewish monotheism. In both of these systems power was the symbol of their supremacy: military power in the case of Rome, law power in the case of Judaism. God chose to reject the power systems of the day and show that his power far transcends the power of men by working through the weakness and folly of the cross to bring about the salvation of humanity and the coming new creation. By choosing the cross to destroy the wisdom of the wise, and the discernment of the discerning, God changes the rules on how he governs time and history. He will use the power and pattern of the cross to accomplish his greatest work, the coming new creation. He will appear to lose on the Good Fridays of life, only to win on Easter Sunday by pulling the ultimate reversal, life out of death. No power on earth has the power to make life out of death, everything out of nothing, strength out of weakness. This power belongs only to God, and it is now the way he rules our personal lives and the history of the world. The cross changes the way the world works. Weakness in Christ is now the path to life-changing power in and over the world.

Paul could have said that God is stronger and wiser than man. However, the message of the cross says more than that. N. T. Wright explains:

> Paul says it the other way round, to make the point with stunning rhetorical effect: God's folly is wiser than humans, and God's weakness is stronger than humans! Of course, it is very easy for humans, when they believe the gospel, to turn it into a way of inflating their own personal or political power, or showing off how clever they are. However, to do so is to undermine the very point of the message.[3]

Paul's message agrees that the sandaled foot of Rome crushed the Savior of the world, but that somehow his death turned everything around, and was about to make everything right again. To say that the cross would end all suffering, all sin, and all death was the kind of nonsense that most right-thinking people of Corinth would reject out of hand. A significant percentage of Corinth, however, fell in love with this message and it's crucified and resurrected hero.

Paul's principle is that the cross makes perfect sense once one realizes how God works. In a world in which human arrogance is the problem, the Father has chosen to work backward, in a way that contradicts human power and arrogance. He will make things out of their opposite. He will

---

3. Wright, *Paul for Everyone*, 12.

win by losing. He will save the world by dying at the world's hands. New creation flows from his apparent defeat, not from the latest slick-talking prophet, politician, or philosopher. The people who will change the world and one day rule the world are the despised of the world. The father will end death, not by preventing it, but rather by transforming and humiliating it through the power of resurrection. Death can no longer hold humanity in its grip. Central to our message of the cross is the medium that God makes everything in the new creation out of nothing, that he works in this world in a way that is opposite to business as usual or human expectations. This is the message of the cross. The death of Christ has now changed all the rules about time, history, judgment, and death. When we preach this message there is no need to add "and this reminds me of a funny story" to hold our audience. The breathtaking scope and shocking originality of the message is all that should be needed.

I didn't grow up in a Christian home. My father had walked away from the Christianity of his childhood and lived for money and the American dream. It was only through a series of "Good Fridays" that his heart was changed and our whole family went in a new direction. Our house burned down. We lost the family lumber business. There was a death in the family. My mother was hospitalized for a critical illness and was on death's door. My father's unbelief melted away, not through the power of logic or the power of some state edict. His heart was changed, and that of the whole family, through the pattern of the cross, used by a sovereign God to bring about the salvation of his lost children. This same pattern is the way he will bring transformation to the whole world and bring about the new creation in its fullness.

This is important for Christians in every age and place to hear. Why do bad things happen to good Christians? What does it mean when we lose the job? What do we do when the kids don't turn out as we hoped? When we can't pay the bills? When our marriage is struggling or sickness brings us low? Does it mean God is punishing us in some way? Does it mean the gospel has failed? None of the above. What it means is that the Father is suffering with us in our Good Fridays, absorbing our pain in order to then bring about an Easter Sunday of new life and power. Such is the Father's love for us, flowing through the cross, that he turns everything for good, even the garbage that happens. That's Rom 8:28 and 1 Cor 1:25. How big is the cross? As big as an infinite and almighty Father, who, because of the cross, is now at work all around us, in ways that contradict conventional power and logic, making us and all things new.

CROSS POWER TWO: THE SON IS AT WORK ALL AROUND US NOW, MAKING US AND ALL THINGS NEW

Cross power is not only the Father's new preferred method of ruling the world, but it is also about his almighty Son and what he has done to bring about the actual salvation of humanity. Note 1 Cor 1:28–31:

> God chose what is low and despised in the world, even things that are not, to bring to nothing things that are, so that no human being might boast in the presence of God. And because of him you are in Christ Jesus, who became to us wisdom from God, righteousness and sanctification and redemption, so that, as it is written, "Let the one who boasts, boast in the Lord." (ESV)

The Father's central act in his new way of ruling the world was sending a savior to die for us and rise with us. The Son is now at work among the nations making all things new. His work on the cross produced not just a new pattern for God's power, but a new intimacy with God through Christ's death and resurrection.

What does this mean? Paul says two big things about cross power and why we should boast in it. The first is about who Jesus is, and the second is about what he has done. First, who is this Jesus that we preach? According to verse 30 he is someone we should boast in. But should we not boast only in God? Precisely Paul's point. The Son who died on the cross was not merely human, but also the divine creator God of Abraham, Isaac, and Jacob. "Time and again," N. T. Wright reminds us, "Paul quotes the phrase 'the Lord' from the Old Testament, where the word refers directly to YHWH, Israel's God, and makes it refer to Jesus the Messiah." Paul does that again here when he speaks of Christ. Wright adds that for Paul, Jesus "is the one 'in whom' Christians possess all the wisdom they need–and the status ('righteousness') of being his forgiven, justified people, and the extraordinary privilege of being set apart for his service ('sanctification') in virtue of his 'redemption' of them from the slavery of sin."[4]

The second big thing about Jesus and his cross is what it does. For Paul, the purpose of Christ's action on the cross is not just forgiveness or justification. His action in the world was to create marital union. That is what the little but all-important phrase in 1:30 says: "In Christ." What does it mean that we are in Christ? It means that whatever Christ accomplished on the cross is communicated to us through this spiritual union with him. If Christ died as the full and final atonement for sin, then our sins are fully and finally atoned for, because we are his and he is ours. Wright elaborates:

4. Wright, *Paul for Everyone*, 17.

> Having him—or rather, being 'in him'—means that you are a genuine human being at last, called to live by God's wisdom rather than that of the world. Exploring what it means to be 'in the Messiah,' so that what is true of him is true of you, is the Christian's basic strength and delight. God has vindicated Jesus in his resurrection; God set him apart for his own service; God accomplished in him the defeat of the great enslaving powers of sin and death. If you are 'in Christ,' a member of the Messiah's family, this 'wisdom, righteousness, sanctification, and redemption' are yours too. And if that doesn't make you 'somebody,' nothing ever will.[5]

The in Christ experience, created by the cross, is one in which Christ binds us to himself forever in an unbreakable union of love and transformation. This union is the fountain from which all other aspects of our salvation flow. From this union comes the gift of righteousness, being justified by faith in what Jesus has done. Those who are in union with him and are justified in him are also sanctified, made progressively and positionally holy and Christlike in their lives. Finally, we are liberated (redeemed) from the powers that have held us prisoner: sin, death, Satan, and the self. It means that I am his and he is mine. It means that we are married. Paul will tell the Ephesian Christians in chapter 5 of that letter that human marriage is a picture or metaphor of a greater marriage between that of Christ and his church.

This marital-like union speaks about the intimacy of mutual ownership and the exchange of goods that is a crucial part of Christian marriage. Our Lord and husband says that he has done all things necessary in time and space to clean up this bride and make her beautiful again, "who became to us wisdom from God, righteousness and sanctification and redemption" (1 Cor 1:30).

Being in daily marital union with him means that what is his is mine and what is mine is his. He takes my misery and gives me his joy. He takes my sin and gives me his righteousness so that I never need worry if I am good enough for this husband. He daily exchanges our sin, misery, depression, and weakness with his fresh and cleansing new joy, new hope, new strength, and new forgiveness. I am his and he is mine. And so let us boast about him and not the world, not ourselves. The cross unleashed all of Jesus into all of his world to bring all of his salvation. The new creation is the new home the bridegroom is preparing for his bride.

---

5. Wright, *Paul for Everyone*, 17.

CROSS POWER THREE: THE SPIRIT IS AT WORK
ALL AROUND, MAKING US AND ALL THINGS NEW

Cross power not only unleashes the Father and Son to work in a new and saving way but also unleashes the Spirit to work with the Father and the Son in applying these benefits to us. The Spirit provides a new way of seeing, which we will discuss more fully in the next chapter. What needs to be said now is that the Spirit is at work all around opening the minds and hearts of the nations to understand this new kind of message. Consider 1 Cor 2:10–13:

> these things God has revealed to us through the Spirit. For the Spirit searches everything, even the depths of God. For who knows a person's thoughts except the spirit of that person, which is in him? So also no one comprehends the thoughts of God except the Spirit of God. Now we have received not the spirit of the world, but the Spirit who is from God, that we might understand the things freely given us by God. And we impart this in words not taught by human wisdom but taught by the Spirit, interpreting spiritual truths to those who are spiritual. (ESV)

Paul points to a new power of persuasion flowing from the cross that is available to the Christian: the Spirit of God. Paul sees the power of persuasion flowing from the new power of the Spirit and the new age of the Spirit. The same Spirit who enabled Jesus to offer up himself as the sacrifice is also the power that enables followers to see and believe the gospel from the inside out.

To think in this new way of the Spirit requires more than conventional logic. Cross power involves a pretty massive paradigm shift from a deep and persistent humanistic way of thinking to a fairly radical new model of reality and of time. More is needed than simply correcting this doctrine or that theological point.

Evangelicalism in America has taken a hit in the twenty-first century, particularly for becoming too political. An overwhelming number of one segment of American evangelicalism, white evangelicals, have aligned themselves with conservative political candidates to the point where the very definition of what it means to be an evangelical seems unclear. To remember our roots, we need to remember not only the theology of the sixteenth-century Reformers but also the main message of the eighteenth-century Great Awakening. Jonathan Edwards, George Whitefield, and John Wesley represented different Christian denominations and theological positions but found their unity in defining true Christianity as an experience of being born again. This expression has now become something of a term of derision by critics of the movement, but what it meant in the 1740s was both fresh and defining. Only an inner work of the Spirit of God, at work all around us, can fill a person with the life-changing presence of God. No amount of good works, social or political activism, correct doctrine, or church participation can transform the heart and destiny of an individual. Edward's sermon, published in 1734 as "A Divine and Supernatural Light, Immediately Imparted to the Soul by the Spirit of God, Shown to be Both Scriptural and Rational Doctrine," captured the central thrust of historical evangelicalism. Only the Spirit of God can give saving knowledge of God in Christ. One characteristic of the Spirit's saving epistemology is that he opens the heart and mind to the beauty and power of the cross. Conventional objections to this symbol of "weakness and folly" melt away in light of the sovereign, Spirit-illuminating work. The cross cleanses the soul from the sin that would otherwise keep the Holy Spirit from indwelling. Because of this cross power, the Spirit now enters and indwells the individual, producing a new kind of Christian: one that is becoming a new creature within, getting ready for the new creation that the same Spirit is preparing outwardly. This is a feature of our message that we must desperately recover. We must be people of the new birth, readied for the future of the new creation and living in the present in a way that is most relevant to that future.

The Spirit now is at work around us, applying the work of the Father and the Son. Both the Father and Son confirm that the Spirit now fills the world with them. The Spirit is opening eyes all around the world, even in the Muslim world, to the power of the cross to bring about the return of the Triune God to our world in grace and transformation. He will open the eyes of students on campus, of loved ones in our homes, of colleagues at work.

What does this mean for Paul and for us? To be spiritual is not to have your head stuck in heaven, but it is to have your eyes open to the Triune God at work on earth. It is seeing the Father, through the new eyes of the heart given only by the Spirit, running down every road, whether in Central Asia or Central Park, to lavishly spread the gift of sonship. It is to see the Son, our husband, ushering us into the joys of sonship with the father. Because of the cross all of the Spirit has been unleashed into all of our world and into all of our lives till kingdom come.

CROSS POWER FOUR: THE FUTURE HAS
BEEN UNLEASHED ALL AROUND, ENABLING
US TO LIVE IN NEW WAYS NOW

Cross power unleashes a new future. It produces a new end to the story of history. History is now hurtling towards, not oblivion, but the new creation, the city of God. We now jump from 1 Cor 1–2 to chapter 15, and the discussion of the resurrection as the crucial part of the gospel we must preach. These opening and closing chapters are the theological framework for the entire epistle. They make it clear that within the brackets of the full gospel of fourfold cross power, we must live our lives of worship and witness in this world. A Triune God through the cross and resurrection of his Son changes the world by ruling in a new way, saving in a new way, helping us see in a new way, and building a new creation not through human power but through cross power. It is that last dimension of cross power that Paul focuses on in 1 Cor 15:1–11:

> Let me now remind you, dear brothers and sisters, of the Good News I preached to you before. You welcomed it then, and you still stand firm in it. It is this Good News that saves you if you continue to believe the message I told you—unless, of course, you believed something that was never true in the first place. I passed on to you what was most important and what had also been passed on to me. Christ died for our sins, just as the Scriptures said. He was buried, and he was raised from the dead on the third day, just as the Scriptures said. He was seen by Peter and then by the Twelve. After that, he was seen by more than 500 of his followers at one time, most of whom are still alive, though some have died. Then he was seen by James and later by all the apostles. Last of all, as though I had been born at the wrong time, I also saw him.
>
> For I am the least of all the apostles. In fact, I'm not even worthy to be called an apostle after the way I persecuted God's church. But whatever I am now, it is all because God poured out his special favor on me—and not without results. For I have worked harder than any of the other apostles; yet it was not I but God who was working through me by his grace. So it makes no difference whether I preach or they preach, for we all preach the same message you have already believed.

Paul summarizes the gospel in chapter 15. The church in Corinth was created by the gospel he preached. The gospel was not just a feeling they had. It was based on historical events of world significance. Jesus, the long-predicted

Messiah, died for our sins and rose again bodily from the grave to conquer death for us as well. These events, as Paul has indicated earlier, have unleashed the very presence of the Triune God into all the earth for all of time. Many reliable witnesses attest to the fact of the resurrection. A new creation is happening all around us, to be realized at the end of time, in which death will be defeated, and eternal life in a renewed world will be enjoyed. Faith in this message is needed to receive this salvation. Wright reminds us of the place of the resurrection in the preaching of the apostles:

> The resurrection's not an isolated supernatural oddity proving how powerful, if apparently arbitrary, God can be when he wants to. Nor is it at all a way of showing that there is indeed a heaven awaiting us after death. It is the decisive event demonstrating that God's kingdom really has been launched on earth as it is in heaven.[6]

This message of future resurrection is based not on how well we behave but on the same faith in the power of the cross that brings about every gift from an infinite and all-loving Father, an ever-present Son, and an eternally indwelling Spirit. Paul's own life as a former persecutor of the church reminded him that the gospel is not something we invent or earn or deserve. The grand conclusion is that the divisions in the church caused by lining up behind favorite preachers is frivolous. The message itself is the star of the show and all of the preachers Corinth has enjoyed preach this same message.

This summary exposed the gaping hole in the Corinthian gospel. Some in Corinth were denying the bodily resurrection by teaching that a spiritual resurrection had already happened and that was all that we should expect. The bottom-line assumption was that dead people cannot be raised, so therefore bodily resurrection was too impossible to be believed. This was another way of denying cross power. They had emptied the cross of its power by their divisions and the assumption that the gospel was, at its heart, yet another human message preached by clever orators. That empty cross made the gospel small and was the root cause for all of the problems that Corinth was experiencing as a church. What was needed was cross power, a new vision of the bigness of the gospel. Cross power changed the way God the Father now rules the world, following the pattern of the cross. Cross power changed our personal destinies by placing us into union with Christ and bringing a full and final salvation to us. Cross power unleashed the Spirit to enlighten, create, empower, and purify the church. However, there was one more dimension of this cross power that Paul needed to display.

6. Wright, *Surprised by Hope*, 234.

Cross power creates a new world where death ends and eternal bodily life flourishes forever. All of God is now at work all around us, making all things new. This dimension of cross power Paul now brings out in chapter 15.

The heart of Paul's discussion of resurrection is in verses 12–20. The main point of this section is captured in verse 15: "if Christ has not been raised, then our preaching is in vain and your faith is in vain." The rest of the chapter unpacks the meaning of the resurrection of Christ as a precursor to our own. Christ's resurrection sets off a chain of events that includes our own resurrection at the time of his glorious and bodily return to earth to reign (v. 23). Our resurrection from the dead is followed by the culmination of history: "Then comes the end, when he delivers the kingdom to God the Father after destroying every rule and every authority and power . . . The last enemy to be destroyed is death" (vv. 14, 26).

What will that resurrection body be like? Paul uses the analogy of the seed and the plant. We are all in a seed state right now: full of future potential, but not yet what we will be. Through being planted (those who die in Christ) we will become the full plant, the full reality that we were always meant to be. Wright comments:

> The new is the transformation, not merely the replacement, of the old. Moreover, since the old is quite obviously not yet transformed, the resurrection, its central feature, cannot yet have happened. Time matters; it was part of the original good creation. Though it may well itself be transformed in ways we cannot at present even begin to imagine, we should not allow ourselves to be seduced by the language of the old song about when "time shall be no more." No: The old field of space, time, matter . . . is to be weeded, dug, and sown for a new crop. We may be tired of that old field: God is not.[7]

What does future bodily resurrection have to do with how we are to live now? Paul ties in this fourth dimension of cross power, resurrection, and new creation, to moral transformation now. "If the dead are not raised 'let us eat and drink for tomorrow we die'" (v. 33). They need to wake up to this gospel reality in order to stop sinning (v. 34). What does he mean by this?

Few theologians have explored the connection between resurrection faith and Christian living as deeply as Oliver O'Donovan in his book *Resurrection and Moral Order*. O'Donovan makes clear that the resurrection of Christ validates creation. God wants to restore earthly life. To take the resurrection seriously then means to take the creation order seriously, the

---

7. Wright, *Surprised by Hope*, 164.

way of life that God wants on earth. O'Donovan draws out the importance of the resurrection for the validation of earthly life:

> In proclaiming the resurrection of Christ, the apostles pro-
> claimed also the resurrection of mankind in Christ; and in
> proclaiming the resurrection of mankind, they proclaimed the
> renewal of all creation with him. The resurrection of Christ in
> isolation from mankind would not be a Gospel message. The
> resurrection of mankind apart from creation would be a Gospel
> of a sort, but of a purely gnostic and world-denying sort which
> is far from the gospel that the apostles actually preached. So, the
> resurrection of Christ directs our attention back to the creation
> which it vindicates.[8]

By "creation" we mean culture and not just nature, human activity in the world. The resurrection calls for a reordering of human activity in the world. Paul ends his chapter with this imperative: "Therefore, my beloved brothers, be steadfast, immovable, always abounding in the work of the Lord, knowing that in the Lord your labor is not in vain" (v. 58). Because of the power of the cross, a new world of eternal bodily life in a renewed world is ours. God will use the loaves and fish of our current human activity to bear witness to this new world coming. Our daily lifestyle is not meaningless. Death is not the end. What we do in our bodies now will affect eternity since the destiny is resurrection to eternal life or to eternal judgment. So live in a way consistent with the life we will lead in the coming new creation. Wright makes this point even more forcefully:

> When Paul wrote his great resurrection chapter, 1 Corinthians
> 15, he didn't end by saying, "So let's all celebrate the great future
> life that awaits us." He ended by saying, "So get on with your
> work because you know that in the Lord it won't go to waste."
> When the final resurrection occurs, as the centerpiece of God's
> new creation, we will discover that everything done in the pres-
> ent world in the power of Jesus's own resurrection will be cel-
> ebrated and included, appropriately transformed.[9]

The cross gives us the power to live in the new age of resurrection now, even as we await the returning king and the renewal of all things.

Corinth had a gospel problem. As a young church, intimidated by the surrounding culture, it was understandable. But it was also destructive. When the gospel becomes small, differences in the church become large.

---

8. O'Donovan, *Resurrection and Moral Order*, 31.

9. Wright, *Surprised by Hope*, 294.

The only antidote is to show how big the cross is. Paul does that by showing that the cross has unleashed all of the Father and all of the Son and all of the Spirit into all of life until the new creation becomes reality. The gospel is as big as an infinite, Triune God. You can't get much bigger than that.

HOW TO CREATE A MOVEMENT: APPLYING PAUL'S GREAT IDEA

What does this mean for leaders today? I would like to end this chapter by spelling out the gospel that we need to teach and practice to get our churches moving again. Many suggested formulae for church renewal today focus on methods and leave the message untouched. After all, is not our gospel unchanging? Have we not uncovered, in the Reformation and in subsequent revivals of the church, the pure gospel of Romans? What is needed is not message-tweaking, but new methods to get this message into the heads and hearts of millennials, Muslims, and masses equally resistant to the good news of Jesus. Paul, in contrast to the methods approach, sees Corinth's problems as a paradigm problem. They were getting bored, not with the whole gospel, but with their incomplete understanding. Paul sees the root problem as an inadequate grasp of the gospel. This inadequate grasp is not just a minor error, but a life-and-death matter, the fount of all other problems in the Corinthian church.

How can a church that preaches the gospel be emptying the cross of its power? How can the church miss the message? Ed Sanders, a leading evangelical theologian, has asked the same question. His answer to this question is troubling but true:

> A gospel which is only about the moment of conversion but does not extend to every moment of life in Christ is too small. A gospel that gets your sins forgiven but offers no power for transformation is too small. A gospel that isolates one of the benefits of union with Christ and ignores all the others is too small. A gospel that must be measured by your own moral conduct, social conscience, or religious experience is too small. A gospel that rearranges the components of your life but does not put you personally in the presence of God is too small.[10]

10. Sanders, *Deep Things of God*, 106.

Humanity in exile
from God

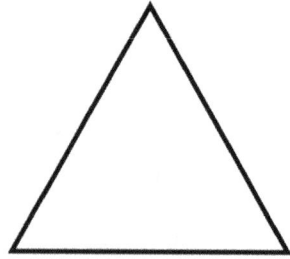

The Eternal Trinity
of Father, Son and
Holy Spirit

For Sanders, a small gospel results from a small view of God. And the only way to get a bigger view of the gospel is to get a bigger view of God. For some that might mean discoursing on his attributes. For Sanders it means rediscovering the Trinity in action. This is Paul's answer too. As we have seen, Paul uses the first two chapters of his letter to deepen and enlarge the gospel message by showing the Trinity in action. A series of diagrams may help us see what preaching a bigger gospel with a bigger view means. A gospel that is only about forgiveness of sins and going to heaven is too small a gospel because it has too small a view of God and his action in the world.

Look at the following series of diagrams. A typical presentation of the gospel begins with humanity's separation from God.

Mankind is unable to breach this gap. The solution must come from God's side. The solution is the cross:

Humanity in exile
from God

The cross as the
bridge to the
Triune God

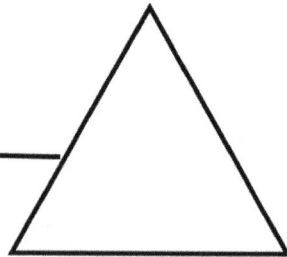

The Eternal Trinity of
Father, Son and Holy Spirit

Because of Christ's cross, alienated humanity, if they will believe, can then cross the bridge of the cross and enjoy forgiveness of sins and restored fellowship with God. This is sometimes stated theologically as being justified by faith. We can picture it as follows:

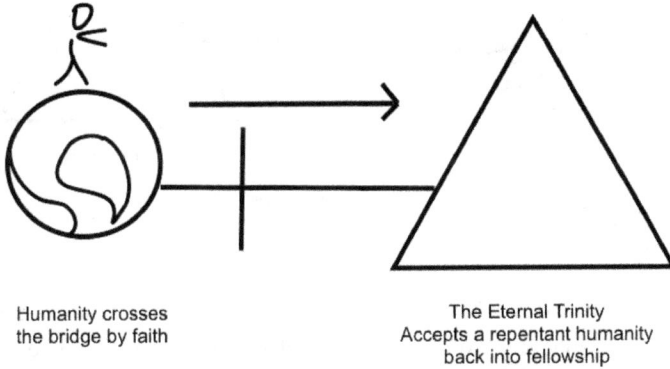

Humanity crosses
the bridge by faith

The Eternal Trinity
Accepts a repentant humanity
back into fellowship

And this is often where the presentation of the gospel stops. Humanity now has a personal relationship with God by faith. Many benefits such as eternal life flow from this bridge of the cross, but is anything being left out? I believe Paul would answer with a vigorous "yes." From his presentation of the gospel as a fourfold cross power that unleashes all of God into all of the world to make all things new, we should add and unpack for our people at least two additional parts of the story.

One part that is missing in the above presentation, but not in Paul's letter, is that cross power not only enables fallen humanity to cross the bridge back to God, but God now crosses the bridge to us. Consider this diagram:

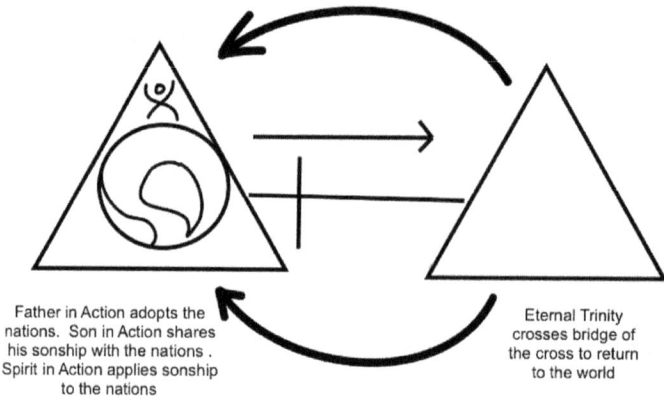

Father in Action adopts the
nations. Son in Action shares
his sonship with the nations .
Spirit in Action applies sonship
to the nations

Eternal Trinity
crosses bridge of
the cross to return
to the world

The cross and its covering of sins allows a holy God to come running back into the world, the whole of the world for the whole of time. The cross unleashes the fullness of the Father and his love everywhere in us and around us. However, the second thing to note about this diagram is where God's action is now centered. God is no longer just far away in heaven land waiting for us to come to him, albeit by grace. God, in his essence, is centered in heaven. God's principle place of action is now here because of the cross. God is here and at work all around us, making all things new. We as the church now work with the all-present and all-active Father, Son, and Spirit, to build towards the new creation:

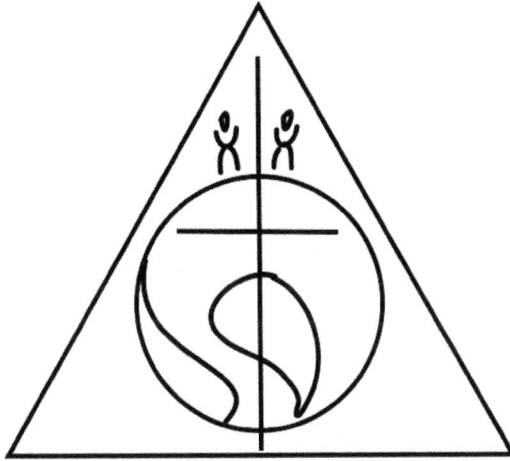

Father, Son and Spirit continue action of
expanding and deepening sonship through
history culminating in the new creation, the end
of evil and eternal life and the reunion of
heaven and eath.

As we live and work, aware that we are surrounded by the good and great Father, an active and involved Savior and Son, and an enlightening and empowering, indwelling Spirit, we can bear witness to the power of the cross and the coming resurrection from the dead and the renewal of all things.

This is the new kind of message that will get our churches moving again. *The gospel changes everything when we show that, through the cross, all of the Father, all of the Son, and all of the Spirit have been unleashed into all of our world, for all of time, to make all things new.*

Oscar Muiru was preaching the simple gospel, in his mind, when he began the revitalization of Nairobi Chapel. However, it was the gospel with a difference. It was a gospel not just about forgiveness of sins as an end in itself, but about the unleashing of God and every spiritual dynamic and gift as a result of the cross and the remission of sins. Preaching cross power changed his church. It can also change ours.

Chapter 3

The Light That Renews

The Spirit as God's Enlightening Presence

"It is love that believes the Resurrection."[1]

—LUDWIG WITTGENSTEIN

READ: 1 COR 2:6—3:4

What was so great about the Great Awakening? I ask this question because evangelicals both in the West and the majority world keep talking about it. Many of us look nostalgically back to the time of Wesley, Edwards, and Whitefield in the eighteenth century as a high-water mark in the history of the movement. The desire for revival and renewal today can be seen in books like *The Next Christendom*,[2] and more recently *Longing for Revival: From Holy Discontent to Breakthrough Faith,* by James Choung and Ryan Pfeiffer.[3] Both Choung and Pfeiffer are campus ministers who are reclaiming the concept of revival for their work with university students.

One of the things that made the Great Awakening great was the theology of revival that emerged from the movement. The central voice in that

1. Wittgenstein, "Ludwig Wittgenstein on the Resurrection," para. 2.
2. Jenkins, *Next Christendom.*
3. Choung and Pfeiffer, *Longing for Revival.*

theology was Jonathan Edwards. For someone like Edwards, awakenings were diverse and complex events that had a single, powerful center—a life-changing encounter with the divine and supernatural light of the Holy Spirit that made the truths of the gospel so real that it produced not only mass conversions, but in the decades that followed, powerful expressions of global mission and social justice.

Edwards's theology of awakening has biblical roots. Some of those roots are found in Paul's theology of the Spirit. And chapters two and three of 1 Corinthians are major statements of that theology. We saw in the last chapter that, for Paul, the solution to theological disunity was a return to a theological core centered on the cross and its power to change the world in comprehensive ways. For the apostle, the real cure for the many issues facing the Corinthian church such as unity, sexuality, food, community, worship, and doctrine, was cross power. Paul calls the church back to this central vision in chapter 1, but more needs to be said. He tackles a related question in chapter 2. If cross power is the answer, why have so many Christians in Corinth turned from it in their pursuit of wisdom and spiritual maturity? His answer is that we must change the way we interpret the message to see the gospel come alive once again in this young church. From 2:6—3:4 he calls for a deep work of the Spirit in our lives to make faith in the gospel possible. Only through the wisdom of the Spirit and its transformative power over my mind and heart can I see the truth of cross power and heal the fractures of the body of Christ. Only then will Corinthian Christians see the power of the cross, the unleashing of death-conquering, sin-destroying, divine love into all the world for all of time, as the greatest power on earth. Only the Spirit can help us see and serve the coming new creation.

In one sense Paul is dealing with the problem of vision. If I am seeing the world around me in a fuzzy way, then I need to have my eyes checked. If I am seeing the gospel in a limited and minimal way, likewise, I need to have some serious work done on the way I see reality. Only with new eyes can I see the reality of a Triune God at work all around me and in me, making all things new, and join him in his work.

What is Paul's great idea in this chapter? *To see and apply the good news of cross power to all of life we must have our hearts and minds transformed by the Spirit of God.* Let's take a closer look.

WHY WE NEED THE RENEWAL OF
OUR MINDS: 1 COR 2:6—3:4.

In chapter 2 of his letter to Corinth, Paul continues to address the problem of theological disunity in the church. In chapter 1, as we have seen, Paul declared that the theological core of the Christian faith and the only foundation for doctrinal unity is a large view of the cross and its power. Cross power not only removes sin but has returned God to our world. All of the Triune God is unleashed into all of the world, for all of time, to make all things new. In chapter 15, he showed that cross power means the resurrection of all from the dead. This means that all of earthly life matters because it matters to God and will be renewed and transformed by God. Cross power is thus the greatest power in the world.

But these are large claims. Conventional wisdom, the way of reason and science, can make no sense of these claims. Surely Paul is exaggerating for effect in his overblown claims about the cross and the resurrection. In response to the skeptics Paul claims that reason, on its own, could never understand, let alone embrace, cross power. It is simply not up to the task. To understand the deep things of God, namely the cross and its power to raise the dead and renew all human life, one needs God. Through the work of the Spirit of God we can recover our theological common ground in the cross and get back to working together to solve the many problems in the church by applying the gospel of the cross to all of life. In 2:6—3:4, Paul gives five reasons why we need the divine and supernatural light of the Spirit to understand cross power. We need the wisdom of the Spirit because 1) human knowledge is transient, limited, and corrupted; 2) the Spirit alone *knows* the depths of God's knowledge; 3) the Spirit alone *communicates* that knowledge to us; 4) the Spirit alone *empowers* us to proclaim that knowledge to others; and 5) the Spirit alone *defines* true spirituality.

First, we need the enlightenment of the Spirit because human knowledge is transient, limited and corrupted. We see this in verses 6–8:

> Yet among the mature we do impart wisdom, although it is not a wisdom of this age or of the rulers of this age, who are doomed to pass away.
>
> But we impart a secret and hidden wisdom of God, which God decreed before the ages for our glory.
>
> None of the rulers of this age understood this, for if they had, they would not have crucified the Lord of glory.

Verse 6 reminds us that though worldly wisdom may be relevant and powerful for a number of things, it cannot comprehend the absolute and the eternal. It is passing away. We can think of countless ideologies of the past that seemed to stop all before them, but which today are mere empty memories. So shall it be with any ideology, any wisdom that says this world is all there is and all there ever shall be. These rules may have their fifteen minutes of fame, but they have no future.

But the transience of human reason is not only faddish, it is epic. We see this in verses 6 and 8, when Paul speaks of the wisdom of "this age." Pauline eschatology saw the cross as creating a new age in history, the "age to come." All humanity now lives in an historical moment in which two great ages overlap. The present evil age overlaps with the age to come, inaugurated by the death and resurrection of Christ. The wisdom of this present age, (that this world is all there is or all there every will be, or that human reason is the arbiter of all truth), is time-bound. The age to come is breaking in and will one day bring an end to the present age. Thinking like the world belittles the cross and its power. It is also thinking that is doomed to fail.

Human reason is not only transient, but also limited. It can only go so far. But divine wisdom can get to the bottom of things. As verse 7 states, "But we impart a secret and hidden wisdom of God, which God decreed before the ages for our glory." Reason is limited to time and to the visible. The Spirit of God as an agent of truth has no such restrictions.

Verse 8 notes a third problem with human reason and its attempt to know ultimate truth: it is corrupted by power. As Blomberg writes, "The 'rulers' refer at least to the religious and political authorities of the day, comparable to Caiaphas and Pilate, who crucified our glorious Lord (v. 8)." Additionally, "they may also refer to demonic powers behind the opposition to the gospel (cf. Eph 2:2, in which Satan is the 'ruler of the kingdom of the air')."[4]

This is Paul's critique of human reason. Christian rationalists elevated human wisdom and knowledge above divine revelation of the gospel. The theological factions had one thing in common—an overconfidence in reason (whether in its logical or mystical forms) as the central path to the truth about God and the world. Paul rejects, not reason, but its claims of supremacy. The cross is both against the arrogance of reason and above the limits of reason. The gospel of a crucified king makes no sense to the person who has not been awakened by the Spirit. When Paul says that only the Spirit of God can know the depths of God's thoughts, he is affirming the necessity of revelation and not reason as the principle way we know ultimate truth. Reason makes a good servant, but a poor master. God has revealed truth about himself through nature and science, but it is limited. Human wisdom based on the limits of human observation is useful, but not ultimate.

4. Blomberg, *First Corinthians*, 29.

Without divine disclosure through the divine and supernatural light of the Spirit we cannot know ultimate truth, namely, the centrality of Christ and his cross as the meaning of everything and the key to the transformation of the world. This is our new hermeneutic, the Spirit, speaking through the apostles about the cross and its powers. This is the key to knowing what God is doing in his world.

Second, we need the divine and supernatural light of the Spirit because he is the only one who possesses comprehensive knowledge of God and his mind (2:9–11). Reason can only see what is in front of us. Only the Spirit knows the depths of God and the ultimate mysteries of his plan and purposes:

> But, as it is written, "What no eye has seen, nor ear heard, nor the heart of man imagined, what God has prepared for those who love him" - these things God has revealed to us through the Spirit. For the Spirit searches everything, even the depths of God. For who knows a person's thoughts except the spirit of that person, which is in him? So also no one comprehends the thoughts of God except the Spirit of God.

As Hays summarizes, "In 1 Corinthians 2:10–13, Paul makes a very simple point: The hidden wisdom of God (Christ crucified) is revealed to us by the Spirit of God."[5] N. T. Wright describes this new hermeneutic of the Spirit:

> How do we know? Because God has given us his spirit. This is another major theme of the letter, introduced here for the first time. Paul relishes the fact that the spirit who is poured out upon believers, bringing them to faith and opening their hearts and minds to the wisdom of the 'age to come,' is God's own spirit, not some lesser being. The spirit within a person–the deep innermost life where thought, feeling, memory and imagination meet–knows best what the person is all about. Even so, Paul declares, God's spirit is like that with God; and this spirit is given to all God's people in the Messiah.[6]

The idea of a crucified Messiah, adds Blomberg, "was not clearly understood in Old Testament times and was still not grasped in Paul's day by those who rejected Jesus."[7]

Third, we need the divine and supernatural light of the Spirit because he alone communicates the depths of divine of knowledge. In verse 12, Paul states, "Now we have received not the spirit of the world, but the Spirit who is from

5. Hays, *First Corinthians*, 45.
6. Wright, *Paul for Everyone*, 2.
7. Blomberg, *First Corinthians*, 29.

God, that we might understand the things freely given us by God." Note that the Spirit doesn't reveal the gospel through a public service announcement. We must receive this Spirit into our lives. This indwelling Spirit of God can then communicate divine truth (cross power) in a way that is not possible by all the usual means of human rhetoric and knowledge, such as science, reason, common sense, experience, intuition, etc.

What does it mean to be spiritual? Paul will talk about possessing divine love in chapter 13, but here being spiritual is receiving the communication of divine truth by the Spirit. The logic of the cross leads to the love that changes the world. Being spiritual means having the Spirit and hearing his message. The Spirit empowers us, but his greater work is waking us up. We should agree with Richard Hays when he says that "Paul and other Christians can speak now about the identity of God not because they have received advanced philosophical instruction or lessons on rhetorical declamation but because they have been taught by the Spirit of God how to speak of God through the word of the cross."[8]

Fourth, we need the divine and supernatural light of the Spirit because he alone empowers his people to make the gospel known through preaching. The mode the Spirit uses to communicate truth to us is the word of God preached and inscripturated: "And we impart this in words not taught by human wisdom but taught by the Spirit, interpreting spiritual truths to those who are spiritual" (v. 13). So it is not Apollos or Cephas or Paul who matter, but the work of the Spirit in equipping and empowering his people to understand the message of the Bible through the lens of cross power.

Does this mean born-again Christians know everything about God and the world? Certainly not. As Wright explains, "It clearly doesn't mean that Christians automatically know everything about God, or why would Paul bother to write letters? It means that they have open access to God's mind—or, as he says in verse 16, to 'the mind of the Messiah.'"[9] This doesn't mean we know everything, but it means he helps us understand how the cross is the secret to understanding what God is doing in the world and in his church. And it also is the key to applying the gospel in any given situation. Taking the way of the cross, the way of divine, sacrificial love, is our true north.

How can I know for sure if the Spirit of God is at work in me either as the preacher or the hearer? The key sign is the cross. The cross is seen by both preacher and hearer as the key to all that God is doing in the world. What should we make of the phrase "interpreting spiritual things to those

8. Hays, *First Corinthians*, 46.
9. Wright, *Paul for Everyone*, 26.

who are spiritual?" Richard Hays believes Paul may be using the term "spiritual" in a slightly mocking sense, referring to those in the Corinthian church who were self-proclaimed spiritual ones. For Hays, Paul is saying, "If you were really as spiritual as you think you are . . . you would understand that our rhetorically unembellished speech about Christ crucified is the message that comes from the Spirit of God."[10]

Fifth we need the divine and supernatural light of the Spirit of God if we want to be a truly spiritual person. Paul takes on the definition of true spirituality in 2:14—3:4:

> The natural person does not accept the things of the Spirit of God, for they are folly to him, and he is not able to understand them because they are spiritually discerned. The spiritual person judges all things, but is himself to be judged by no one. "For who has understood the mind of the Lord so as to instruct him?" But we have the mind of Christ. . . . But I, brothers, could not address you as spiritual people, but as people of the flesh, as infants in Christ. I fed you with milk, not solid food, for you were not ready for it. And even now you are not yet ready, for you are still of the flesh. For while there is jealousy and strife among you, are you not of the flesh and behaving only in a human way? For when one says, "I follow Paul," and another, "I follow Apollos," are you not being merely human?

Paul does two things in these verses: he defines what a truly spiritual person is and what she is not.

Let's begin with what a spiritual person is not. They are not like everybody else. Verse 14 talks about the natural person as one who finds the gospel of cross power nonsensical. They are *psychikoi,* having a merely human soul or psyche. Hays describes the mindset of the average person. *Psychikoi* "refers to human beings living in their natural state apart from the Spirit of God and therefore unenlightened and blind to the truth. They just don't 'get it.'" He adds that "it refers to those who belong to the old age; it emphatically does not refer to less advanced Christians."[11] Note the irony. The spiritual elite are in fact the spiritual infants. Hays picks up this paradox:

> Thus, Paul is not coining fresh categories in order to classify the relative spiritual maturity of his readers; rather, he is turning the tables on the spirit-enthusiasts, placing them at the bottom of their own scale of religious achievement rather than at the top, where they suppose themselves to belong. They consider

10. Hays, *First Corinthians,* 46.
11. Hays, *First Corinthians,* 46.

themselves mature and spiritual, but Paul replies with a put-down: sorry, you remain immature and fleshly.[12]

The problem in Corinth was a super spirituality that was a smokescreen for human arrogance. Because cross power and cross power alone has unleashed the Triune God into the world, it also means that the Spirit of God, the Third Person of the Trinity, has been unleashed to reveal to those who have rejected the sufficiency of human reason or intuition the nature of reality—God at work, making all things new through the cross.

Wright comments on this distinction between spiritual and carnal. Rather than constructing an elaborate taxonomy of degrees of spirituality, he is making fun of those that make such classifications:

> There is, in fact, a very subtle shift from 'merely human' (2.14) to 'all too obviously human' (3.1), to 'very determinedly only-human' (i.e., actually resisting the spirit, not merely showing no evidence of it) (3.3). Paul is not suggesting that each of these words refers to a different level of Christian (or sub-Christian) experience, or to a different type of person. He is insisting that all of them alike are 'unspiritual'–and that the Corinthian church, insofar as it is indulging in personality cults, is showing strong evidence of exactly that. This is why he hadn't been able to give them stronger, deeper, richer teaching; they weren't ready for it, and their present factional fighting shows that they still aren't.[13]

I believe Blomberg is correct to interpret the term *psychikoi* as "the man without the Spirit." "In other words," he writes, "this is a person in his ordinary, unredeemed state of earthly existence, which he inherited from the Fall."[14] Carnality then does not refer primarily to sexual sin or being a neophyte Christian. Carnality at its root is the abuse of power. Carnality is "living in rivalry and disunity within the church."[15] Paul warns us that any Christian can slip back into worldly thinking at any moment and thereby lose their mind, the mind of Christ.

Second, if Paul has exposed what false spirituality is, then what is true spirituality? Real spirituality, real Christianity, is not a feeling that exalts, but a vision that unites. To be a Christian is having the Spirit open our eyes to God's love as the greatest power in the world, a love that suffers and dies to liberate the beloved from sin and death and not stroke the ego and pander

---

12. Hays, *First Corinthians,* 47.

13. Wright, *Paul for Everyone,* 31.

14. Blomberg, *First Corinthians,* 30.

15. Hays, *First Corinthians,* 48.

to human self-reliance. As Blomberg writes,"'Spiritual' must therefore mean not merely having the Spirit but having the Spirit in charge."[16] And what does it look like when the Spirit is in charge? The cross is everywhere:

> The spiritual (or mature) person is the one who accepts the crucified Christ as Savior, over against the natural (and therefore immature) person who rejects him. Christians' behavior in any age needs to match their status; they must learn the truth that "we never . . . move on from the cross of Christ—only into a more profound understanding of the cross."[17]

What about the Christian who falls into worldly ways of thinking? Is Paul saying that he or she is unsaved or unregenerate? It is possible for a genuine believer to so grieve the Spirit through spiritual pride and trust in human power that they are temporarily blinded to the truth of cross power and actually see reality as the world does rather than as God does. They need to be revived, not regenerated. The same gospel of cross power that regenerates also revives, and so Paul is confident that by preaching cross power in chapters 1 and 15 he will see both works of the Spirit happen in the Corinthian Christian community.

Paul's equation is that true spirituality equals cross-eyed seeing and living. If I have moved beyond the cross, then I have moved beyond life in the Spirit and beyond the profound center and depth of the Christian message. In the rest of his letter Paul will apply cross power to other issues beside disunity: sex, culture, food, community, truth, love, men and women, theology—all will get the cross treatment. But he spends time on the disunity issue because it goes to the root problem of the church—moving away from cross power. If I am fighting for power, then I am a living contradiction of the one who rejected the way of power and followed the way of sacrificial love.

In summary, Paul, in 2:6—3:4, delivers his second great idea: *To see and apply the good news of cross power to all of life we must have our hearts and minds renewed by the Spirit of God.* Paul gives his reasons for his view. Human knowledge is transient, limited, and corrupted. The Spirit alone *knows* the depths of God's knowledge. The Spirit alone *communicates* that knowledge to us. The Spirit alone *empowers* us to proclaim that knowledge to others. The Spirit alone *defines* true spirituality.

As he presents his case, Paul also exposes the lie of a Christian spirituality that tries to move beyond the cross to more spiritual or lofty themes. To leave the cross behind is to leave the Spirit of God behind. To such spiritual

16. Blomberg, *First Corinthians*, 38.

17. Blomberg, *First Corinthians*, 31.

elites "Paul delivers a splash of cold water on their faces, which were burning with what they supposed to be spiritual ardor. 'Wake up,' he says. 'Stop
fighting with each other; you are acting like spoiled babies, not like people
who have received the Spirit of God.'"[18]

APPLYING PAUL'S GREAT IDEA

How should our churches today apply this great idea? Pentecostalism, with
its 500 million adherents, has captured much of the discussion of what the
Spirit of God is doing in his world and what we must do to get in step with
the Spirit. Yet as powerful as this global movement has been, we need to
hear again what Paul is saying about a true work of the Spirit and what true
spirituality looks like. Consider these five applications of Paul's great idea.

Application 1: Seeking gospel unity

We need to make unity the test of spiritual maturity. Christians can disagree
on many things. They may disagree about politics, denominational distinc-
tives, and modes of worship. But there should be no debate on the core of
the gospel that through the death and resurrection of Christ my salvation
and the new creation of the world has been accomplished. We need to get
back to basics in our congregations, particularly if we have seen cracks in
the unity of the body. Hays reminds us: "The real measure of spiritual maturity is unity and peace in the community."[19]
    One of the debates in African Christianity in the late twentieth century
concerned Christian unity. Many African evangelicals were challenged by
the need for a united witness with other Christians. Central to this discussion was Nigerian Byang Kato, who as secretary general of the Association
of Evangelicals in Africa gave a clear message: no unity in the dark. We need
to talk. We need to listen. But at the end of the day, we need to unite only
around the cross and its power as the mark of the Christian. We must not
split hairs over every doctrinal difference, but we must keep the main thing
the main thing.

18. Hays, *First Corinthians,* 49.
19. Hays, *First Corinthians,* 49.

Application 2: Promoting true spirituality

Second, we need to redefine spirituality for followers of Jesus. We are not here to critique the diverse forms of spirituality today from new age to Eastern to even secular expressions. But what we must critique as kindly, but as clearly, as we can is the nature of Christian spirituality. It may appear weak and mundane against some of the heroic spiritual disciplines practiced by members of other religions, yet we must be straightforward about the fact that Christian spirituality is cross-centered. Only the faith, hope, and love that comes from cross power deserves to be called Christian spirituality. We may learn much from other traditions, but what we cannot do is swap our centers. As Wolfgang Schrage, writing on true spirituality as cross spirituality, has stated:

> the Spirit that teaches understanding to the Christians is not some kind of spirit of field, forest, and meadow, nor is it a natural magic potency that produces enthusiasm; rather, it is the spirit of the crucified Christ. Thus, this spirit is to be measured by the cross, and it is therefore unavoidably a critic of all self-directed wisdom and likewise of all elite wisdom.[20]

One recommended resource for promoting this kind of spirituality is *The Gospel-Centered Life* by Robert Thune and Will Walker. Its chapters and exercises lay out a vision of Christian spirituality that is deeply rooted in Paul's teaching about the cross.[21]

Application 3: Christian hope

Paul's discussion of the wisdom of this age versus that of the age to come reminds us that our view of time and eternity affects our view of truth. The gospel only makes sense against the backdrop of eternity. If this life is all there is, as Paul observes in 1 Cor 15, then our faith is vain, and we are without hope. In the words of Abraham Heschel, we must begin to see time as "eternity in disguise."[22] In other words, we need to get our eschatology back. Hays reminds us that the gospel is "a message about God's plan from before the ages to bring God's people through the present time of conflict to eschatological glory. Only in that frame of reference does the cross make sense, and only in that frame of reference will the divisions in the church be

---

20. Quoted in Hays, *First Corinthians*, 47.
21. Thune and Walker, *Gospel-Centered Life*.
22. Heschel, *Sabbath*, 25.

seen in their proper light."[23] When was the last time your church did a series on the Christian view of hope? We need to avoid the narrow eschatologies that seemed obsessed with predicting the tribulation and identifying the antichrist. But the kind of healthy and biblical eschatology explored in a book like *Surprised by Hope,* by N. T. Wright, will help our churches flourish.

Application 4: Discovering a new theology of power

Paul makes clear the connection between theology and power. Theologies of the left and of the right are both prone to cashing in the chips of theological correctness to win control over institutions and influence. The result is the kind of power struggle Paul describes in Corinth. Only certain types of theology help avoid the abuse of power. A theology of the cross is one of the only approaches to biblical truth that humbles all parties in the conversation. Paul shows in Phil 2 that a theology of the cross in which Jesus "emptied himself" trades in the love of power for the power of love. According to N. T. Wright:

> The Christian message from the very beginning challenged the world of power, including social and political power, with the message of God's superior kingdom unveiled in Jesus' death and resurrection. Paul doesn't want the Corinthians to imagine that he is talking simply about a religious experience that won't have anything to do with the real life of politics and government. He wouldn't want us to imagine that either. Let us not settle for a gospel which allows the world's power-games to proceed without challenge.[24]

Application 5: Preaching for conversion and regeneration

Central to the great idea we are exploring is the necessity of a personal awakening by the Spirit in order to know God, experience the cross, and live a cross-centered life full of cross power.

What does this awakening look like? A new birth. When Jonathan Edwards published his revival sermon on a divine and supernatural light in 1733, he captured the essence of what it means to be a biblical Christian. Edwards's main idea was that "There is such a thing, as a spiritual and divine light, immediately imparted to the soul by God, of a different nature from

23. Hays, *First Corinthians,* 50.

24. Wright, *Paul for Everyone,* 26.

any that is obtained by natural means."[25] This divine light is a work of the Spirit, who in the work of regeneration "unites himself with the mind of a saint, takes him for his temple, actuates and influences him as a new, supernatural principle of life and action. There is this difference; that the Spirit of God, in acting in the soul of a godly man, exerts and communicates himself there in his own proper nature."[26]

The Spirit gives no new doctrine but makes the message of the cross come alive. Edwards explains this point:

> This spiritual light is not the suggesting of any new truths, or propositions not contained in the Word of God. This suggesting of new truths or doctrines to the mind, independent of any antecedent revelation of those propositions, either in word or writing, is inspiration, such as the prophets and apostles had, and such as some enthusiasts pretend to. But this spiritual light that I am speaking of, is quite a different thing from inspiration: it reveals no new doctrine, it suggests no new proposition to the mind, it teaches no new thing of God, or Christ, or another world, not taught in the Bible; but only gives a due apprehension of those things that are taught in the Word of God.[27]

This enlightening work moves beyond giving light only to the mind and gives a sense of the heart. "Thus there is a difference between having an opinion that God is holy and gracious, and having a sense of the loveliness and beauty of that holiness and grace," Edwards writes. "There is a difference between having a rational judgment that honey is sweet, and having a sense of its sweetness."[28] This sense of the heart makes the cross and resurrection so beautiful to the believer that he or she falls in love with the doctrine. The truth of the gospel thus becomes rooted in the heart and not just the mind.

Can this light change our behavior? Can it help us live differently in everyday life? Edwards ends his sermon by saying that only this light produces divine love in the heart, the essence of true holiness:

> But this light, as it reaches the bottom of the heart, and changes the nature, so it will effectually dispose to an universal obedience. It shows God's worthiness to be obeyed and served. It draws forth the heart in a sincere love to God, which is the only principle of a true, gracious and universal obedience. And it

25. Edwards, *Sermons of Jonathan Edwards*, 123.

26. Edwards, *Sermons of Jonathan Edwards*, 124.

27. Edwards, *Sermons of Jonathan Edwards*, 125.

28. Edwards, *Sermons of Jonathan Edwards*, 127.

convinces of the reality of those glorious rewards that God has promised to them that obey him.[29]

We must preach and seek this experience of new birth and the new light that it gives. If you have grown tired of hearing about being born again or have lost faith that it can produce any real transformation in a life, then I would encourage you take up Edwards's sermon and read it to be refreshed in the awesome power and necessity of the divine and supernatural light which alone can produce genuine faith, authentic hope, and lasting love.

Application 6: Practicing a new hermeneutic

Finally, Paul's great idea calls us to a new way of seeing Scripture and the world. Conversion is not only about the change of heart but the change of hermeneutic, one's way of interpreting the world. Hermeneutics isn't merely about objectively reading reality. It is about power. It is embedded with self-interest and self-glory. Only a hermeneutic of divine love can free us from the hermeneutics of power and control. Many of us, however, have been so brainwashed by the Enlightenment that we read Scripture and interpret in very secular ways with little spiritual insight or power. As N. T. Wright observes:

> Enlightenment thought rejected Jesus's resurrection, but not because of a new scientific awareness that dead people do not rise. Everybody has known from earliest times that dead people stay dead. The Enlightenment's real reason for the rejection was that, if Jesus had risen from the dead, his resurrection would be the turning point of world history—a status the Enlightenment claimed for itself. There cannot be two such turning points. Here lies the crucial epistemological battle. The Enlightenment was in thrall to the split-level epistemology that, by insisting on hard facts and creaming off everything else into a subjective sphere, realized Francis Bacon's maxim that "knowledge is power."[30]

What does this have to do with the Spirit and the hermeneutic of divine love? To change the world we need a new hermeneutic: one that can redeem hedonism and redeem science and technology. Paul points the way forward. A hermeneutic of the Spirit is a hermeneutic of divine, transforming love. To see the word through pneumatic glasses is not only to see the

---

29. Edwards, *Sermons of Jonathan Edwards*, 140.

30. Wright, "Loving to Know," para. 6.

world the way God sees it, but to see it in a way that treasures what we see and empowers us to lay down our lives for the world.

Only the Spirit, God's indwelling love, can help us see the world with new eyes and live in that world in new ways. Cross power is not only a spiritual revolution, but also an intellectual one. The resurrection opens our eyes to see the depth of God's love for all things—death will not have the last word—and his love for persons. Through the enlightening work of the Spirit, our eyes, transformed by the love unleashed at the cross, can at last be opened to the beauty of the world and the inviting outline of the coming city of God.

Chapter 4

Leaders Who Renew

"The first responsibility of a leader is to define reality. The last is to say thank you. In between the two, the leader must become a servant and a debtor."[1]

—MAX DUPREE

READ: 1 COR 3:5–4:21

The fire that saved Chicago

In 1871, downtown Chicago was destroyed by a fire. The predominantly wooden buildings acted like kindling for the out-of-control blaze that claimed 300 lives, destroyed over three square miles of the city center, and left 100,000 people homeless. Whether it started in Mrs. O'Leary's barn, as tradition has it, or somewhere else, this devastating fire changed the way modern cities would be built. No one did more to bring about this architectural revolution than William LeBaron Jenny. Jenny vowed to prevent such a disaster from ever recurring and found that terra cotta, a mixture of

1. Dupree, *Leadership Is an Art*, 11.

sand and clay, was fire-resistant. Jenny incorporated it into his buildings. He pioneered the use of steel and glass, eventually building the first skyscraper in the world in 1885. Jenny was a master builder who not only saved a city from a repeat of the tragedy of 1871, but made cities all over the world safer because of his breakthrough approach to urban architecture.[2]

In chapters 3 and 4 of his First Letter to the Corinthians, Paul turns his attention to what could be called the "builder" model of leadership. He continues his discussion of strife in the church. At the root of the conflict is human pride: boasting about men. His argument in chapter 1 was that cross power removes any reason for humans to boast. Boasting makes no sense when it is clear that we were the problem and God alone was the solution. Our salvation is utterly dependent upon the work of God in Christ. His argument in chapter 2 is that even our knowledge of what God did in Christ is dependent on God. Only through the divine and supernatural light of the Spirit, and not through unaided human wisdom, can we know Christ and his power in a saving way. So, no boasting in the achievement of salvation and no boasting in our insight into this salvation.

Paul now turns his attention to a third possible area for human boasting—the act of teaching and leading. Maybe salvation was a work of God. Maybe we need the Spirit to bring the truth to the heart. But surely, when it comes to the public teaching of these truths, doesn't good rhetorical skill make all the difference in whether our churches grow or not? Between the work of Christ and the work of the Spirit stands the work of the teacher/leader. Here the human ego inserts itself as the real cause of effective ministry. As Gordon Fee notes: "At issue is their radically misguided perception of the nature of the church and its leadership, in this case, especially the role of the teachers."[3]

Paul uses a series of metaphors to describe the church and, consequently, the way humans can partner with God, without destructive pride, in the building and perfecting of the Christian movement. He employs a farming metaphor in 3:5–9, a building metaphor in 3:10–15, and a temple metaphor in 3:16–17. But it is the building metaphor that dominates these verses. The act of building the temple extends rather than replaces the building metaphor. The farmer-leader metaphor in 3:5–9 enriches the builder-leader metaphor, but does not negate it. For that reason, I'd like to propose that Paul is primarily presenting a builder-leader model in these chapters.

What is the great idea that Paul shares with the church in these verses? It is a word about cross-powered leadership: *leaders who renew are leaders*

2. Craven, "Biography of William Le Baron Jenney."

3. Fee, *First Epistle to the Corinthians*, 128.

who build to last. How then does Paul describe the builder-leader in 3:5—4:21? Paul gives us a rounded portrait of this leader in eight snapshots. Let's take a closer look at how leaders can build to last.

EIGHT WAYS TO BUILD TO LAST

Snapshot 1: The builder-leader is a servant, not a boss (3:5–7)

In verse 5, Paul writes: "What then is Apollos? What is Paul? Servants through whom you believed, as the Lord assigned to each." The builder-leader is not the boss. He or she is fundamentally a servant under orders. Yes, Paul and Apollos and the other teachers were crucial in cultivating belief in the hearts and minds of Corinthian Christians. But their role was dominated and directed by the Lord. They served his express will, and they performed specific roles and tasks in building that belief.

The servanthood Paul has in mind is not servanthood in general, but Christlike servanthood in particular. Christ's life and death, as described in chapter 1, is the model of the servant and builder that Paul unfolds here. The primary task of apostolic servants is that of growing the people of God. Thus, he uses a farming metaphor in 3:6–7. They serve alongside God as co-laborers, but their work would be nothing without the God who makes things grow (v. 7). The gospel is never far from Paul's thoughts on leadership. "The cross," Fee reminds us, "is not only the paradigm of the gospel, and of God's ways that stand in contradiction to human ways, but it also serves as the basic model for ministry. It stands as the divine contradiction to a merely human understanding of the role of leaders, such as the Corinthians were exhibiting."[4]

In ministry today, we need to be builder-leaders who know our calling and follow the pattern of our King Jesus, who became a servant to build the new people of God. There is no room for an arrogant CEO mentality among those who lead Christ's church. We are never in charge of the great project of creating a new people for the new creation. We are not capable of changing hearts or changing the world. We are co-workers who work alongside and under the authority of the ultimate builder "who gives the growth" (v. 7).

4. Fee, *First Epistle to the Corinthians*, 131.

Snapshot 2: Builder-leaders don't take shortcuts (3:10–15)

In 3:10–15, Paul explicitly uses builder terminology to describe his leadership model. The actual term he uses is our word for architect (*archetekton*). It's a combination word from *tekton*, "a skilled builder," and *arche* from "chief" or "primary." This kind of builder-leader is also described as *sophos*, or "wise." The master-builder described here, therefore, is not just a day laborer but one that is highly trained and highly responsible for the building project.

One characteristic of the wise architect is the selection of the best building materials available. No matter how great the design is, without the right materials, the building will fail. Jesus has laid the foundation of this new building of God (v. 11). Nothing can shake this foundation. Jesus built to last. Because this new building, the city of God, is eternal, the materials with which one builds matter. If we build with the ideas and attitudes of the world, "the present evil age," with its pride and unbelief, then we are building with the "wood, hay and straw" that will not last (v. 11).

There is another way to build. Cross power produces the divine love and Spirit empowerment that makes it possible to build with these golden and enduring materials. As Paul will say in chapter 13, without love, what we do amounts to nothing. Note that he is not saying that carnal Christians will miss out on eternity because of the way they minister, but he is saying that they will have little to show for their earthly ministry if they followed the wisdom of the world rather than the wisdom of the cross. "It is the 'work' that is consumed (because it was built of perishable material) and not the laborer herself/ himself."[5]

Richard Hays offers a helpful illustration of what Paul is teaching:

> We might think of what happens in California earthquakes. Some buildings that have been properly constructed to withstand the shocks remain standing, while others that have not been built according to sound principles of seismic engineering come tumbling down, with sometimes tragic results. Rather than an earthquake, Paul uses the image of fire, a traditional Old Testament image for God's judgment, but his point is the same: A cataclysm is coming that is going to test the structural integrity of our construction work, so we should build with great care.[6]

5. Fee, *First Epistle to the Corinthians*, 144.
6. Hays, *First Corinthians*, 53–54.

Should we make anything out of the list of building materials? Can we find conceptual equivalences for the gold, silver, jewels, and the wood, hay, and straw? Hays warns against this. "The six different building materials, perhaps arranged in descending order of value (3:12), have no special significance beyond the fact that the last three are combustible, and the first three are not."[7] The real point of these materials is to contrast two kinds of builders: those who build to last and those who do not.[8]

Snapshot 3: Builder-leaders see their work as sacred (3:16–17)

Paul reminds builder-leaders not only to use the right materials but to remember the kind of building we are constructing. We are not just building bowling alleys or beach cabanas, we are helping to build the ultimate dwelling place of God on earth.

> Do you not know that you are God's Temple and that God's Spirit dwells in you? If anyone destroys God's Temple, God will destroy him. For God's Temple is holy, and you are that Temple.

Leaders in the church are building a sacred residence. "Paul is here reflecting on the church as the corporate place of God's dwelling."[9] In the new creation, which has been inaugurated with the death and resurrection of King Jesus, God himself is making his home with redeemed humanity. He will dwell with them on a renewed earth. This temple is the city of God, the new Jerusalem, so majestically described in Revelation 21. Leading the church in a reckless way can get one removed from ministry ("if anyone destroys God's Temple, God will destroy him," v. 17). If we forget whose temple we are building—God's not ours—we will render ourselves irrelevant for his mission.

Hays brings out the significance of Paul's claims about the church here:

> Thus, when Paul now transfers this claim [that the church is God's Temple] to the community of predominantly gentile Christians in Corinth, he is making a world-shattering hermeneutical move, decentering the sacred space of Judaism (cf. John 4:21–24). How can Paul possibly assert that the church has replaced the Temple? He believes that the Spirit of God is

7. Hays, *First Corinthians*, 55.

8. Hays also references Robertson and Plummer: "As Robertson and Plummer (64) rightly observe about 1 Corinthians 3:12–15, there is not "the remotest reference to the state of the soul between death and judgment" (*First Corinthians*, 55).

9. Fee, *First Epistle to the Corinthians*, 146.

> present in the community and that the community is now the
> place where praise and worship are rightly offered up to God.
> The Spirit of God no longer can be localized in a sacred build-
> ing: it is to be found in the gathered community of God's elect
> people in Christ.[10]

Builder-leaders do not need to put on special robes to sense the sacredness
of his or her calling. They need only remember the gospel: the Triune God
is unleashed fully into the world by the cross of Christ to live with his people
now and forevermore.

Snapshot 4: Builder-leaders think outside the box (3:18–22)

Paul returns to the fundamental conflict between the wisdom of the world
and the wisdom of the cross in 3:18–22. The main characteristic of human
wisdom is "boasting in men" (v. 21). That is the "box" that characterizes all
fallen thinking. The wisdom of effective builders is the wisdom of the age
to come, that "God through Christ was reconciling the world to himself" (2
Cor 5:19), thus beginning a new and final stage in human history. To think
in light of the coming new creation is to think outside the box of worldly
thinking and human pretension.

What will this contradiction of conventional wisdom look like in
practice? It doesn't mean we reject beautiful facilities, educated leaders, or
efficient administration. It does mean, though, that we believe that only
the Spirit of God can knit together the threads of our human work into a
tapestry of divine glory. And the Spirit will not work outside of the gospel.
Without confidence in cross power as the driving force for building up the
people of God and bringing in the new creation, we will quench the Spirit
empty the gospel of its power, and develop churches that are irrelevant to
his mission.

Gordon Fee applies Paul's teaching on wisdom to the need to learn
from other Christians who may not be from my "tribe":

> The Corinthian error is an easy one to repeat. Not only do we all
> have normal tendencies to turn natural preferences into exclu-
> sive ones, but in our fallenness we also tend to consider ourselves
> "wise" enough to inform God through whom he may minister to
> his people. Our slogans take the form of "I am of the Presbyte-
> rians," or "of the Pentecostals," or "of the Roman Catholics." Or
> they might take ideological forms: "I am of the liberals," or "of

10. Hays, *First Corinthians*, 57.

the evangelicals," or "of the fundamentalists." And these are also used as weapons: "Oh, he's a fundamentalist, you know." Which means that we no longer need to listen to him, since his ideology has determined his overall value as a spokesman for God. It is hardly possible in a day like ours that one will not have denominational, theological, or ideological preferences. The difficulty lies in allowing that it might really be true that "all things are ours," including those whom we think God would do better to be without. But God is full of surprises; and he may choose to minister to us from the "strangest" of sources, if we were but more truly in Christ and therefore free in him to learn and to love.[11]

What does Paul mean in 3:21 that for those who reject worldly wisdom "all things are yours?" Hays suggests that Paul is alluding to a well-known aphorism of philosophers: "In order to appreciate the impact of this conclusion, we need to know that it was a universal maxim of Greco-Roman popular philosophy—particularly among the Cynics and Stoics—that "the wise man possesses all things."[12] Paul is insisting that given the death, resurrection, and current rule of Christ preparing history for the new creation, it is the church and the wisdom of the cross that possesses all things because we possess the future.

Snapshot 5: Builder-leaders work for an audience of one (4:1–5)

In chapter 4, Paul reminds his readers that the model of leadership and ministry he is describing is one of servanthood and accountability. But accountability to whom? He is not consumer-driven. He will not let his critics in Corinth bind his conscience with their criticism. His sense of calling and esteem comes from God. He is not a slave to the praise or blame of men. He adds in verse 3, "I do not even judge myself." We talk about leaders who are their own toughest critic. Even this way of thinking means boasting in men because it makes human judgment (my own!) supreme. Only God can judge his builders. Only the boss gets to evaluate his team. And we must await his final judgment of our work when the Lord returns (v. 5). On that day, our hidden motives and agendas will be revealed, and our work judged by the Lord of the city of God.

So to prepare for that day, we need to turn from the distortions and deceptions of human judgment and see our work in light of eternity. This eternal perspective will keep us working in great humility and dependence

11. Fee, *First Epistle to the Corinthians*, 155–56.

12. Hays, *First Corinthians*, 60.

on him and his power. As Fee comments: "Paul says that the Corinthians are to regard him and Apollos in the terms just described, as servants. But his new point is that although he 'belongs' to them (since he is Christ's servant for them), he is not accountable to them. What is required of household stewards is faithfulness (v. 2), and only the master of the house can make that determination (vv. 4b, 5c)."[13]

Snapshot 6: Builder-leaders build by the book (4:6)

The apostle warns ministers to "learn by us not to go beyond what was written." If I become arrogant and think my way is better than God's way, I can neglect Scripture, marginalize the gospel, and turn my ministry into a Babel project, full of human pride to make my name known. There is no room for boasting. Everything we bring to ministry is a gift from God to be used according to the Scriptures and in the power of the Spirit.

Commentators acknowledge the challenge of interpreting the phrase "not going beyond what was written." There are several possibilities, but the one most-recommended view takes its cue from the reference to *gegratptai* (writings), which almost always in Paul's letters refers to the Old Testament Scriptures. So the injunction should be taken as "live according to the Scriptures."

Snapshot 7: Builder-leaders build with blood, sweat, and tears

In 4:8–13, Paul makes it clear that following the book doesn't mean smooth sailing. Effective ministry involves plenty of pain and suffering. Nothing is accomplished without sacrifice. That is true of the gospel, and it is true of our ministry as well. In verse 8, with evident sarcasm, Paul describes the mentality of the troublemakers: "Already you have all you want: Already you have become rich! Without us you have become kings." Paul wants them to be full of the riches of God, but he knows there is only one path to glory— the way of Good Friday leading to Easter Sunday. Cross power thus is not only the message we preach, but the pattern of our work.

What of the leaders in whom the Corinthians boast: Paul, Jesus, Apollos, Peter—what was the cost of their ministry? Paul pulls out the receipts in verses 9–13:

> For I think that God has exhibited us apostles as last of all, like
> men sentenced to death, because we have become a spectacle to

13. Fee, *First Epistle to the Corinthians*, 158.

the world, to angels, and to men. We are fools for Christ's sake, but you are wise in Christ. We are weak, but you are strong. You are held in honor, but we in disrepute. To the present hour we hunger and thirst, we are poorly dressed and buffeted and homeless, and we labor, working with our own hands. When reviled, we bless; when persecuted, we endure; when slandered, we entreat. We have become, and are still, like the scum of the world, the refuse of all things.

Paul presents the upside-down thinking of the cross, where going down is the way up and where dying makes one genuinely alive. What does this cross pattern accomplish in ministry? It leads to the flourishing of the local church. If ministry is so hard then why doesn't Paul just give up and find a new job? Cross power keeps him in the game. Good Fridays of disappointment and loss will always lead to Easters of resurrection power, spiritual progress, and church flourishing. Getting used to this is key to builders who last and who build to last.

How can we apply this difficult text to our churches today? Gordon Fee suggests two important applications. The first application concerns putting ourselves in the shoes of the Corinthians:

We need to become more aware of the Corinthian side of this text than we tend to. That is, we try desperately to identify with Paul, when in fact we are probably much more like the Corinthians than any of us dare admit. We are rich, well-filled, etc.; and all too often that blinds us to our desperate needs. As Barrett notes (p. 113), between Paul's and the Corinthians' views of ministry "there can be little doubt which conception . . . corresponds more closely to the Lord's command (e.g., Mark viii. 34f.)."

The second application involves rethinking our relationship with a fallen world:

Perhaps if we were truly more like our Lord, standing more often in opposition to the status quo with its worldly wisdom and more often in favor of justice, we too would know more about what it means to be scum in the eyes of the world's "beautiful" or "powerful" people.[14]

14. Fee, *First Epistle to the Corinthians*, 182.

Snapshot 8: Builder-leaders emulate apostolic builders (4:14–21)

Not only do builder-leaders follow the Old Testament (4:6), but they follow the apostles:

> I do not write these things to make you ashamed, but to admonish you as my beloved children. For though you have countless guides in Christ, you do not have many fathers. For I became your father in Christ Jesus through the gospel. I urge you, then, be imitators of me. That is why I sent you Timothy, my beloved and faithful child in the Lord, to remind you of my ways in Christ, as I teach them everywhere in every church. Some are arrogant, as though I were not coming to you. But I will come to you soon, if the Lord wills, and I will find out not the talk of these arrogant people but their power. For the kingdom of God does not consist in talk but in power. What do you wish? Shall I come to you with a rod, or with love in a spirit of gentleness? (ESV)

Paul asserts three ways in which ministers of the gospel then and now can emulate apostolic builders. First, he calls us to follow their model. In verse 16, he tells them to "be imitators of me." Follow the same pattern of life and work he has described in these chapters. Paul even sent Timothy to teach them more about the way cross-powered ministry should be conducted (4:17).

Second, seek apostolic feedback. Even though Paul has warned against submitting one's work to the judgment of men, he does encourage them to submit to apostolic authority and criticism. Note verses 18 and 19: "Some are arrogant, as though I were not coming to you. But I will come to you soon if the Lord wills, and I will find out not the talk of these arrogant people but their power." Paul is not going to do a theological audit only. When he comes, he will do a power audit of the church. Are they building up the church or tearing it down? Are they deepening unity, or are they sowing division? Love is the test of effective ministry.

Thirdly, accept apostolic rebuke. Paul indicates that if their approach to ministry does not change, he will come with a rod (4:21). Paul wants to come in love and a spirit of gentleness (4:21b), but he has the right and authority as God's builder to admonish those who are not building well.

These then are the snapshots of the builder-leader. In these eight ways, Paul seeks to apply cross power to the way we lead and use power in the church. His great idea? *Builder-leaders build to last.* And the only way they can build to last is by building in a way that is different than the world, follows the pattern of the cross into suffering, emulates apostolic builders, and seeks to please the Lord of the building and not a human audience. How can we learn how to build to last as we work within the church around the world today? Let's explore some possible applications of this great idea.

EXPLORING APPLICATIONS

Let me conclude by suggesting five ways that we can build to last in our specific ministries.

Application 1: Character matters—The power of humility

One of the classic texts on organizational effectiveness is *Good to Great: Why Some Companies Make the Leap . . . And Others Don't*,[15] by Stanford professor Jim Collins. One of the many principles Collins identifies is the level-five leader, someone who combines deep personal humility with a passionate commitment to do the right thing for the company and customer. Level-four leaders are more common. They are ego-driven leaders that love the limelight and do what will win them the accolades of their peers. But level-four leaders are seldom successful for long. Eventually, their own self-orientation gets in the way of doing the right thing in the right way.

Paul describes the level-five leader in 1 Cor 3–4. Corinthian house churches were awash with level-four leaders. That's why there was so much strife. Spiritual pride and one-upmanship were dividing the church. What was needed was humility. Rick Warren famously defined humility as not thinking less of yourself, but thinking of yourself less.[16] Paul might add that humility is not only thinking of yourself less, but thinking of God more. God is the one who makes things grow. The Corinthian church is part of his global temple that he is preparing for his eternal and glorious dwelling with humanity. Whatever gifts or offices of ministry we have are from him and not from ourselves.

David Brooks defines humility as "freedom from the need to prove you are superior all the time."[17] How do I know when I am leading from an attitude of pride and not humility? One of the telltale signs for me is contempt. Contempt is looking down on others, discounting their contribution, exaggerating their weakness, and downplaying their strengths. Contempt is "the feeling that a person or a thing is beneath consideration, worthless, or

---

15. Collins, *Good to Great*.

16. Warren, *Purpose Driven Life*, 148.

17. Brooks, quoted in Choung and Pfeiffer, *Longing for Revival*, loc. 1912 of 3765.

deserving scorn."[18] It doesn't take too much imagination to predict what contempt will do in a church or Christian organization. Not only does it demoralize team members, but it produces a spirit of enmity that cripples the effectiveness of ministry.

But how do I get humility? Cross power can produce humility in the heart. As we internalize the Phil 2 journey of our Lord from privilege to poverty, and sacrifice all for the sake of our salvation, we expose the lie that only the loud and the proud win the race. The Spirit of God, the power that raised Christ from the dead, is turned off by pride, but turned on by humility. To leaders, Paul is saying clearly, repent of contempt, turn from pride, and walk after the one who, though equal with God, emptied himself and became a servant even to death.

Application 2: Become your own best critic

Criticism is one of the toughest things to take in leadership. Whether one is leading a Bible study or a megachurch, criticism can rob the leader of joy, motivation, and confidence. Paul deals with the criticism problem in chapters 3–4. He warns against the extremes of being blown away by criticism or becoming deaf to it. Instead, an effective leader must become one's own best critic by engaging in an ongoing internal dialogue with God. Only God has the right to judge, but he may speak through others, and he may speak through conscience.

One reason many avoid this internal dialogue with God is because they have a wrong view of what it means to do ministry. Whether we are in full-time paid ministry or volunteer in the church, we must avoid thinking of what we do as just another job. Richard Hays elaborates: "Paul's call to self-scrutiny should be taken with the utmost seriousness. Our habit of thinking of ministry as a 'profession' is likely to produce serious distortions in our conception of the church and our role within it. Are we using the church as though it were ours, or as though it were an instrument for the advancement of our own careers or causes?"[19]

We must be introspective because we will be judged—not our salvation, but our relevance to his mission. Hays states:

> Teachers and preachers should read and deal with the full passage, making clear that it is not about "purgatory" or about individuals but about the church's structural wholeness; at the same

18. Choung and Pfeiffer, *Longing for Revival*, loc. 1872 of 3765.

19. Hays, *First Corinthians*, 61.

time, we should emphasize that the passage portrays a God who will not tolerate pride and divisiveness. Judgment and grace are inseparable elements of the whole biblical message. Without the reality of judgment, there would be no grace at all, but only benign divine indifference.[20]

Criticism is never easy to take, but when we channel criticism, whether from the congregation or our conscience, into a conversation with our Almighty and all-loving Father, it becomes a constructive and life-giving exercise that can remotivate and reinvigorate one's ministry.

Application 3: See your role as an ambassador (not a king) of reconciliation

Paul will write to the Corinthian church in the future about the centrality of the "ministry of reconciliation" and of church leaders as "ambassadors" who promote reconciliation wherever they find themselves (2 Cor 5). But we don't have to wait until the second letter to hear Paul address the role of the leader as a peacemaker rather than a troublemaker. That theme is implicit in the chapters before us. House church leaders were acting as though rival house churches were competitors for the spiritual market share of Corinth. Effective leaders seek to build cooperative, not competitive, relationships with other churches as best as they can. Hays pushes this point:

> The passage contains an urgent call for the unity of the church. All our denominational and interdenominational divisions are in the last analysis simply silly; where squabbles persist, it is a sure sign that we are putting human wisdom and human boasting in the way of God's design to build a unified community. We are acting as though the various churches were franchise operations like McDonald's and Burger King and Wendy's, each hustling for a market share.[21]

We don't need to fall into "co-operitis," where we are hesitant to do anything unless we are doing it in concert with others. At the same time, when it comes to serving our cities, engaging in global ministry, or meeting the needs of the marginalized and refugees in our communities, there are great opportunities for cooperation that should not be missed. Working side by side with other churches can be a significant step in displaying a visible unity in the body of King Jesus and strengthening our witness to the world.

20. Hays, *First Corinthians*, 63–64.
21. Hays, *First Corinthians*, 62.

Application 4: Let God take the heat

Richard Hays reminds us that the passage before us is not just a critique of human leadership. It is also a celebration of divine leadership:

> The passage's conclusion points again to the cosmic scope of the gospel message. The God whom we worship rightly claims us because he is the creator and Lord of the universe. Because we are in Christ, we participate in the reality of God's dominion and therefore are set free from anxiety and petty scrambling for human approval. Paul and Apollos and Cephas here (v. 22) symbolize any group allegiances that trick us into groveling around before human authorities or trying to manipulate people into joining our party. We all belong to God; if we believed that and acted on it, it would simplify our lives enormously—and, at the same time, heal our divisions.[22]

When we throw ourselves all-in for ministry, we may feel the exhilaration that can come from having a purpose. But we can also feel the pressure for results. Burn out happens when we take all of the pressure of work on our own shoulders. God is building his church around the world. We are his partners, but his junior partners. Let him take the heat.

Paul is frank about the pain and suffering that go with an effective ministry. But he does not call for stoicism and the stiff upper lip. He calls for faith in the good news that the God that turns Good Fridays into Easter Sundays for his people will do it for you and in your ministry.

Application 5: Lead along the "U" curve

Life and ministry don't follow straight lines. For those outside of Christ, life may look like an inverted "u," more like an "n" shape. We start low in childhood and then reach our peak physically and career-wise somewhere in our adulthood. But then it is all downhill until death.

Because of the gospel of King Jesus, life for his followers is u-shaped. It is a series of journeys from success to sacrifice, from high to low. But at the bottom of the "u," if we hold on to our Lord for dear life, he lifts us up in new and greater ways. Even our own physical death will follow the "u" curve, where we will descend into the jaws of this final enemy only to be raised in a new body and a transformed inner being for life eternal in the kingdom of God. He brings us low only to lift us high.

---

22. Hays, *First Corinthians*, 64.

Luther spoke of churches of the cross versus churches of glory. Churches of glory are those that love success and attention and the praise of men. What they hate is suffering, marginalization, criticism, and failure. They will do anything to avoid these things, even changing the gospel so that only the triumphalist notes are sung. Luther contrasted churches of glory with churches of the cross. Churches of the cross endure suffering and contempt, knowing that it will not last forever and that the same Lord who died and rose from the dead will lift these churches of the cross up eventually and fill them with fruit and effectiveness. When I think of the evangelical movement in the United States and in many parts of the world in the 1920s and 1930s, when nonevangelical churches were full and conservative churches were relegated to the margins, I marvel at the reversal we have seen in the century since. But evangelical success today can produce a pride and triumphalism that will lead to the bottom of the "u" where God must do the radical surgery of humility before we can be lifted up to relevance for his mission once again.

Chicago's 1871 fire may have ruined a city, but it may have saved thousands more from a similar fate. New builders arose who changed their attitude, changed their materials, and, in so doing, helped to change the urban world we know today. Paul is calling for a similar paradigm change. We need to hear that call today. Builder-leaders of the new world unite!

Chapter 5

A Renewed Community

Practicing Our Citizenship in the New Creation

"Hope is the ability to hear the music of the future; faith is the courage to dance to it today."[1]

—PETER KUZMIC

READ: 1 COR 5:1—6:11

I will never forget living in Kenya following the 2007 presidential election. The incumbent corrupted the vote-tallying process and stole the election. Through the first six months of 2008, Kenya was traumatized by a horrific explosion of interethnic violence. Kenyans of one tribe slaughtered Kenyans from the neighboring tribe. What I found especially distressing was the realization that the majority of Kenyans (the same ones engaging in such horrors) were professing Christians. As I interviewed leaders across the country, I heard story after story of pastors encouraging and blessing the young men to go and engage in Joshua-like conquest of "those people" from the other ethnic community. The church of Kenya had no voice to call for reconciliation between parties in the conflict because everyone was aware

1. "Inspirational Quotes," 9.

that some of the burning of homes and slaughter of "others" was being done in Jesus' name. This is the bitter fruit of superficial and ineffectual discipleship. Transformation of deep-rooted convictions did not take place at any more than the surface level, and thus, in a time of crisis, these Christians did not see reality from the perspective of Jesus. Instead, the default setting that dominated the thinking and behavior in the crisis was the same ethnic-based "life-world"[2] that shaped their minds and hearts since early childhood. Instead of seeing persons from other ethnic communities with the eyes of Jesus, Kenyan Christians often perceived threatening enemies who were the ancient foes of "our kind of people."

Have you ever been upset by this question: Why, in the name of Jesus, do those who profess obedience to Jesus' teaching do things that are in such sharp contrast to his ideals? Christians are people of the resurrection who are filled with the Spirit. We really are living in God's new creation. However, throughout the global church today, Christians are schizophrenic. We have divided minds and hearts, and when crisis erupts, professing Christians often behave in ways which are antithetical to the example and teachings of Jesus. When we Christians do seriously incongruous things, we throw up major road blocks which can hinder seekers from encountering Jesus. John Stott said that "the greatest hindrance to the advance of the gospel worldwide is the failure of God's people to live like God's people."[3]

Certainly this stunning incongruity, which is the fruit of ineffectual approaches to discipleship, is not only a crisis in Africa. Among many American "evangelicals"[4] there is evidence that very little transformation has taken place. Aside from one hour on Sunday morning, the majority of us seem to think and act like folks who are "red, white, and blue" all the way to the bone. What Martin Luther King, Jr. said half a century ago still is true: "We must face the fact that in America, the church is still the most

2. "life-world" refers to the "common sense knowledge" which is the knowledge I share with others in the normal, self-evident routines of everyday life. It provides a coherent meaning structure. Sociologists choose this label as opposed to "worldview." Worldview is typically seen as being more thoroughly cognitive and is normally learned through formal means. The "life-world" is a shared world. It is "pre-reflective." See Berger and Luckmann, Social Construction of Reality.

3. John Stott, in his last published sermon, quoted by Oh, "Gospel Strategy of Christ-Like Leadership," para. 1.

4. The "brand" evangelical has now become tragically misunderstood in the US in the twenty-first century. Popular use in the media does not grasp theological distinctions. Thus this strong, historic label is increasingly useless in communicating in public contexts. When this label is used in this chapter, I will be referring to its historic significance rather than the current sense. The Lausanne Movement is the custodian of the evangelical tradition in this era (see www.lausanne.org and study the Lausanne Covenant). On the definition of evangelical, see Hindmarsh, "What Is Evangelicalism?"

segregated major institution in America. At 11:00 on Sunday morning when we stand and sing and Christ has no east or west, we stand at the most segregated hour in this nation."[5]

Three decades ago, Brueggemann wrote, "The contemporary American church is so largely enculturated to the American ethos of consumerism that it has little power to believe or to act."[6] This remains true today. When we confront upheavals and we feel that our prosperity is threatened, we do not perceive with the mind of Christ. In crisis, we revert to "me first and America first"—the way of thinking that shaped us as we were socialized in our culture of origin.[7] As a result, we have lost our voice and are not seen as credible agents of love and justice. Today the US church is failing to be salt and light.

The great ideas which can liberate us in the twenty-first century are rooted in Paul's Spirit-inspired guidance to this young Christian community. Let's explore 5—6:11 as a case study of how a pastoral leader provides skilled spiritual direction which guides a community as they shift toward becoming a new-creation community. If we are to flourish as persons, each one of us must unlearn the values and worldview of our before-Christ culture and be formed by the new-creation community vision.

5. King, "MLK at Western," 22.

6. Brueggemann, *Prophetic Imagination,* 11.

7. As I write this in 2020, the polling data continues to reveal that 75 percent of US "evangelicals" are doggedly supportive of a US president whose words and decisions in the first three and a half years of his administration have been to a shocking extent 100 percent antithetical to the clear teachings of Jesus (Shellnutt, "White Evangelicals Are Actually for Trump," paras. 2 and 8). While we say we believe the Bible, we are loyal in our embrace of a leader who models a lifestyle of greed and conspicuous consumption (what Jesus called "mammon worship"), a man who proudly denigrates women as toys, is off the charts as far as mendacity is concerned, actively promotes hatred and white supremacy, and looks for a diversity of ways to crush the poor and the aliens. Compared to a previous LifeWay Research survey conducted in the months leading up to the 2016 election, more white evangelicals say they plan to vote for Trump in 2020 (73 percent to 65 percent). President Trump's advantage among evangelicals, however, comes primarily from white evangelicals (73 percent) (Earls, "Evangelical Vote Once Again Split," para. 9). Trump did not win the 2020 election. For a careful analysis of this cultural-political phenomenon see Posner, *Unholy.*

GREAT IDEA: LEADERS SHAPE COMMUNITY
THROUGH RESOCIALIZATION BY THE SPIRIT

Paul is guiding the resocialization process in 1 Cor 5–6

Paul's letter is pastoral counsel which responds to the issues as they surface in his interaction with the believers from Corinth. Keep in mind that
the Christian movement is moving into new territory as a result of Paul's
evangelistic efforts (see Rom 15:18–20) and these friends in Corinth are
relatively new to this movement. As is normal and inevitable, the new
Christ-followers come into Christ[8] with all their old Corinthian paradigms.
These recent converts do not come out of a long history of Judeo-Christian
social values. Life as they have known it in pagan Corinth prior to their
conversion seems normal. This is not a case of "backsliding," as old-time
Christians used to say; newly baptized disciples still have all the old values deeply rooted in them. So coming into Jesus requires a comprehensive
immersion into the culture of the new creation. Please be sure to notice
that this is about a community. Our Christian life is not merely a private,
personal relationship experience.

What do we mean by *resocialization?* Here is our working definition
which undergirds this great idea: resocialization is a process which takes
place over time and through which a community comes to embrace new
values, explanatory options, and attitudes. It is a journey we take together
which transforms our original values and assumptions about life and gives
us new ways of seeing everything. For followers of Jesus, our deepest identity and most profound sense of belonging must become the reality that we
are in Christ.

In chapter 5, Paul intervenes in a sensitive scandal involving sexual
immorality on the part of professing believers in the young church. Observe
in verses 2 and 6 that Paul confronts the community (not the sinner). He
rebukes them for misguided pride. "And you are proud! Shouldn't you be
deeply saddened instead? Shouldn't you have thrown out of your church
the man doing this?" (v. 2; the pronoun "you" is plural in these texts). "Your
bragging is not good. It is like yeast" (v. 6).

We should think for a moment about reasons for such an attitude of
tolerance. It is plausible to infer that a gnosticlike value system[9] was a part of

8. The phrases "into Christ" and "in Christ" are identified with quotation marks to
highlight that these expressions are Paul's preferred way of referring to persons who are
born-again believers. (Paul does not use that expression, although he would not object.
He very rarely uses the word "Christian.")

9. Strictly speaking, there is no genuine Gnosticism in its developed form until the

the worldview that the Corinthian converts brought with them from the old culture. In much Hellenistic thought and culture, the physical body was devalued and what took place in this discounted material realm was regarded as of no consequence for the enlightened. Equally plausible is an explanation that traces the attitude to a distorted understanding of the "freedom" of the truly "wise" man according to the ideas in popular Hellenistic philosophy.[10]

Let me summarize the key ideas emphasized by Paul as the apostle takes this problem and guides the community on the discipleship journey.

Resocialized to become a community rooted in our union with Christ

In chapter 5, we discover Paul reinforcing again the value that the Corinthians are to see themselves as a community bound to one another in Christ. The entire community of believers must deal with this scandal since what affects one family member affects all of us. "Don't you know that just a little yeast makes the whole batch of dough rise? Get rid of the old yeast. Then you can be like a new batch of dough without yeast. That is what you really are. . ." (vv. 6–7).

We in the West have difficulty accepting that we are woven into a corporate family. These early Christians were shaped by a culture which had a different sense of what it means to be a person. Their paradigm is much closer to reality. "Paul is saying then that individual Christians in their corporeal existence are the various body parts of the corporate personality of Christ through which the life of Christ is expressed."[11] One implication of such a consciousness of our interconnectedness as persons was a sense that since we together are a body, then our body (i.e., community) must guard itself against disease or pollution.

---

second century AD. But many of the themes and values that would be synthesized into second-century gnostic systems were in circulation in diverse cultures in ancient Hellenism. See Yamauchi, *Pre-Christian Gnosticism* for a careful review of historical data.

10. Words and phrases such as "the enlightened," "the wise," and "freedom" are specialized words and phrases in Hellenistic philosophy, which was popular entertainment in Corinth and therefore seems to have influenced the Corinthian community. See Hays, *First Corinthians*.

11. Clapp, "Tacit Holiness," 68.

Resocialized to become a community which experiences the presence of the risen Christ

Paul reminds them that they are a community which lives together with the risen Jesus who is mystically present among them. Paul reinforces the reality of the Lord's presence in verse 4: "So when you come together, I will be with you in spirit. The power of our Lord Jesus will also be with you." Jesus is present when we gather. And because Jesus is present when we gather, we are a community which can discern the mind of the Lord and can hear his voice. This is also true of us today. Most of us who were socialized in North America were formed to operate in a naturalistic life-world. Engaging with spiritual forces and beings is not normal. This is a huge paradigm shift for most of us as we learn to live in the new creation. But Father, Son, and Holy Spirit are actually among us when we gather. C. S. Lewis wrote, "His presence, the interaction between Him and us, must always be the overwhelming dominant factor in the life we are to lead within the Body; any conception of Christian fellowship which does not mean primarily fellowship with Him is out of court."[12]

Resocialized to become a community which makes wise decisions

Paul also emphasizes that the gathered community can judge truthfully and lovingly through the power of Jesus. Note that in verses 4–5 it is the community gathered in Jesus' presence which is urged to deal with this "brother." It's not a grand jury situation. It's a mystical gathering in the Spirit. To grasp the discernment process at work here, we must imagine house church dynamics. Let your mind picture a community of twenty-five or thirty persons who have shared deeply in all aspects of life for six months or a year or more. We have shared our common meal together weekly. We have learned together and walked together. We know each other's names and families. We have borne one another's burdens. We share our finances as needed.

Then as weeks pass, we become acutely aware that something has changed in the life of one of our brothers. He rarely joins us for the *agapē* meal these days. When he participates, he is guarded and evasive. He does not pray when we call on the Father together. He no longer confesses sin or expresses a need for prayer. We are all troubled by his demeanor.

The friend who was always closest to this brother, attempts to draw near to him and break through his recent defensiveness. But this friend's inquiries are rejected. We see less and less of the brother and his attitude

12. Lewis, *Weight of Glory*, 35.

to all of us is increasingly hostile. He refuses to listen to the counsel of his community and eventually the truth surfaces. He is involved in a messy immoral tryst. We attempt to sit down with him one-on-one. But he rebuffs the invitation. To a greater and greater degree, his heart becomes hard and he is insensitive to the counsel of friends and elders. Finally he is defiant and will not agree to meet with any from the family of Jesus.

This is the setting we must keep in mind as we seek to read the chapter 5 situation. It's not dealt with by the elders in a closed-door session. This is a family being devastated by one of us who is walking away on a path of self-destruction.

Resocialized to become a community which speaks truth in love in order to restore

The teaching in chapter 5 that is most upsetting to many of us in our none-of-your-business culture is Paul's counsel that the community should confront this brother as an act of love. "When you come together like this, hand this man over to Satan. Then the power of sin in his life will be destroyed. His spirit will be saved on the day the Lord returns" (v. 5). We immediately recoil from the language, "Expel the sinful brother." It sounds so antithetical to Jesus' ethic of love. It brings to mind the horrors of the Inquisition. But German pastor-theologian Dietrich Bonhoeffer helps us rethink this emotional reaction.

> Reproof is unavoidable. God's Word demands it when a brother falls into open sin . . . Where defection from God's Word in doctrine or life imperils the family fellowship and with it the whole congregation, the word of admonition and rebuke must be ventured. Nothing can be more cruel than the tenderness that consigns another to his sin. Nothing can be more compassionate than the severe rebuke that calls a brother back from the path of sin. It is a ministry of mercy, an ultimate offer of genuine fellowship, when we allow nothing but God's Word to stand between us, judging and succoring. Then it is not we who are judging; God alone judges, and God's judgment is helpful and healing . . . we serve (the brother) even when we must speak the judging and dividing Word of God to him, even when, in obedience to God, we must break off fellowship with him . . . He who accepts the ministry of God's judgment is helped."[13]

13. Bonhoeffer, *Life Together*, 107.

Paul urges the Corinthians to be a community which speaks the truth in love. We must realize that it can be a loving act to dis-illusion someone who is caught in a self-destructive trap. With a liturgical refrain, Paul calls to mind the reality that this is a community which has been set free from the slavery of old ways. "Christ our Passover has been sacrificed for us. Therefore, let's feast !" (vv. 7–8).

Resocialized to become a community which never withdraws from its witness to the world

Paul addresses a sometimes confusing aspect of our new identity as God's holy community. We are called to be "in the world, but not of the world" (John 17). He affirms that we are a community that is free to be involved with others in our society and to follow Jesus' example and welcome "sinners."[14] Paul helps the Corinthians avoid a dead-end misunderstanding of separationism: "I wrote a letter to you to tell you to stay away from people who commit sexual sins. I didn't mean the people of this world who sin in this way. . . . I didn't mean those who cheat or who worship statues of gods. In that case you would have to leave this world!" (vv. 9–10). We have a long history of misunderstanding the teaching of the apostle, even as these Corinthian believers did. Hauerwas explains Paul's emphasis:

> Paul does not fear the pollution of the church by contact between the Christian and the non-Christian, but he does think that the disguised presence within the church of a representative from the outside, from the cosmos, that should be 'out there,' threatens the whole body . . . The body of Christ is not polluted by mere contact with the cosmos or by the body's presence in the midst of the corrupt cosmos.[15]

So a church that follows Jesus' teaching and example is a community that embraces sinners.

Yet simultaneously, Paul says we are a community with clear boundaries and a definite sense of belonging. An authentic community discerns who is in and who is an outsider. Paul clarifies this identity issue: "But here is what I am writing to you now. You must stay away from anyone who claims to be a believer but does evil things. Stay away from anyone who commits sexual

14. Why do I have quotation marks around "sinners?" Jesus is described as a "friend of sinners" in Luke 15:1–2. There is a note of irony in Luke's Gospel. Persons looked down on in the society were the ones most responsive to God's invitation. Who really are the "sinners" in God's eyes?

15. Hauerwas, "Sanctified Body," 27.

sins. Stay away from anyone who always wants more and more things. Stay away from anyone who worships statues of gods. Stay away from anyone who tells lies about others . . . Don't even eat with people like these" (v. 11).

So in chapter 5, Paul skillfully, lovingly addresses this sin problem and turns it into an opportunity for formation of the church on the pathway to becoming a radical community of resurrection people. His guidance is founded on the cross and resurrection of Jesus.

Resocialized to become a community which makes the tough decisions inside the church and not outside it

In 6:1–8, the presenting issue is believers bringing lawsuits against other believers and using the Roman court system. Richard Hays argues[16] that there is, in all likelihood, an issue of socioeconomic class warfare within the Corinthian church, since courts in Roman society were so readily manipulated by the wealthy (as they are now in the USA). Hellenistic culture created a highly stratified society—like a caste system. Upper-class members of the community were socialized to assume that their privileged situation and the resulting injustice were normal. But the attitude expressed by the Corinthian Christians of higher socioeconomic status by their determination to exploit the poorer members of the church is, "in Christ," the complete antithesis of the "mind of Christ" (see Phil 2).

So another core value of the new-creation community is at stake here. The value is that in Christ there is no rich-versus-poor or slave-versus-freeman. This core value is on display in the Jerusalem church described in Acts. The dynamics of that community seen in Acts 4:32–35 are not evidence of some kind of end-of-the-world fanaticism. The fact that "there were no needy persons among them" (v. 34) is the result of the comprehensive "oneness" noted in verse 32a, which was the result of a radical change in the human heart brought about by the filling of the Holy Spirit. It is hard to imagine a more profound change of a person's heart than the one reflected in the words, "no one claimed that any of his possessions was his own" (v. 32b). This freedom to let go of possessions is central to being the new-creation community and reflects the vision of the early church which was that it was the community in which God's covenant values[17] were to be fulfilled "on earth as it is in heaven."

---

16. Hays, *First Corinthians*, 93.

17. The first Christian community described in Acts is a community which sees itself as the eschatological fulfillment of God's new covenant promises to Israel. It was therefore necessary for these early believers to embody in their practices the

For Paul as well, the process of forming a new-creation movement demands embracing a new value system that mimics the ways of Jesus. Paul reframes this lawsuit challenge in chapter 6 in light of the Jesus story (which is *reality*). The community must guard this new identity and guard against behaviors that will tend to drag everyone back into the old system of death. There is a need for vigilance since a new identity and corresponding value system is fragile in the early period of formation. The old ways, i.e., demanding what is mine, still seem so normal.

Resurrection-age living is a way of life in which Jesus' values are gladly embraced. A—perhaps *the*—central value of Jesus' way is beautifully described in Paul's letter to the new-creation community in the very Roman town of Philippi[18]:

> In his very nature he was God. Jesus was equal with God. But Jesus didn't take advantage of that fact. Instead, he made himself nothing. He did this by taking on the nature of a servant. He was made just like human beings. He appeared as a man. He was humble and obeyed God completely. He did this even though it led to his death. Even worse, he died on a cross! (2:6–8 NIRV)

The value system which flows out of Jesus' example is made explicit in the verses just prior to this summary of the new framing story:

> . . . agree with one another. Have the same love. Be one in Spirit and in the way you think and act. By doing this, you will make my joy complete. Don't do anything only to get ahead. Don't do it because you are proud. Instead, be humble. Value others more than yourselves. None of you should look out just for your own good. Each of you should also look out for the good of others.

---

inauguration of the new age because they experienced the resurrection and the pouring out of the Spirit. They really experienced the fulfillment of Jer 31:31–34. Empowered by the Spirit, they could do what the covenant with God required and make the Year of Jubilee a reality in their new creation community. They put into practice Deut 15:8, 10: "do not be hardhearted or tightfisted toward your poor brother . . . Give generously to him and do so without a grudging heart . . . I command you to be openhanded toward your brothers and toward the poor and needy in your midst." This was the beginning of the new creation. Therefore they welcomed God's word and let the alternative value system become the new normal.

18. I heartily recommend the thorough exegetical study by Michael J. Gorman, *Cruciformity: Paul's Narrative Spirituality of the Cross*. Gorman demonstrates that Paul's "master narrative" (5) is presented in Phil 2, and that this brief but rich poetic description of the center of Jesus' life and ministry is foundational to everything Paul believes concerning God, himself, spirituality, and ministry. Gorman refers to the value system which flows out of the "Jesus-narrative" as "cruciformity"(88).

As you deal with one another, you should think and act as Jesus
did. (2:2–5 NIRV)

In view of this central moral value demonstrated in Jesus' life, taking
a believer (brother) to court is evidence of a present-evil-age value system.
Hauling you before the Roman judge says, "I must get what is mine, no
matter what. I have power to abuse and coerce you. I will not be deprived."
But Paul reminds his friends (and us) that we are "eschatological people."[19]
We are being transformed through resocialization to embrace the reality
that already we have begun to live this resurrection life according to the
new-creation ethical standards in our radical community. We are people
of the Spirit and therefore have been given the capacity for knowing the
mind of Christ (remember 1 Cor 2:16). Paul wants Christians to accept
that we are called to "rule over" creation in God's new age. (v. 3) But the
assignment to rule is not an opportunity for arrogance and expressions of
present-evil-age power.

Note that there is nothing intrinsically evil about the principle of a
government establishing a justice system. To sue is "to use a legal process by
which you try to get a court of law to force a person that has treated you un-
fairly or hurt you in some way to give you something or to do something."[20]
This is morally acceptable in the present-evil-age realities. However, bringing a suit against another Christian in the Roman law courts in Corinth
brought a huge amount of shame on the reputation of the Christian movement. In Paul's day, the church was a new religious movement, and an
often-misunderstood phenomenon in the cities of the empire. There were
lots of rumors circulating around the cities of the empire about this strange

19. Quite often, New Testament scholars will employ this word "eschatological."
Eschatology refers to the study of the end times. By calling the Corinthian church an
eschatological community, we are meaning that even now in this time prior to the end
of history as we know it, people who are "in Christ" are enjoying in a limited, but very
real, sense the blessings of God's new creation. Today, even while the present evil age
continues, Christ-followers taste the age to come and are partners with God in transforming today's world into the new world that God intends.

20. *Merriam-Webster*, s.v., "sue," https://www.merriam-webster.com/dictionary/sue.

"cannibalistic cult."[21] To add further scandal by taking to the courts to solve our conflicts is missiologically[22]counterproductive. This is also true today.

However, there are situations in which seeking justice from a government's judicial system is required. In itself, going to court is not sin. It is often a tragic necessity when the church is dysfunctional and failing in its calling to be a community which discerns Jesus' voice. For example, in far too many cases abused women must seek from the court system protection and justice in their society since churches far too frequently represent the same abusive patriarchy that exists in the pagan culture. In this case, the woman who needs justice is not wrong to appeal to the courts. Her church family has failed her. When we fail to pursue the resocialization process then the old ways still seem quite normal.

So why is choosing to sue another Christ-follower in a pagan court a bad idea? Paul is confident that the believing community has amazing resources for dealing with day-to-day conflicts, since it is indwelt by the Holy Spirit (6:1B–4). Paul revealed in chapter 2 that Christians have access to deep wisdom. It is based on this experiential reality (the Spirit really is present in the community) that Paul sees the incongruity of going to pagan judges for justice. He writes:

> Why not take it to the Lord's people? Or don't you know that the Lord's people will judge the world? Since this is true, aren't you able to judge small cases? Don't you know that we will judge angels? Then we should be able to judge the things of this life even more! So suppose you disagree with one another in matters like this. Who do you ask to decide which of you is right? (NIRV)

Note this assumes we do have conflicts among Christ-followers. This is inevitable in community. We disagree. We hurt and harm each other. But the new thing that must be evident in Christ is that when we are wronged or when we do wrong, we have better ways of sorting things out than the

21. One of the most scurrilous charges against early Christians was that they practiced ritual cannibalism. These charges were common enough that numerous second-century writers felt constrained to refute them. The earliest explicit reference we have comes from Justin Martyr in Palestine around the year AD 150. A few decades later in North Africa, Tertullian employed mock exaggeration to refute the claims: "Come! plunge the knife into the baby, nobody's enemy, guilty of nothing, everybody's child . . . catch the infant blood; steep your bread with it; eat and enjoy it" (*Apol.* 8.2).

22. By "missiological," in this context, we mean that such public disgrace has a negative impact on the church's mission. The church's mission is to be a working model of the power of Jesus to reconcile and to bring shalom. In current conversation a missional church is a community of God's people that defines itself by, and organizes its life around, its real purpose of being an agent of God's mission to the world.

normal course of events in the present evil age. Litigation violates the new-creation ethic. Even if you win the settlement, you lose. This is not Jesus' way (see again Phil 2). We must be resocialized into this upside-down way of thinking: "When you take another believer to court, you have lost the battle already. Why not be treated wrongly? Why not be cheated? Instead, you yourselves cheat and do wrong. And you do it to your brothers and sisters. Don't you know that people who do wrong will not receive God's kingdom? Don't be fooled" (1 Cor 6:7–9 NIRV).

So for these reasons, Paul urges the community members to opt for the better way. He grounds this counsel in the eschatological identity of the community. He reminds his friends, "You Christians are those who inherit the kingdom of God."[23] People professing to be in Christ who are persisting in the ways and values of the present evil age are demonstrating that they are *not*, in reality, members of the resurrection community. Jesus says that behaviors (referred to as "fruit") reveal the true heart condition in Matt 7:16–20.

In 5:1—6:11, we have observed the work of a skilled spiritual director guiding a community as they transition to new-creation living. Notice how each life issue that is faced becomes an opportunity for going further along in the journey toward becoming a radical community. We are grateful for the inspired wisdom given to Paul because we understand that today the pastoral leader's challenge and privilege is to nurture this kind of process of in-depth discipleship (resocialization) among the members of the new-creation communities where we are called to serve.

WHY IS RESOCIALIZATION BY THE SPIRIT URGENTLY NEEDED TODAY?

Encountering the risen Lord Jesus through the Holy Spirit by faith is an experience of breathtaking significance. The New Testament writers are unanimous in testifying that when a person responds with openness to the outpouring of love on the part of the Father, Son, and Holy Spirit, a transformation takes place in the life of that one who embraces the truth. The impact of this encounter is comprehensive and truly epic. Paul expresses it this way:

23. Maybe you notice that sometimes we refer to God's future promised utopia as the "kingdom of God," and sometimes I've been calling it "new creation." The two different ways of referring to this glorious hope are interchangeable, since they are both biblical descriptions of the same future reality. What God has planned for his creation—and us—is so amazing and beyond us that there is no one precise expression that can capture it all. So, different Bible writers use different language to attempt to open our eyes to the glory of it.

"if anyone is in Christ, the new creation has come (alternative translation, "that person is a new creation"[24]). The old has gone, the new is here!" In 1 Corinthians 6, he lists several degenerate behaviors as examples of those which can disqualify a person from God's kingdom. Then Paul reminds the Corinthians that they are living evidence of how God can transform a person. "And that is what some of you were. But you were washed, you were sanctified, you were justified in the name of the Lord Jesus Christ and by the Spirit of our God" (6:11). Jesus himself famously described conversion as equivalent to being born again! Biblical teaching envisions a transformation of identity at the deepest level and grants the grace of acceptance into a new family identity. Faith (in a New Testament sense) must involve public allegiance to the risen Lord and initiation into the new-creation community.[25] This realignment is another dimension of God's grace—not a penalty or an additional obligation. God's commitment to our healing and flourishing is so great that he places us in a new family which nourishes us in the ways of new-creation living.

We must go back to our Bibles and reexamine the New Testament models of conversion.[26] Our evangelism must invite pagans to begin a lifelong journey in relationship with the Triune God and his community (rather than the much-too-common modern approach that often seems merely a one-off transaction which issues the "saved" individual with a get-out-of-hell-free pass.) For the past 100 years, the most common Western version of the so-called gospel invitation is individualistic and reductionist when compared to the spiritual dynamics described in the New Testament. Thus, it can be difficult for us to embrace the nonnegotiable place of the re-socialization journey because we have been shaped by a highly privatized[27] idea of salvation in Christ.

24. The Greek text of 2 Cor 5:17 simply says, "if someone (is) in Christ—'new creation.'" Various English translations convey different senses of Paul's terse statement. It is possible that Paul is referring to the radical personal transformation of an individual convert, or possibly that believing in the gospel results in a person being incorporated into the new creation age/community, as in Col 1:13–14.

25. Water baptism plays a vital role in the New Testament conversion experience. It is the public pledge of faith in, and allegiance to, Jesus as Lord, and also the rite of initiation into the people of the risen Lord. See the classic study by George Beasley-Murray, *Baptism in the New Testament*.

26. In popular evangelical jargon, we often talk of "getting saved." But that's not a phrase the Bible's writers use. Paul uses various expressions to express the multidimensional impact of the work of Christ for us. As we said, his preferred expression is to say we are "in Christ." For an excellent study on rethinking conversion, see Smith, *Transforming Conversion*.

27. Privatization in sociology refers to a social process by means of which members of a community perceive reality as having two distinct spheres of social interaction, i.e.,

We evangelical Christians often use the language of "making disciples," (borrowing language from Jesus and his early followers, who were commonly referred to as disciples). But in reality the process undertaken for formation of the members of the faith community is typically superficial, formal, and relationally barren (and too often seen as optional). It often bears more resemblance to a classroom than to a family environment. Even the content of disciple-making is too often restricted to the spiritual domain and compartmentalized, addressing exclusively concerns of religious behavior and conformity within the narrowly confined sphere of church-centered rules and expectations. Our discipleship curriculum too often explains how one can be a good church-goer rather than a transformed Christ-follower. In many cases, the values and intuitive assumptions of one's original worldview remain unaltered. Rarely is there an expectation or invitation to embrace Jesus' radical new utopian vision of the kingdom.

Discipleship is learning to live according to the way of Jesus in partnership with the Holy Spirit and fellowship with Jesus' community. In this new-creation community, we are "putting off" old ways that we learned from our culture of origin (Col 3:5–10). Jesus is Lord now. The risen Jesus teaches a superior value system that reveals the way to abundant life—God's perfect will. This change process is resocialization.

What exactly is resocialization?

How can a new believer embrace her/his identity as a new creation? I'm employing a sociological concept in explaining Paul's pastoral work in order to help us think about our own activities in a fresh light. The sociology of knowledge is a branch of the discipline of sociology which has helped me appreciate the challenges involved in resocialization. It sheds light on why we so often fail to see Rom 12:2 lived out, i.e., Christians "being transformed by the renewing of our minds." The sociologists who reflect on how we know what we know explain that there is a dominant view of reality which prevails in any society. Within my culture or tribe, this is viewed as a true understanding of the way things really are. The man on the street in any given society holds certain unquestioned assumptions about the nature of reality which provide order to his/her life. Of course, if I get to know a

public and private. Os Guinness, in his 1983 book, *The Gravedigger File: Papers on the Subversion of the Modern Church*, argues that privatization represents a truncation of Christian faith. Jesus is Lord of all reality, not merely a socially bound "private" dimension of life. When Christians accept the idea that their faith is a "personal and private matter," the impact of Jesus and his authority is tragically shrunken (Guinness, *Gravedigger File*, 74–86).

different tribe/culture, I may be surprised to discover that they see life quite differently. But among all the members of my family, village, clan, community, or tribe, the certainty of our assumptions is simply taken for granted.

Because we absorb these ways of seeing and interpreting during the earliest years of life, we say that one is socialized into this life world. Our way of seeing is not reflected on, but rather it is made up of the everyday information which allows a person to live her/his everyday life. These matters are not taught to us in a formal school setting. We absorb them by just being and paying attention in a family environment. Examples of such givens might include what a normal dwelling place looks like, what kind of food is desirable versus disgusting, what a female is supposed to look like and act like, which roles in our group are high status versus low status, etc.

My family of origin also teaches me how we all view "the others." Kenyan consultant and sage Sunny Bindra explains this:

> Think about it. Do you detest a group of people based on their faith, their tribe, or their colour? Where does this hatred come from? Is it from personal experience of bad deeds committed against you, or in your presence? I am willing to wager that in most cases it is not. Most of us are taught to hate. By elders and parents; by teachers and role models; by politicians and rabble-rousers. By weak minds and twisted ones.[28]

So why did I take you on that little detour into the mysteries of the sociology of knowledge? Because for me, this insight into the way the Spirit uses the community in shaping one's thinking helps me explain a serious problem for our Christian movement. The problem we observed at the outset is that many who profess obedience to Jesus and his word do things "in the name of Jesus" which are in such sharp contrast to these ideals.

The insights of the sociology of knowledge help us to figure out why our discipling process seems to be producing disappointing results. The sociologists tell us that there must be relationally intense social frameworks in order for resocialization to take root. Lacking such a context, home reality (that is, the life world of my culture of origin) persists. Our disciple-making therefore faces a huge challenge. Peter Berger says, resocialization "always presupposes a preceding process of primary socialization; that is, that it must deal with an already formed self and an already internalized world. It cannot construct subjective reality *ex nihilo*. This presents a problem because the already internalized reality has a tendency to persist."[29] This means that in the absence of a relationally intense resocialization experience, one's prereflective life world

28. Bindra, "Who Taught You to Hate?," para. 6.
29. Berger and Luckmann, *Social Construction of Reality*, 146.

remains the dominant influence on behavior (especially in seasons of crisis and threat to identity and well-being.)

Since we don't get zapped by the Spirit as we pray the Sinner's Prayer, and instantly become people who grasp and live out the reality of the new creation on the day of our conversion, this challenge is ongoing. This is your primary task as leader of a local church today. And it never stops being necessary—if there is a steady stream of new believers. In fact, a truly dynamic church is always dealing with messy sin problems because new converts do not yet know how to follow Jesus when they come into Christ. If your church is free from scandals, that likely means that you are not seeing people come to Christ.

I've served as a missionary in Africa for the past twenty years and we missionaries have seen the need for resocialization very clearly when evangelizing persons from an African pagan environment. Western missionaries have joyfully welcomed new believers to the Christian family and insisted on the need for a thorough worldview makeover in order to free the former pagan from the bondage to what we regarded as a degenerate culture of origin.

But consider me. I also was formed 100 percent by my culture of origin. I was born into a white, middle-class family in New York in the 1950s. This context taught me everything about everything. It gave me the concepts and metaphors and explanations to navigate daily living. I did not get these concepts from any formal classroom experience. Life in this social world shaped me. (This is why we talk of it as socialization.) Because everybody within my social world explained experience according to the same socially constructed paradigm, we all agreed that what we knew was certainly reality. In my particular culture of origin we were shaped to be thoroughly individualistic, anti-supernatural, and materialistic. My culture taught me "might makes right," and that one's life goal should be "looking out for number one." I was shaped to know that "what's good for America is good for God," and that "God helps those who help themselves." In my life world, talk of invisible, supernatural beings was obviously mere superstition.

This cultural formation happens to all of us no matter which society forms us—Mongo, Luo, Croat, Welsh, Tamil, Hmong, Slovak, etc. Since my own way of seeing life was shaped by 1950s America, all my thinking was purely American. When I come into Christ, Paul says I enter the new-creation life. God's salvation involves more than an isolated soul getting a free pass to heaven. When I came into Christ, all the old paradigms had to be revised.

Is it possible for a resocialization process to bring deep change?

Is it ever possible for somebody like me to think and act more like Jesus and less like an American? Jesus commands us to undertake this transformation and the research in the sociology of knowledge says that it is possible. But the transformation process is demanding. Sociologists tell us that when the resocializing process requires an actual transformation of the individual's home reality, the discipleship process must be as relationally intense as the process that shapes us at the beginning of our lives.[30] This means we will fail to form Christ-followers if our spiritual formation experiences and strategies are too reliant on classrooms, lectures, sermons, and readings.

Paul's letters are inspired by the Spirit with the intent to mentor the first-century disciples as they struggle to unlearn the values and worldviews of their before-Christ culture and be formed by the new-creation narrative into a radical community. Like these early Christ-followers, our challenge also is to learn to experience all of life in light of Jesus' resurrection. Reality is not what my American culture taught me when I was a little kid. We need to get acclimated to the truth concerning Jesus, who is *now* "living, reigning and acting . . . He is alive, Lord over all time and space. He is alive, to come again to bring all things to the Father."[31] For me to get it and begin to discover how to do life, I need to be immersed in a family that eats, sleeps, talks, and walks resurrection life.[32] This is why Paul is so consistently pressing home the issues of community. Malcolm Gladwell, a British-born writer for *The New Yorker*, understands the necessity of community. He affirms the genius of John Wesley when he writes: "Wesley realized that if you wanted to bring about a fundamental change in people's belief and behavior, a change that would persist and serve as an example to others, you needed to create

---

30. Berger and Luckmann, *Social Construction of Reality*, 146: "The formal processes of secondary socialization are determined by its fundamental problem . . . When the process requires an actual transformation of the individual's 'home' reality it comes to replicate as closely as possible the character of primary socialization . . . secondary socialization becomes affectively charged to the degree to which immersion in and commitment to the new reality are institutionally defined as necessary. The relationship of the individual to the socializing personnel becomes correspondingly charged with 'significance,' that is, the socializing personnel takes on the character of significant others *vis a vis* the individual being socialized. The individual then commits himself in a comprehensive way to the new reality."

31. Purves, *Resurrection of Ministry*, 87.

32. "Plausibility structure" is how sociologists refer to this community function. A way of perceiving is given greater credibility when all the members of my group agree on the same way to interpret an experience.

a community around them, where those new beliefs could be practiced and expressed and nurtured."[33]

The risen Jesus teaches a superior value system that reveals the way to a flourishing life. Jesus' way of seeing life is, on a range of issues, at odds with those of America. He says, "Do not store up for yourselves treasures on earth . . . No one can serve two masters . . . You cannot serve both God and money" (Matt 6:19, 24). Jesus says there's a better way to deal with enemies than to try to kill and destroy them. He teaches us, "Love your enemies, do good to those who hate you, bless those who curse you, pray for those who mistreat you . . . Do to others as you would have them do to you . . . Be merciful, just as your Father is merciful" (Luke 6:27-28, 31, 36).

On many occasions, Jesus teaches us that we ought to prioritize the concerns of the poor in our midst. In the new-creation value system, we seek opportunities to serve those at the bottom of society. In Matthew 25, Jesus tells us that compassionate service to "the least" (vv. 40, 45) is behavioral verification of his life within us.

Jesus' great respect for the dignity of women must transform our cultural patriarchalism and inherited gender bias. Jesus' example shows us how to love and respect females rather than to see women as objects to be rated on a scale of one to ten and groped, existing merely as a means to satisfy a man's own animal urges. Remember his encounters with the Samaritan woman at the well and the woman caught in adultery recorded in John 4:1–42 and 8:2–11. Think of how he shattered the cultural barriers by welcoming Mary as a disciple (Luke 10) and appointing her as "apostle to the apostles" following his conquest of death (John 20).

The extent to which we North American evangelicals have resisted Jesus' way and have been substantially conformed to this world requires that we acknowledge that our current efforts at discipleship are inadequate. Although there are noble exceptions, in general we who claim to be seeking Christlikeness in all things, desire and cherish to a remarkable degree the identical things, experiences, and lifestyle of every other US citizen. Our five-star lifestyles are characterized by conspicuous consumption. "We buy things we do not want to impress people we do not like."[34] We revere and support the same dissipated celebrities as our neighbors. Because we evangelicals are, like many Americans, obsessed with our guns,[35] we are much more inclined to shoot our enemies than to love them[36] (Jesus' teachings notwithstanding).

---

33. Gladwell, *Tipping Point*, 173.

34. The quote is attributed to various sources.

35. See Shellnutt, "Packing in the Pews."

36. An extreme expression of this value appeared via the social media hashtags

The sad incongruities mentioned above provide behavioral evidence that resocialization into the values of the new creation inaugurated by Jesus' death and resurrection has not taken place beyond the surface level. We are not a distinctive community devoted to Jesus and his values.

WHAT MUST CHANGE IF WE ARE TO BECOME NEW-CREATION COMMUNITIES?

In order to put this great idea into practice, there are several paradigm shifts that must take place in our contemporary ways of being church and doing ministry.

Stop going to church to listen to lectures!

Three decades ago, philosopher John Alexander wrote an article titled, "Stop Going to Church; Start Being the Body."[37] Alexander observed that the very common expression we say without thinking, "I'm going to church," would have sounded particularly odd in the ears of a first-century Christ-follower. Church is not something you go to. When American churches gather on Sunday mornings, the paradigm of what goes on and who does what and how it gets done is an auditorium-based, lecture hall kind of gathering:

> Our Enlightenment heritage has left us with a rationalistic, mind-oriented approach to everything . . . Where did our present practice of centering our church meetings on a lecture (called a sermon) come from? It was imported from the surrounding society, especially from the schools. The Reformers—Luther, Calvin, and others—were academics. They were trained by listening to lectures. They judged correctly that their followers needed more information. So using the pattern current in Western society, they made their lectures/sermons the focal point of the church meeting they led . . . Jesus seldom used this approach, preferring a more personal and effective approach in

---

#welcomesign and #theriverattampabaychurch following a mass shooting at a Baptist church in Texas. A Florida church responded to the atrocity by posting a sign which read: "Welcome to The River at Tampa Bay church—right of admission reserved. This is private property. Warning: please know this is not a gun free zone—We are heavily armed—any attempt will be dealt with deadly force—Yes we are a church and we will protect our people.—the Pastors." See Aaron, "After Deadly Church Shooting."

37. Alexander, "Stop Going to Church," 43–44.

which he always accompanied his words with deeds . . . The New Testament shows us a much wider range of church expression.[38]

In our evangelical tradition, people come to a sacred building of some sort and sit in straight rows, facing the platform. The structure does not foster life-on-life sharing or eating a meal together. We attendees are really just an audience. The present auditorium-based model seems so obvious to us and it seems like what Christians have always done. But this paradigm will not result in the formation of a distinctive new-creation community.

Start being the church by practicing "one-anothering" by the power of the Spirit.

When we read Paul's letter to Corinth, the picture that instantly pops into our minds is of a gathering that obviously must have looked just like our meetings. But I am quite certain that if you had visited Corinth in Paul's day, and if you managed to locate the family home in which this new community of Christ-followers was gathering, what you experienced would have been dramatically different. It would not have been on Sunday morning, since the members who were slaves did not have a free day for church-going. The Christ-followers who gathered would not have been seated quietly on rows of benches all facing a stage. Rather, it would seem that everybody had something to say or do. Most crucially for Paul, based on what we learned in chapter 5, the gathering of these Christ-followers was a mystical gathering, with the risen Jesus in the center. When they came together, they experienced an in-depth connection with one another and with Jesus. They all ate a meal together—with Jesus. Since *he* was the priest, they all came eager to hear his voice and experience his power.

I believe that the churches of North America must creatively follow the Spirit of Jesus in exploring fresh, relevant ways of gathering together. Deep transformation rarely happens in large crowds. We need to imagine a fresh model that resembles the coming together of an extended family for the purpose of sharing a special feast. Throughout the global church, many congregations are organizing diverse forms of small groups or cell groups or house churches to respond to this need for deeper community.[39] When we are coming together, we need to organize the gathering in such a manner

---

38. Kraft, *Christianity with Power*, 43.

39 An overview of these phenomena can be found in Hadaway et al., *Home Cell Groups and House Churches*. Howard Snyder has urged us to recognize the urgency and power of a small-group system for church renewal (Snyder, *Radical Wesley and Patterns for Church Renewal*).

that we can all actively do the "one anothers,"[40] since we are family and we are "members of one another." The Holy Spirit commands us to engage in a wonderful collage of more than twenty specific behaviors as an in-Christ family. We are exhorted to "serve one another in love," to "be of the same mind with one another," to "accept one another," to "confess sins to one another," to "bear one another's burdens," to "speak truth to one another," to "wash one another's feet," and to "forgive one another."

That is not a comprehensive list of the one-anothers[41] but it is clear that the paradigm of a radical community in the New Testament writings is intensely relational and intimate. This is what we do in Christ. When we come together, our gatherings must create social space for *koinonia*, which is best translated as "sharing a common life in the Holy Spirit." God has given churches wonderful freedom to invent fresh forms for meeting together. There is no rule book in the Bible on how the officially sanctioned churches will organize themselves. But the forms that we use to organize our coming together must maximize the opportunity for us to do these one-anothers.

Getting saved necessarily includes being incorporated into God's radical holy community. This is a gift of *grace*. God's commitment to our healing and flourishing is so great that he places us in a new family which nourishes us in the ways of new-creation living.

> As a newborn baby breathes and cries, so the signs of life in a newborn Christian are faith and repentance, inhaling the love of God and exhaling an initial cry of distress. And at that point what God provides, exactly as for a newborn infant, is the comfort, protection, and nurturing promise of a mother. "If God is our father, the church is our mother." The words are those of the Swiss Reformer John Calvin . . . it is as impossible, unnecessary, and undesirable to be a Christian all by yourself as it is to be a newborn baby all by yourself.[42]

To nurture the process of resocialization and shape a radical new-creation community is your great challenge and privilege if you are a Christian leader.

---

40. There are a number of books available which explore the "one another" texts in the New Testament. Consider: Getz, *Building Up One Another*; Sittser, *Love One Another*; Banks, *Paul's Idea of Community*.

41. See George, *Prepare Your Church for the Future*, 129–31, for a total list of "one anothers." Summary available online at: http://storage.cloversites.com/wakarusamissionarychurch/documents/59one_another_scriptures.pdf.

42 Wright, *Simply Christian*, 210.

Chapter 6

Sexual Renewal

Transforming Marriage and Morality in Light of the New Creation

The Bible holds such a high celebrative view of human sexuality
. . . We exist as male and female in relationship. Our sexualness, our
capacity to love and be loved, is intimately related to our creation
in the image of God. What a high view of human sexuality . . . their
masculinity and femininity are the handiwork of God, as is their
passionate affection. Their differences also unite them; they are male
and female but also one flesh.[1]

RICHARD FOSTER

READ: 1 COR 6:12—7:40

In book two of C. S. Lewis's enchanting space trilogy, his robust imagination brings to life a character who has never been damaged by the fall. When the protagonist lands on Perelandra (Venus), he encounters an enthralling wonder, the Green Lady. As Lewis's mind describes this uncorrupted person, he

1. Foster, *Money, Sex, and Power*, 91, 94.

exposes (by contrast) just how damaged we all are by the universal effects of the fatal choice of our primal ancestors. The Green Lady is serene, beautiful, and mindful. There is no guile in her, and thus her words are transparent. She possesses courage which flows from the total absence of fear. She is pure, like a clear, cold mountain spring. She is in complete ecological harmony with her paradiselike environment. And she is thoroughly joyful and even playful. All of her beauty finds its source in her unequivocal trust in "the King" (God). The Green Lady is powerfully appealing (in a nonsexual way) and delightful.

Lewis's bountiful capacity for describing the good life—and his Christian faith—as an enticing invitation to joy had a remarkable impact on many of his Oxford students. Lewis scholar Alan Jacobs, in his book *The Narnian: The Life and Imagination of C. S. Lewis*, describes the lasting influence of Lewis's generous character and imagination on the British theater impresario and essayist, Kenneth Tynan. In the last decade of his life, Tynan wrote (after reading *That Hideous Strength*), "How thrilling he makes goodness seem—how tangible and radiant!" Lewis's imaginative portrayals of goodness and love seduced Tynan throughout his exceptional life.[2]

Deep in your gut, how do you perceive goodness? As the philosopher Simone Weil remarked, "Imaginary evil is romantic and varied; real evil is gloomy, monotonous, barren, boring. Imaginary good is boring; real good is always new, marvelous, intoxicating."[3] I raise the question at the outset because this chapter is concerned with sex. The presenting issues in 1 Cor 6–7 concern sexual immorality. Part of me thinks that this is a bit unfortunate, since it reinforces the misperception that Christians are obsessed with sexual misconduct.[4] As Richard Mouw writes, "We Christians have to work to overcome the long-standing impression that our message about human sexuality is primarily negative—that we want to keep people from doing enjoyable things."[5] Why don't we get worked up about domestic violence, or environmental degradation, or the fact that 1 percent of the world's elite own 50 percent of the world's wealth? In truth, we do care deeply about all these profoundly sinful problems, since the three that I mentioned are totally at odds with God's new-creation agenda.

But it is also undeniable that sexual behaviors really do matter greatly. Our sexuality can be a source of indescribable elation when lived according

2. Jacobs, *Narnian,* 312.

3. Weil, *Gravity and Grace,* 62.

4. Mouw, *Uncommon Decency,* 106. Also see Gerson, "Last Temptation," para. 43, where he argues that there exists ". . .the damaging impression that Christians are obsessed with sex. . ."

5. Mouw, *Uncommon Decency,* 104.

to God's intention or so terribly destructive and traumatizing when we arrogantly decided to write our own rules of the game. An honest assessment of modern Western societies reveals that our cultural prejudice which affirms that all forms of genital sexual expression are valid and must never be inhibited is *not* giving birth to a free and fulfilled society of love and peace and satisfaction.

If one is to receive the teachings of 1 Corinthians concerning sexuality as something other than anti-PC, puritanical, and censorious, one must treasure a solid conviction that God is unwaveringly *good,* and that his ways are the way to human flourishing and joy. One's predisposition will color how a person receives these teachings. Decades ago, Pastor A. W. Tozer wrote: "What comes into our minds when we think about God is the most important thing about us."[6] To hear this teaching on sex and respond with joy and gratitude depends on your view of God.

The writer of Ps 19 grasped that receiving God's revelation was a priceless gift. He celebrates the goodness of God's revelation. The Bible, as God's word, is comprehensive wisdom for all of life—present and eternal (after death).

> The law of the LORD is perfect, reviving the soul; the decrees of the LORD are sure, making wise the simple; the precepts of the LORD are right, rejoicing the heart; . . . the ordinances of the LORD are true and righteous altogether. More to be desired are they than gold, even much fine gold; sweeter also than honey, and drippings of the honeycomb . . . in keeping them there is great reward. (Ps 19:7–11)

This inspired writer was convinced that revealed knowledge of God's instructions was a priceless treasure. So again, what do you think about God? Are you really convinced that God is good? Or are you slightly suspicious that God is really a prude? Do you fear that he is uptight, anal-retentive, frustrated, stern? Do you see God scouring the earth with a furrowed brow perpetually shouting, "Cut that out?" Or do you possess a deep confidence that God is good—joyful, alive, life-giving?

There is another related question with which one must come to grips. Do you think God is intelligent? Do you think he knows how life works? Does he grasp biology? Do you think he's smart enough to grasp human sexuality? Philosopher Dallas Willard writes:

> Our commitment to Jesus can stand on no other foundation than a recognition that he is the one who knows the truth about

6. Tozer, *Knowledge of the Holy,* 9.

our lives and our universe. It is not possible to trust Jesus, or anyone else, in matters where we do not believe him to be competent . . . And can we seriously imagine that Jesus could be Lord if he were not smart? If he were divine, would he be dumb? Or uninformed? Once you stop to think about it, how could he be what we take him to be in all other respects and not be the best-informed and most intelligent person of all, the smartest person who ever lived?[7]

The big issue here is not first about sex; it's about God. God's agenda in giving us teaching regarding sexuality (remember, God thought it up!) is to mark off a pathway by means of which we can actually get a taste of real love. The Scripture's teachings are not primarily about boundaries and restrictions. The guidance we receive can lead us to an experience of uncorrupted intimacy and it can root out fear and shame. God's ways give life!

Here is the great idea which we discover in this unit—*Resurrection people truly love bodies because God made them, owns them, redeemed them, and will transform them.*

FRAMING THE TEXT AND DISCERNING THE APOSTLE'S APPROACH

Paul's way of teaching, which can be called "task theology," means that Paul responds to the issues as they surface in his interaction with the believers from Corinth. This is a real letter set in a specific historical-cultural context. We are reading somebody else's mail. Paul's agenda is to reframe the particular issues, and thus guide the community through a step-by-step resocialization process.

Here, in the second half of chapter 6, the presenting issue again concerns sexual immorality. It seems that some community members were enlisting the services of prostitutes on a regular basis. This was just normal male behavior in that ancient Hellenistic seaport city. Furthermore, the practice was given philosophical/theological justification as being an expression of authentic freedom.

Cultural background for rightly interpreting 6:12–20

The culture that formed some subsets of the Corinthian community prior to their coming into Christ was a culture that saw surrendering of personal

7. Willard, *Divine Conspiracy*, 94.

prerogatives as objectionable. Richard Hays argues that a common Hellenistic understanding of wisdom placed a great emphasis on personal freedom. Hence the mantra of the Corinthians, "I am free to do anything." We will watch as Paul shrewdly destroys their "community-destroying insistence on autonomy . . . [as] the emphasis lies not on what is legally allowable but on the sovereign authority of the individual over all external constraints."[8] In the light of the evidence of Stoic-Cynic tendencies in their culture, "The enlightened *wise* person is free to do anything he or she chooses. This is consistent with the idea that the *sophos* is a 'king' to whom all things belong . . ."[9]

In addition, as Hays reminds us, the cultural world of Corinth had some big differences from the ethical expectations of modern societies:

> Prostitution was not only legal; it was a widely accepted social convention. "The sexual latitude allowed to Corinthian men by Greek public opinion was virtually unrestricted. Sexual relations of males with both boys and harlots were generally tolerated." (Talbert, 32). Thus the Corinthian men who frequented prostitutes were not asserting some unheard-of new freedom; they were merely insisting on their right to continue participating in a pleasurable activity that was entirely normal within their own culture. The Corinthian *sophoi*, seeing the body as transient and trivial, have concluded that it makes no difference what we do with our bodies . . . sexual gratification? None of this makes any difference, they say, because it concerns only external physical matters, which are of no lasting significance.[10]

Paul is passionate about shaping the new-creation community. As was the case in chapter 5 and earlier in chapter 6, Paul acknowledges the offense only briefly. He does not get into any details, nor does he mention names. There is actually no direct confrontation of the sinner. Also, as a skilled spiritual director, Paul does not simply pronounce the letter of the law by quoting from Leviticus 18 or the Jerusalem letter sent out by the council (reported in Acts 15:20). He wants to nurture this community toward maturity and not keep believers at the level of mere blind obedience to a command that declares, "Thou shalt not . . ."

Paul discerns that it's a teachable moment which he can use to explain a whole new way of seeing really foundational life issues. Paul discerns that his friends in Corinth must discover that embracing this new way of living under Jesus' values is crucial to restoring what it means to be fully human

8. Hays, *First Corinthians*, 101.

9. Hays, *First Corinthians*, 101 (italics original).

10. Hays, *First Corinthians*, 102.

and fully alive. Following Paul, we must frame this issue in light of the new story which defines reality.

Following the apostle's counsel, step by step

Chapter 6, verse 12 launches into this dialogue. Watch a brilliant mind and caring pastor begin his assault on distorted teaching. First, he must challenge the normal way of answering the question: What does it mean to be "free?" Here are verses 12–13, set out as dialogue:

> Quoting Corinthian mantra: *Some of you say, "I have the right to do anything."*
> Paul's counterproposal: *But not everything is helpful.*
> Quoting Corinthian mantra: *Again some of you say, "I have the right to do anything."*
> Paul's counterproposal: *But I will not be controlled by anything.*
> Quoting Corinthian mantra: *Some of you say, "Food is for the stomach, and the stomach is for food. And God will destroy both of them."*
> Paul's counterproposal: *But the body is not meant for sexual sins. The body is meant for the Lord.* (NIRV)

Paul is remarkably well-informed in his response. He cleverly rebuts the *sophoi* by using another philosophical term they would have known: "not all things are *beneficial*." The word translated "beneficial" (*sympherei*) has a history in Hellenistic popular philosophy. Hays summarizes Paul's argument: "the extreme Corinthian position is bad philosophy: the wise person will not act in self-indulgent ways but will seek to act in accordance with an enlightened understanding of human good."[11]

Paul's second counterproposal, "But I will not be controlled by anything," is evidence of some deep psychological insight. Once again he mines the resources of Hellenistic popular thought. When Paul responds with the words, "I will not be dominated by anything," he is drawing on the motifs common in the culture. Hays explains that "this too sounds like a Stoic argument: the wise person will not surrender control to anything or anyone. The danger is particularly great that the person seeking to exercise freedom through promiscuous sexual activity will end up as a slave to passion."[12]

Paul's insight here is more than mere rhetorical jousting. He discerns that there is a pseudofreedom that is, in reality, slavery. Jesus, of course,

11. Hays, *First Corinthians*, 103.
12. Hays, *First Corinthians*, 103.

said it very directly: "Everyone who sins is a slave to sin" (John 8:34). And existentially we actually know this to be true. Dallas Willard probes more deeply into the operations of the "slave-trade":

> "Free love," as it is euphemistically but falsely called, along with the various forms of perversion, are simply an extension of bodily worship . . . But it turns out that sensuality cannot be satisfied. It is not self-limiting. That is partly because the effect of engaging in the practices of sensuality is to deaden feeling. This awakens the relentless drive, the desperate need, simply to feel, to feel something . . . The drive to self-gratification opens up into a life without boundaries, where nothing is forbidden—if one can "get away" with it. . . . They are willing slaves of their feelings or appetites. (Rom 1:18). They "want what they want when they want it," . . . If they do not get it they become angry and depressed, and are a danger to themselves and others.[13]

Paul takes up the issue of true new-creation freedom in chapters 8–10 in much more depth. We have addressed the authentic freedom issue there.

TEN REASONS WHY GOD IS PRO-BODY (KEY IDEAS IN VV. 15–20)

1. God raised Jesus from death in a new body.

The breathtaking reality of Jesus' bodily resurrection in history is the ground of our respect for the human body. Gordon Fee writes: "The affirmation of the resurrection in verse 14 . . . serves as the theological basis for Paul's basic assertion which controls most of the argument (v. 13) . . . 'the body is for the Lord and the Lord is for the body.' . . Our resurrection is predicated on the resurrection of Christ."[14]

2. God will raise whole persons and in new-creation life we will live in resurrection bodies.

Paul will teach at length in chapter 15 that Jesus' resurrection body is the definitive prototype of what the future resurrection body of the Christian will be like. In chapter 15, Paul uses the metaphor of "first fruit"[15] to say that

13. Willard, *Renovation of the Heart*, 53.

14. Fee, *First Epistle to the Corinthians*, 256.

15. "First fruit" is a metaphor based on an Old Testament sacrificial ritual that God

the transformation of Jesus' body following his death is a manifestation in time of what will take place for all those in Christ at the end of history. Paul assures us: "if the Spirit of him who raised Jesus from the dead is living in you, he who raised Christ from the dead will also give life to your mortal bodies because of his Spirit who lives in you." (Rom 8:11)

3. *Your own physical body is a member (body part) of Messiah Jesus.*

In chapter 10, Paul speaks of our union with Christ, saying, "Because there is one loaf [*in Holy Communion*], we, who are many, are one body, for we all share the one loaf." In Rom 12:4–5, Paul writes: "For just as each of us has one body with many members, and these members do not all have the same function, so in Christ we, though many, form one body, and each member belongs to all the others."

4. *When you have sexual intercourse with a person, you become profoundly one with that person.*

Paul stands firmly with Moses and Jesus and affirms the reality first revealed in Gen 2, when God originally invented sex. Man and woman become "one flesh." The physical act is profound and unitive. Intercourse can never be just a one-off tension-reliever (purely physical).

5. *By means of your own physical body, you are united to the Messiah in Spirit.*

We can only relate to other persons via our bodies. The physical body is the external you. Our spiritual union with Jesus Christ cannot be compartmentalized and separated away from our physical life lived in our physical body (that is Gnosticism). Paul was thoroughly Hebrew in his thinking about the human person. The person is an indivisible whole, and all aspects of the personality operate as one in real life.

---

instituted to teach trust and gratitude. Hebrews were instructed to bring the very first produce from their annual harvest to the sanctuary and celebrate God's faithfulness. They were affirming by faith that God would surely give a full and bountiful harvest.

6. Sexual intercourse is so profound and significant (and good) that if you prostitute yourself by having sex with a prostitute, you are actually doing damage to yourself.

Paul does not say that sexual sin is more heinous or worthy of judgment than other transgressions. But he explains that sexual immorality is a deeper sin in this sense—it has a damaging impact on your own personality. Other types of sins are external to the deep self. There is an abundance of empirical evidence to support Paul's teaching.

7. Your physical body is a temple.

A temple is a dwelling place for God to come and be present. Paul teaches that Christ lives within us in many of his writings. For example:

> You, however, are not in the realm of the flesh but are in the realm of the Spirit, if indeed the Spirit of God lives in you. And if anyone does not have the Spirit of Christ, they do not belong to Christ. But if Christ is in you, then even though your body is subject to death because of sin, the Spirit gives life because of righteousness. And if the Spirit of him who raised Jesus from the dead is living in you, he who raised Christ from the dead will also give life to your mortal bodies because of his Spirit who lives in you. (Rom 8:9–11)

Because God chooses to make his dwelling place in this world within our bodies, we are, therefore, temples.

8. God has given you the Holy Spirit and he now lives within your physical body.

Paul easily shifts his language back and forth from saying "Christ is in you" to saying the "Holy Spirit is in you." This is not evidence of confusion or of theological imprecision. It reveals his awareness of the dynamics of the Trinity. For example: "Now it is God who makes both us and you stand firm in Christ. He anointed us, set his seal of ownership on us, and put his Spirit in our hearts as a deposit, guaranteeing what is to come" (2 Cor 1:21-22). Or again, "You, however, are not in the realm of the flesh but are in the realm of the Spirit, if indeed the Spirit of God lives in you. And if anyone does not have the Spirit of Christ, they do not belong to Christ" (Rom 8:9).

9. You are not actually the owner of your physical body. It belongs to God.

God created each person. He is the true owner of all that he made. We are stewards of the physical body that he gave to us. The Psalms celebrate this as a wonderful reality: "The earth is the Lord's, and everything in it, the world, and all who live in it" (Ps 24:1), and "Know that the Lord is God. It is he who made us, and we are his" (Ps 100:3).

God delegated to each of us the freedom to make choices about who our bodies (still owned by God, but managed by us) will serve. Writing to the Romans, Paul urges us to choose to recognize the true owner. "Therefore, I urge you, brothers and sisters, in view of God's mercy, to offer your bodies as a living sacrifice, holy and pleasing to God—this is your true and proper worship." (12:1) Earlier in his writing, he expresses the importance of the physical body: "Therefore do not let sin reign in your mortal body so that you obey its evil desires. Do not offer any part of yourself to sin as an instrument of wickedness, but rather offer yourselves to God as those who have been brought from death to life; and offer every part of yourself to him as an instrument of righteousness" (Rom 6:12–13).

10. God bought your body by paying an infinite price. Jesus gave his life for you. Redemption includes gaining possession of your body.

Peter the apostle writes: "For you know that it was not with perishable things such as silver or gold that you were redeemed from the empty way of life handed down to you from your ancestors, but with the precious blood of Christ, a lamb without blemish or defect" (1 Pet 1:18–19).

These are the reasons why we know that the Lord is pro-body. "God honored the Master's body by raising it from the grave. He'll treat yours with the same resurrection power. Until that time, remember that your bodies are created with the same dignity as the Master's body. You wouldn't take the Master's body off to a whorehouse, would you? I should hope not" (6:14–15 MSG). This means (as it will in the future) we are free to delight in the gift of a physical body and to honor God with this remarkable gift.

I hope you were paying close attention to the way Paul handled this sensitive issue. He did not just issue a "Thou shalt not" and command obedience. He is wise enough to know that that has limited effectiveness when it comes to restraining sin. Rather, Paul is working to teach this new community to think in a totally different way about the value of our human bodies.

He realizes that if we think differently as a community, that this dynamic can have a very powerful impact on our behavior.

CHAPTER 7: GUIDANCE REGARDING MARRIAGE CONCERNS RAISED BY THE CORINTHIANS

First Corinthians 7 is very down-to-earth (interesting phrase!) wisdom and counsel for living new-creation life in-between times. Recall N. T. Wright's summary of the narrative which orients us to reality:

> . . . with Easter and Pentecost the remaking of God's creation of space, time and matter has already begun. One of the primary places where this remaking is to be seen and known is in Christian holiness, which is not a matter of observing rules and regulations but of Christians taking proper human responsibility for a bit of the created order, their own bodies, and working at making them reflect the image of God as they were made to . . . (see Rom. 8:29) God has already begun the ultimate, final work of new creation; by baptism and faith you have left behind the old order of sin and death, and by God's Spirit within you, you have God's own resurrection power to enable you, even in the present, to resist sin and live as a fully human being at last; you must therefore live in the present, as far as possible, like you will live in the future.[16]

Framework for interpreting text of chapter 7

Chapter 7 begins with the words, "Now for the matters you wrote about . . ." It seems that in addition to the delegation of representatives from Corinth who visited Paul in Ephesus, that some members of the Corinthian community had composed a letter that was carried to the apostle. So in chapter 7 (and 8, 11, and 12), Paul is responding to issues raised in the letter from Corinth seeking counsel.

It is important to observe that Paul is not giving a new-creation rule book. This counsel is not a set of case laws. It is not a new *Halakah*[17] (although too often we interpret it as case law, mimicking the Pharisees'

16. Wright, *Surprised by Scripture*, 94.

17. *Halakah* is a Hebrew word that refers to a collection of rabbinic laws. *Halakah* means "walking," and the goal of the rabbis (the traditions of the elders) was to discover a biblical text which provided instruction on right conduct for every conceivable life situation. The Talmud is the collection of this systematic exegetical tradition.

approach). There is no need for such. We have the Spirit within us who is the resurrection power. (Ezek 36:25–28 is fulfilled!) We are living in the presence of the risen Jesus. So together, as his partners, we are able to walk and discern. Will we make mistakes? Yes. But "now there is no condemnation 'in Christ Jesus.'"

When Paul receives the letter from his spiritual children in Corinth, he discerns that we need the mentoring of a spiritual Father to navigate this new terrain. Therefore, Paul undertakes the work of developing a new vision of the spiritual life. Practicing resurrection happens in the relationships and activities of day-to-day life. This is a radical new approach to being spiritual.

What are the assumptions of the Corinthians?

For many of these recent converts, embracing a dualistic, gnostic-style otherworldliness, or what we might refer to as hyper-spirituality, would seem like the obvious way to give expression to having been "raised with Christ and seated in the heavenly realms" (Col 3:1) There was a strong pull toward so-called spiritual practices which encouraged a convert to opt totally out of life and be holy (like we find in 2 Thess 3). This worldview, which is referred to as dualism, was pervasive in the Hellenistic culture. When we talk about dualism, we are referring to a way of seeing reality in which all the stuff of the created, physical world is regarded as lower, corrupted, less real, enslaving, and evil. This includes the physical universe and, since our bodies are part of this material realm, everything we desire, do, or experience with these flesh-and-blood bodies is downgraded. In sharp distinction to the lower realm of the material world, there exists the higher dimension of the spirit or soul.

Paul's alternative creation-affirming spirituality

The apostle will offer an alternative vision of authentic spirituality rooted in God's good creation and the bodily resurrection of Jesus. He will teach that new-creation living takes place as we engage in the nitty-gritty challenges of daily life. Paul gives counsel so we can live in the present, as far as possible, like you will live in the future." Being spiritual is all about daily issues like sex and marriage, vocational choices, courtship, friendship, and social status.

The first matter taken up by Paul (7:1–16) in response to the letter he received from Corinth challenges the thinking of some who have argued for the cessation of sexual relations within marriage on the basis of their slogan: "It is good for a man not to have relations with a woman." This phrase does not represent Paul's teaching, but is a quotation from the Corinthians' letter to Paul.[18] Let's examine this fascinating discussion more carefully.

The Corinthians' position is summarized: "Sex is evil" (belonging to the realm of "the flesh") (7:1)

Now for the matters you wrote about: "It is good for a man not to have sexual relations with a woman."

Recognize that 7:1b is a quote from the Corinthians' letter to which Paul takes issue. Paul himself is not saying that sexual relations are bad. Some members of the Corinthian community saw abstinence as more spiritual. Paul disagrees. Some scholars have suggested that Paul is dealing with some super-spiritual women who reject sexual intercourse with their husbands now that they are made new. In their way of thinking, the spiritual life is just to enjoy ecstasy and pray. Gordon Fee explains the thinking underneath this rejection of normal marital relations: "[*some Corinthian women*] think of themselves as having already realized the "resurrection of the dead" by being "in spirit" and thus already as angels (cf. 11:2–16; 13:1), neither marrying nor giving in marriage (cf. Luke 20:35)."[19]

Paul's counsel to two married believers—enjoy the goodness of sexual relations (7:2–7)

> But since sexual immorality is occurring, each man should have sexual relations with his own wife, and each woman with her own husband. The husband should fulfill his marital duty to his wife, and likewise the wife to her husband. The wife does not have authority over her own body but yields it to her husband. In the same way, the husband does not have authority over his own body but yields it to his wife. Do not deprive each other except perhaps by mutual consent and for a time, so that you may devote yourselves to prayer. Then come together again so that Satan will not tempt you because of your lack of self-control. I say this as a concession, not as a command. I wish that all of you were as I am. But each of you has your own gift from God; one has this gift, another has that.

18. Paul quotes his dialogue partners on a number of occasions in his letters as he teaches the believers. We saw this back in 6:12, and we will see it in 8:1, 4, and 10:23.

19. Fee, *First Epistle to the Corinthians*, 269 (italics mine).

Be sure to recognize Paul's stress on the mutuality of responsibility between husband and wife. This is a revolutionary perspective in Paul's culture. Eugene Peterson expresses this well in *The Message*: "The marriage bed must be a place of mutuality—the husband seeking to satisfy his wife, the wife seeking to satisfy her husband. Marriage is not a place to "stand up for your rights." Marriage is a decision to serve the other, whether in bed or out."

Paul does agree that there can be brief periods where we might decide to abstain from normal sexual relations as a spiritual discipline—a sort of fasting. He offers a "concession" (v. 5) and proposes a brief interlude of abstinence, which is limited and mutually agreed upon.

Embracing God's diverse gifts (7:7)

> Sometimes I wish everyone were single like me—a simpler life
> in many ways! But celibacy is not for everyone any more than
> marriage is. God gives the gift of the single life to some, the gift
> of the married life to others. (MSG)

Paul sees both marriage and singleness as a *charisma*. The word translated as "gift from God" is the word *charisma*. He is emphasizing that both marriage and singleness are expressions of God's grace. "I wish that all of you were as I am. But each of you has your own gift from God; one has this gift, another has that" (v. 7). Paul personally delights in his charisma. He will say several times in this section that he wishes everybody was single like he is. But he also is clear that this grace is not given to all.

To those whose marriage has been dissolved by death (7:8–9)

> I do, though, tell the unmarried and widows that singleness
> might well be the best thing for them, as it has been for me. But
> if they can't manage their desires and emotions, they should by
> all means go ahead and get married. The difficulties of marriage
> are preferable by far to a sexually tortured life as a single. (MSG)

Paul seems to focus here on those who are not currently married, but who once were, and thus those who may not share his charisma of freedom from sexual need. Paul has a preference for singleness but also gives a truly realistic bit of counsel.

Two Christians married to each other must not end the marriage through divorce (7:10–11)

> To the married I give this command (not I, but the Lord): A wife must not separate from her husband. But if she does, she must remain unmarried or else be reconciled to her husband. And a husband must not divorce his wife.

We must recall that Paul is responding to the Corinthian view of spirituality. Paul clarifies that his words here (v. 10) are based on the direct teachings of Jesus (Matt 19:9). It is important to make note that Paul first addresses the wife. It is possible that this is because it was more common for Corinthian women to adopt this "spiritualized eschatology."[20] But it also again shows respect for the wife's decision-making responsibility. This is quite shocking in the Hellenistic culture.

A Christian married to a non-Christian must not seek to end the marriage (7:12–16)

> To the rest I say this (I, not the Lord): If any brother has a wife who is not a believer and she is willing to live with him, he must not divorce her. And if a woman has a husband who is not a believer and he is willing to live with her, she must not divorce him. For the unbelieving husband has been sanctified through his wife, and the unbelieving wife has been sanctified through her believing husband. Otherwise your children would be unclean, but as it is, they are holy. But if the unbeliever leaves, let it be so. The brother or the sister is not bound in such circumstances; God has called us to live in peace. How do you know, wife, whether you will save your husband? Or, how do you know, husband, whether you will save your wife?

In reading this pastoral guidance, we should always recall that we are dealing with a first-generation situation as far as being in Christ is concerned. The Christian movement is so new in the Corinthian context that it is likely that all members are former pagans who only encountered Jesus and the

---

20. Fee, *First Epistle to the Corinthians*, 12. Fee notes that the Pauline communities may be familiar with Luke's collection of Jesus' teachings and that Luke 20:35 may be especially prized by some female members (" . . . in the resurrection of the dead they will neither be married nor given in marriage . . . they are like angels . . ."). These eschatological women believe they are now experiencing a kind of ultimate spirituality in which they live above the mere material existence of the present age.

gospel within that past year or two. Thus, in most cases, it is a situation where there were two pagans who were married as pagans. Then one of the spouses joined this new movement and was transformed by the Spirit of Jesus. Now the marriage relationship is dealing with a very different dynamic. Undoubtedly some especially spiritual Christians felt that it was no longer acceptable for them to be united to an unbelieving partner. No doubt such a spiritual person felt encumbered or perhaps polluted by the attachment with a pagan partner.

But Paul counsels the believer to continue in this marriage. He teaches that it is the holy person in Christ who will have a substantial influence on the unbeliever. He even says that the Christian spouse will make the pagan holy ("to make holy"—*hagiazō*).[21] Paul's idea is that because of this marriage bond, this pagan is "under the influence" of the Holy Spirit because she/he is continuously involved with a person who belongs to Jesus. It seems that holiness is contagious.

Paul is always conscious of the potential impact of personal relationships. He sees every relationship as an evangelistic opportunity. He thinks that persons in whom the risen Jesus dwells will radiate cross power and thus be an attractive advertisement for God's grace. "You never know, wife: The way you handle this might bring your husband not only back to you but to God. You never know, husband: The way you handle this might bring your wife not only back to you but to God" (MSG).

However, Paul is a realist and agrees that if the non-Christian spouse should choose to end the "mixed-marriage," then, in such a situation, the abandoned believing partner will not be "enslaved."[22] Paul emphasizes that we are called to be people who seek shalom, which is God's peace (v. 15).

A primary value of Paul which will be applied to various life situations (7:17)

And don't be wishing you were someplace else or with someone else. Where you are right now is God's place for you. Live and

21. The biblical word "holy" (translated from Greek *hagiazō*) does not primarily refer to a person's good behavior. To be holy in the Bible is first about God's choice to take possession of a person or an object or a people group. The chosen person is set apart as belonging to God—but not necessarily saved. An unbelieving spouse is set apart and privileged due to that one's ready access to the gospel of God.

22. Paul uses the word *dedoulōtai*, from *douloō*, meaning "to be a slave, to be under bondage," which indicates that the believing spouse who is deserted has no further obligation to the prior marriage.

obey and love and believe right there. God, not your marital status, defines your life. Don't think I'm being harder on you than on the others. I give this same counsel in all the churches. (MSG)

Throughout the rest of chapter 7, Paul will urge that we continue to live in the life circumstances in which we were functioning when God called us. Thinking missiologically, Paul urges each of us to see our situation as the Lord's assignment for us.

The heart of this teaching—seek to be a fully devoted (pure) follower of the risen Lord

In the second half of this dialogue between Paul and the Corinthians, Paul's counsel is quite clear-eyed and practical. He has one huge priority which he will affirm over and over. The essence of this section is found most clearly articulated in verses 32–35, which is the pathway to freedom:

> Those who use the things of the world should not become all wrapped up in them. . . . I don't want you to have anything to worry about. A single man is concerned about the Lord's matters. He wants to know how he can please the Lord. But a married man is concerned about the matters of this world. He wants to know how he can please his wife. . . . His concerns pull him in two directions. . .
>
> I'm saying those things for your own good. I'm not trying to hold you back. I want you to be free to live in a way that is right. I want you to give yourselves completely to the Lord. (NIRV)

In Paul's thinking and experience, this is about freedom to enjoy God unencumbered. Paul knows that true freedom is enjoyed in being Jesus' slave (*doulos*). This is counterintuitive in every culture. Yet if we are honest, our self-centered pursuit of freedom is not delivering the desired results. Richard Foster exposes our lack of single-minded focus and the resulting stress this creates:

> We dash here and there desperately trying to fulfill the many obligations that press in upon us. We jerk back and forth between business commitments and family responsibilities. While we are busy responding to the needs of child or spouse, we feel guilty about neglecting the demands of work. When we respond to the pressures of work, we fear we are failing our family. In those rare times when we are able to juggle the two successfully, the wider

issues of nation and world whisper pestering calls to service. . .
. What will set us free from this bondage to the ever spiraling
demands that are placed on us?[23]

TENSIONS AND BALANCES FOUND IN 1 COR 7
WHICH CHARACTERIZE LIFE IN CHRIST

Chapter 7 is a passage about living with tensions or living with a new-creation
balance. Jesus' words in his final prayer express the tension that his followers navigate. He spoke of our being in the world, but not of the world (John
17:15–18). This requires maintaining a delicate balance in Christian living.

Our master narrative is about living with paradox and being honest
about the opposites. We truly live resurrection now; but clearly, the present
evil age is real and is the arena for redemption and mission.

- On the one hand, sex is good. It is not unspiritual. Every married person should meet her/his mate's sexual needs. We are free to serve one
  another. We submit to one another out of reverence for the Messiah
  (as revealed in 7:1–5).

- But on the other hand, beware and be honest that the urge toward
  sexual immorality is powerful and still lurking to destroy you.

- On the one hand, Paul loves his freedom from domestic responsibility.
  He can be fully devoted to Jesus and his mission.

- But on the other hand, Paul affirms that marriage is a good gift
  (charisma).

- On the one hand, marriage is a very challenging relationship because
  we are "one flesh" with our partner. We must do everything possible to
  enjoy a marriage that reflects and manifests shalom (God's peace and
  harmony). If at all possible, a Christ-follower should not be the one to
  dissolve a marriage with a pagan spouse.

- But on the other hand, we must not try to force a pagan to stay enslaved if that pagan demands to get out. This freedom is how we pursue shalom.

- On the one hand, to persons classified as slaves in the Roman Empire's
  system, Paul says you can be God's free agent even if your ID card
  says "slave" (v. 21). But if the option to change your legal standing is
  given—go for it!

23. Foster, *Freedom of Simplicity*, 77.

- On the other hand, Paul exhorts "free" citizens in the Roman Empire's system to use the status to be a "slave" of Jesus (v. 22).

- On the one hand, don't opt out of day-to-day life. Paul's own example in Corinth was to work his trade (Acts 18).

- But on the other hand, don't get tempted by the seductions of commerce and accumulating stuff (vv. 29–31).

Paul urges that we always think missiologically about our choices in relationships. We can have an eternal impact. Be Jesus' "slave" (*doulos*) in every situation (*doulos* is Paul's self-designation and his highest calling—see Phil 1:1). Life in Christ, energized and guided by the Spirit who raised Jesus, is a life of balance. But we discover this balance by pursuing a single-eyed priority. "I want you to give yourselves *completely to the Lord*" (v. 35).

HARVESTING THE TEACHING OF CHAPTERS 6 AND 7

Paul's agenda is to guide young Christ-followers who are seeking to enjoy life in Christ in the midst of "the country of death." Paul and his spiritual children are walking together along this journey and it is a journey that no one has walked before. The Christian movement is still in its earliest years and there is very little precedent for navigating this pathway in a pagan center like Corinth. Chapters 6 and 7 offer the necessary guidance from a father who knows with certainty that his counsel is based on insight which he has received from the Spirit (see Paul's comments in vss. 25, 40: ". . . I think that I too have the Spirit of God.").

In chapters 6 and 7, Paul seeks to bring about a paradigm shift in relation to the traditional worldview of Hellenism. New-creation thinking about life is radically distinct (holy). Paul challenges two serious distortions which those new to the community bring along from their culture of origin: a twisted notion of freedom, and a gnostic-style dualism that despises or trivializes the physical body. Salvation, according to the Bible, is not an escape from existence in a material realm to the realm of ideas and spirit. As biblical Christians we hope for the future resurrection of the body (rather than looking forward to "immortality of the soul.").[24]

24. On "immortality of the soul," Fee explains how Jesus' resurrection transforms the viewpoint of the prevailing culture: "This affirmation (resurrection of the body) stands in bold contrast to the Corinthians' view of spirituality, which looked for a 'spiritual' salvation that would finally be divested of the body . . . Out of such a view developed the idea of the 'immortality of the soul' . . . This is a totally pagan view . . . In stark contrast to the Greek view, the OT declares that at creation, God looked on the universe that he had made and pronounced it good. The final consummation looks to

Paul teaches that when we are aligned with the new-creation narrative, we embrace a worldview in which spirituality is about day-to-day living, not some special holy vocation or setting (like being a monk or missionary or attending a church service and doing spiritual stuff). Henri Nouwen says:

> Jesus does not respond to our worry-filled way of living by say-ing that we should not be so busy with worldly affairs. He does not try to pull us away from the many events, activities, and people that make up our lives. He does not tell us that what we do is unimportant, valueless, or useless. Nor does he suggest that we should withdraw from our involvements and live quiet, restful lives, removed from the struggles of the world. Jesus asks us to shift the point of gravity, to relocate the center of our atten-tion, to change our priorities. Jesus wants us to move from the "many things" to the "one necessary thing." . . . He speaks about a change of heart . . . This is the meaning of "Set your hearts on his kingdom first."[25]

Remember the great idea—*Resurrection people truly love bodies because God made them, owns them, redeemed them, and will transform them.* The Creator designed us for wholeness and created our sexuality to be a source of delight. The wisdom of God revealed in this apostolic counsel regarding sexuality is "an expression of the beautiful mind of God,"[26] and reveals the pathway to a flourishing life. We can summarize some key themes as follows:

- Sexual purity is a core value of the resurrection community. This is because God is pro-body (6:13) and our physical bodies are temples, as taught in 6:19. Purity is valued because purity is the path to human flourishing.

- Paul urges that we always keep the mission of the community in view in decision-making. He guides his children to regularly ask, "What is the gospel impact of my choice?"

- Paul's overarching priority in relationships is that we should seek free-dom to serve Jesus totally unencumbered. He believes we can continue in our circumstances while enjoying a new freedom. Marital status is irrelevant to this highest priority. In Paul's teaching, either living as

---

a new heaven and a new earth; and in that new order the body will be raised so that God's people will experience the final wholeness that God intended" (*First Epistle to the Corinthians*, 256–57). See also Wright, *Surprised by Hope,* and Cullman, *Immortality and Resurrection.*

25. Nouwen, *Making All Things New*, 41–42.

26. Willard, *Divine Conspiracy*, 141.

a married person or as a single person is equally okay. Each Christ-follower must discover what her/his own gift and calling is. Paul affirms that God gives a charisma to every person.

- Mutuality, respect, and mutual responsibility between men and women are new-creation values. Paul repeatedly addresses women and men as equally free and equally responsible to love and serve. (The way he addresses the Corinthians is an application of Eph 5:21, "submit to one another out of reverence for Christ.") His stress on the way both a husband and wife must serve each other by meeting the spouse's sexual needs is countercultural. Paul clearly affirms that sexual intercourse in marriage is a good gift, following Gen 2:22. Paul will not permit dualism to destroy marriage relationships.

APPLYING THE SPIRIT'S WISDOM AMIDST TODAY'S SEXUAL INSANITY

Can we find some ways to apply Paul's sometimes strange and confusing teaching? Is it too remote for today?

Needed—a robust theology of the goodness of sexuality

This chapter began by inviting us to do a gut check, not specifically about matters of sexuality, but rather about our confidence in God's goodness. We listened to Ps 19 and heard the psalmist celebrate his discovery of God's revealed wisdom. In a similar vein, we read David's ecstatic delight over his possession of God's truth in Ps 119: "You are good and what you do is good; teach me your decrees" (v. 68); "I rejoice in following your statutes as one rejoices in great riches" (v. 14).

Perhaps one of the most urgently needed gifts that Christ-followers could give to Western culture today would be for the church to articulate and live a joyful theology of the goodness of sexuality. The intimacy and pleasure of holy sexual intercourse in a covenant relationship is God's good gift. As the psalmist affirms: "I will walk about in freedom, for I have sought out your precepts" (119:45).

Western culture is psychotic when it comes to matters of sex. And the results flowing from our self-inflicted blindness to truth are devastating. US culture regards any restriction of an individual's freedom for sexual experiences of any kinds as anathema. Certainly as a society we are living with a conspiracy of denial and fantasy. People are miserable and countless lives are broken as a result of uninhibited sexual expression. Despair and alienation are prevalent motifs in our art and literature.

In current technological society, we experience epidemic levels of loneliness and alienation. To attempt to sooth the pain of loneliness, we substitute genital sexual expression for authentic intimacy. This fails and we end up broken, shamed, degraded, and alienated.

God's community can offer a delightful alternative if we study, embrace, articulate, and live the teachings of Scripture. Theologian Marva Dawn has cast a compelling vision for what she calls "Sexual Shalom." She observes that, as persons, we are created by God as sexual—and *good!*—beings and we can only and always relate to another as sexual beings (gender-based). We relate in real life through our bodies and these bodies are sexually differentiated. This has potential to bring great delight and deep satisfaction. She writes:

> Shalom starts with the recognition that God is a gracious God. The Creator designed us for wholeness and created our sexuality to be a source of delight. . . . Shalom, based in the character of God and flourishing in the intimacy of the Christian community, enables us to be truly at peace with others and with ourselves. . . . God's people need to recapture the biblical sense of the community, for all of us together are required to build in the Body the sexual Shalom we seek. We need the whole community to love us, to support us, to teach us, to guide us, to rebuke us, to forgive us, to bring to us God's healing. The Church must be the Church. . . . Then we will have the peace within ourselves that instills courage to resist our society's false notions of genital sexuality.[27]

Giving genital sex its holy and delightful place in life leads to joy

The intimacy and pleasure of holy sexual intercourse in a covenant relationship is God's good gift. "God has designed sexual intercourse as the special sign of a permanent commitment between a man and a woman, a covenant that takes them beyond themselves and their own sexual pleasure into the larger realm of seeking the purposes of God's kingdom."[28]

Our psychotic culture needs guidance and positive examples. "The assumption in our society is that genital sexual expression is the 'be-all and end-all' of human existence."[29] Richard Foster speaks truth into the madness:

27. Dawn, *Sexual Character*, 164.
28. Dawn, *Sexual Character*, 165.
29. Dawn, *Sexual Character*, 5.

In fact, what we call sexual needs are really not needs at all but wants. The body needs food, air, and water—without these, human life cannot long survive. But no one has yet died from a lack of sexual intercourse. Many have lived quite full and satisfying lives without genital sex—including Jesus. So sexual intercourse is a human want, not a human need, and the difference is significant.[30]

Sexual intercourse involves something far more than just the physical, more than even the emotions. It produces a profound union that the biblical writers call "one flesh":

We esteem genital sexuality as a beautiful and powerful reality which calls forth the person in the depths of his or her being . . . it is not something superficial. The unique friend—the husband or the wife—is not simply a partner in a sport. He or she is the beloved, the chosen one of the heart, to whom one entrusts that which is most intimate in one's body and in one's heart. The exercise of sexuality leads to a new relationship. . . . The most authentic Christian version does not deny, condemn, or devalue genital sexuality; on the contrary, it sees it as a reality so beautiful and so profound that it can be lived fully and most humanly only if the two persons recognize the bonds which unite them forever; these are a covenant, founded on the covenant of each one with God.[31]

Forgiveness and healing for failures

It's a tragic reality that discussions of God's life-enhancing instructions concerning the gift of sexuality bring to the surface feelings of guilt in so many. Rejecting God's ways can create a lot of anguish. So let us return again to the good news concerning cross power:

Our culture is rife with sexual idolatry . . . *but* God's grace is larger than our idolatries and misunderstandings . . . God's

30. Foster, *Money, Sex, and Power*, 152. Foster continues: "Genital sex outside of marriage is wrong because it violates the inner reality of the act; it is wrong because unmarried people thereby engage in a life-uniting act without a life-uniting intent. . .Intercourse signs and seals—and maybe even delivers—a life-union; and life-union means marriage" (118).

31. Vanier, *Man and Woman, He Made Them*, 122. Vanier adds: "The values of gift and communion implied in the gestures of love carry with them something absolute . . . In the Christian vision, this mutual gift of the man and the woman, this new bond through the body and genital sexuality, is so profound that it is acknowledged as the image of that which unites Christ with his Church" (122).

love and forgiveness are larger than our rebellion. Shalom for Christians is based on the assurance that in Jesus Christ we are totally forgiven and set free from our human propensity to make ourselves (and our sexual fulfillment) gods.[32]

In order for the power of the gospel words concerning hope, forgiveness, and healing to be experienced in our word-resistant culture, our churches must become grace-saturated communities. We are invited to submit to the Spirit of Jesus and partner with Jesus in becoming new-creation families. Paul has cast the vision for the church in his writings: "as God's chosen people, holy and dearly loved, clothe yourselves with compassion, kindness, humility, gentleness and patience. Bear with each other and forgive one another if any of you has a grievance against someone. Forgive as the Lord forgave you. And over all these virtues put on love, which binds them all together in perfect unity" (Col 3:12–14).

Marva Dawn's compelling vision of "sexual shalom" describes the healing power of communities saturated with God's love. Dawn writes:

> The friendships of the Christian community will also be a source of healing and strength for those who have been broken by the lack of sexual shalom in our world. The love of Christ at work in the members of his Body will seek to enfold and encourage homosexuals who suffer profoundly in their loneliness or confusion, victims of abuse, those who have been abandoned or rejected in divorce, children of unpeaceful homes, women who grieve an abortion, single persons who long to be married but find no godly companions, teenagers who are overwhelmed by peer pressures, persons in troubled marriages, and any others who need the gifts of genuine friendship.[33]

Nurturing such "sexual shalom" through the power of the Holy Spirit can be a "tangible and radiant" expression of God's goodness, for as Dawn says, "The world around us is longing for the truth and security, the delight and fulfillment of sexual shalom."[34]

---

32. Dawn, *Sexual Character*, 163, 164 (italics ours).

33. Dawn, *Sexual Character*, 167.

34. Dawn, *Sexual Character*, 168.

Chapter 7

A Renewed Humanity

Holiness and Human Flourishing
in New-Creation Perspective

"A Christian is a perfectly free lord of all, subject to none. A Christian is a perfectly dutiful servant of all, subject of all, subject to all."
MARTIN LUTHER[1]

READ: 1 COR 8–10

What is the best way to wreck a church? What is Satan's preferred strategy for derailing the kingdom movement? I do not pretend to understand the mind of Satan. I do know, as Paul tells us, that the enemy of God is exceedingly clever and typically "masquerades as an angel of light." Satan is too cunning to come right out and hit us with blatant perversity. We might be on to him if he overplays his hand. I would like to propose an unscientific hypothesis regarding the number one cause of church weakness, pathology, loss of vitality, and death. I suggest that the number one tactic is to foment interpersonal conflict among fellow believers—squabbling, slander and

1. Luther, "Treatise on Christian Liberty," 251.

gossip, mutual recriminations, unwillingness to forgive, and harsh criticism of fellow disciples.

Particular local churches are fragile entities. It is absolutely true that The Church is invincible and cannot be destroyed (as Jesus says in Matt 16:18 and Paul affirms in Phil 1:6, "He who began a good work in you (plural) will carry it on to completion."). However, there is an abundance of tragic empirical evidence that specific local churches in many cases cease to exist. We have many historical examples, like the seven churches in Asia Minor mentioned in Rev 2–3. Take a walk around England or northern New England or Western Europe and you will see what were once great cathedrals and church buildings with flourishing ministries, but which today are museums, gift shops, or mosques. All of us can think of a particular church which has completely ceased operations. What are the reasons why a church stops being a church?

Sometimes substantive doctrinal controversies over core Christian beliefs can create division and conflict. Recall the challenges faced by the early Christian leaders such as Athanasius and the controversies in Alexandria.[2] Sometimes scandals involving pastoral leadership can cripple a church. These are nowadays so frequent that no illustration is needed. Sometimes money issues bring strife. There are many cases in which changing racial demographics in an urban neighborhood in a US city causes congregations to divide or even die. Although there can be many causes, I am still sticking to my hypothesis: the number one reason is interpersonal conflict among fellow believers—good old-fashioned bickering.

In C. S. Lewis's penetrating classic, *The Screwtape Letters*, the titular "senior demon" gives this advice to his nephew, Wormwood, about his tempting of a new Christian:

> ". . . if your patient can't be kept out of the Church, he ought at least to be violently attached to some party within it. I don't mean on real doctrinal issues; about those, the more lukewarm he is the better. . . . the real fun is working up hatred between those who say 'mass' and those who say 'Holy Communion' when neither party could possibly state the difference between [the two]."[3]

In view of this ever-present peril, the pastoral counsel in chapters 8–10 is some of the most urgently needed wisdom that we as Christ-followers

---

2. See the classic by Jaroslav Pelikan, *The Christian Tradition: A History of the Development of Doctrine,* for an analysis of the doctrinal controversies of the second and third centuries involving Athanasius and other Church Fathers. Also see Irvin and Sunquist, *History of the World Christian Movement.*

3. Lewis, *Screwtape Letters,* 75.

can ever receive. This is not just about some now-irrelevant cultural practice regarding clean-versus-unclean holiness codes in ancient Hellenism. Although the presenting problem the Corinthians wrote to Paul about had to do with eating meat offered to idols, Paul's guidance given to the community in these three chapters reframes the original issue. He exposes what are inevitable human dynamics which can express themselves with devastating results—division, arrogance, bitterness, a sense of moral superiority, and factionalism.

The great idea which is revealed in chapters 8–10 is: *The greatest exercise of true freedom (and the greatest evidence of genuine divine wisdom) is the free act of renouncing my rights for the sake of a fellow Christian. This is Jesus-style love.*

In exploring chapters 8–10, we will observe Paul showing us "the better way"—the way of *agapē*. As we learn to live together in Christ, we learn a way of life in which Jesus' values are gladly embraced. A, perhaps *the*, central value of Jesus' way is applied in day-in, day-out relationships in chapters 8–10. That applied value says: "None of you should look out just for your own good. Each of you should also look out for the good of others. As you deal with one another, you should think and act as Jesus did. . ." (Phil 2:4–5). As a Christ-follower, I want to learn to love like Jesus. Many of his teachings are counterintuitive. But he is Lord and he is brilliant. Obedience to Jesus leads to maximum human flourishing. So following his example, I determine to pursue shalom for *you*—even if I must sacrifice in this pursuit. Paul is a powerful guide for us, since in chapters 8–10 he offers his own lifestyle as a model. He dares to say: "Follow me, as I follow Christ. (11:1).

DISCOVERING WISDOM IN 1 COR 8–10

We are accustomed to seeing the contents of the Bible divided into chapters and verses. We know that the chapter divisions and verse numbers are not inspired by the Spirit who guided the apostolic writers. It is important in following the author's spiritual direction to absorb chapters 8–10 as a unit, and not permit artificial breaks and boundaries to intrude into our reading and thinking.

First Cor 8:1 introduces the presenting problem: "Now about food sacrificed to idols":

In the letter delivered to Paul from his friends in the Corinthian community, they raise a question regarding the matter of eating *eidōlothutōn*, the meat that has been in the pagan temples of Corinth. The nature of this problem raised by these early Christians is not obvious to those of us in the twenty-first-century West. This is one of those issues in Scripture that requires that we who are unfamiliar with ancient Hellenistic culture do some historical investigating in order to understand the situation arising in a very different culture.[4]

Let me summarize a few aspects of the situation in Corinth. In his exploration of the ancient world of Corinth, Professor Ben Witherington III, explains that some, if not most, of the meat available in the local city market had a history of being a temple sacrifice.[5] "The word *eidōlothuton* ("idol food," 8:1, 4,7, 10; 10:19) is not a pagan term, since pagans would hardly call their gods 'idols.' It is rather a polemical term that arose in early Christianity for the sacred food eaten in pagan temple precincts after a sacrifice."[6] Archaeological excavations have revealed that several temples in Corinth had dining rooms where feasts were held on many occasions, including birthdays. Temples served as the restaurants of antiquity. "Most of the *nouveau riches* of Corinth owed their money to maritime commerce. . . . It was necessary for such people to maintain their social contacts in order to keep their businesses going."[7] A typical business luncheon would be held in a pagan temple. Research also reveals that the poorer person in an ancient city like Corinth did not often eat meat. Meat was relatively expensive. "If the poor got meat, it was likely at such a feast as part of a celebration involving eating in temple precincts or as a bequest given by the more well-to-do in honor of a god."[8]

So the eating of this previously sacrificed meat was a complex matter with spiritual, social, economic, and cultural implications. As is common

4. There are excellent study resources which can be accessed by all students of the Bible (no need to be a full-time scholar). See, for example, Keener, *IVP Bible Background Commentary*. Also, see two short and very readable historical fiction sources: Banks, *Going to Church in the First Century*, and Witherington, *Week in the Life of Corinth*. In addition, there are fine commentaries written for nonspecialists, such as Witherington, *Conflict and Community in Corinth*.

5. Witherington, *Conflict and Community in Corinth*, 189.

6. Witherington, *Conflict and Community in Corinth*, 189.

7 Rostovtzeff, *The Social and Economic History of the Roman Empire*, 172. See also, Meeks, First *Urban Christians*, 67–70.

8. Witherington, *Conflict and Community in Corinth*, 189. See also Witherington, "Not so Idle Thoughts about *Eidōlothuton*," 237–54.

in Paul's letters, when he addresses a matter raised by some members of the church he will begin the dialogue by quoting statements that represent the viewpoint of some of these Corinthians.[9] He does this in 8:1, "We know that 'We all possess knowledge.'" At least one segment of this community was quite proud of the fact that they "possessed knowledge" (gnōsis).[10] Wisdom and knowledge were highly prized in ancient Corinth. Paul brought genuine gnōsis of the true God when he brought the message of the Christian gospel. In fact, what this segment of the church was claiming as knowledge was true teaching which they had learned from Paul (especially the ideas in verses 4–6). The theological content was absolutely true. But there was a serious problem with the arrogant attitude. This is a persistent peril for people who embrace truth. The temptation to pride is always lurking close by. For this reason, Paul immediately challenges their contention, "We all possess knowledge," with a counterclaim which warns us of the danger.

8:1–3: "But knowledge puffs up while love builds up. Those who think they know something do not yet know as they ought to know. But whoever loves God is known by God."

Are you observing the discernment exercised by Paul and his skillful reframing of the issue? The presenting problem concerned the consumption of idol meat. But Paul discerns that the real peril facing the community is pride. The attitude of the members who possess the truth can be a source of division and conflict and can cause harm in the community. They may be right, but they are also wrong. Paul rebukes the mantra of this group right at the beginning of the dialogue. What is the danger inherent in being "enlightened?" It "puffs up."[11]

The nonnegotiable positive dynamic that any community requires is that it be "built up" (see ch. 12 and 14:3–5, 26 on *oikodomei*, and Eph 4:29).[12] Paul regards "being built up" as a priority value and a guide to genuinely community-enriching behaviors. What is truly enabled by the Holy

9. Since Paul's letters are actual correspondence, he frequently interacts with the churches by quoting the opponents, as in 6:12–13; 7:1; 15:12.

10. Refer to the earlier discussions of gnōsis in previous chapters (2 and 6).

11. On being "puffed up," see Hays, *First Corinthians*, 137. "Paul has already used this vivid metaphorical verb several times in the letter, urging the Corinthians not to be 'puffed up in favor of one against the other' (4:6), warning them not to be puffed up against his own apostolic authority (4:18–19), and castigating them for being puffed up about (or in spite of) the case of incest in their midst (5:2)." This also previews what Paul will say about love in chapter 13:4–5. Love is the antithesis of being puffed up.

12. Dunn, *Jesus and the Spirit*, 293–96.

Spirit will bring about "edification" since the Spirit's purpose is to "build the Temple of God" according to Eph 2:21–22. "Whatever does not build up, whatever word or action destroys the congregation's unity or causes hurt to its members . . . that word or action fails the test of *oikodome*, and should be ignored or rejected."

Paul turns the tables on the know-it-alls. It is not what I know, but the reality that *God knows me!* What we boast in, according to Paul, is loving God in response to God's grace demonstrated at the cross. "Let him who boasts, boast in the Lord" (1:31). Paul affirms the priority of love over arrogant possession of true knowledge. The greatest good is to love God and be known by God.

8:4–8: Is food that has been sacrificed safe?

In 8:4, Paul again picks up the issue of eating food sacrificed to idols which people living in Corinth must deal with on a recurring basis. It is significant to observe that Paul does not just give a command. He could have produced a copy of a letter with the "signatures" of the members of the Jerusalem Council (see Acts 15:29). In the letter from the council to the gentile churches, there is specific mention of avoiding meat offered to idols (*eidōlothuton*). But Paul's goal is not to put them under law, but to lead them to maturity which involves Spirit-guided moral reasoning grounded in Jesus' teachings. He wishes to guide them to embrace new-creation values.

In 8:4b–6, Paul articulates the essential theological knowledge that drives this conflict. The Corinthians are correct in their understanding. Paul agrees. (Notice that he does not call this group "the strong." He does not frame this issue as "weak" versus "strong.") There are two key theological affirmations which are in play in this situation: First, an idol is nothing. This is a strong theme in many Old Testament prophets, for example Isa 44:9–20. Second, there is one real God (again a confession rooted in Old Testament Scripture, i.e., Israel's *shema*.)[13]

However, Paul discerns that there are diverse sensitivities within the Corinthian family. "But not everyone possesses this knowledge" (8:7). Paul has returned to the community-centered dynamics once again because of his commitment to our being formed into a new-creation community characterized by oneness. So although the know-it-all Corinthians proudly affirm, "We all possess knowledge," Paul counters with, "Not all possess

13. Notice the statement "one God and one Lord." This is an implicit affirmation of the Trinitarian divine nature here in embryonic form. The deep mystery regarding God's triunity is assumed, but not developed or elaborated.

knowledge," since he is aware of the diversity of knowledge and experience within the church.

Paul recognizes that we are all shaped by our culture and that this early formation results in different perceptions of what is moral versus immoral or clean versus unclean (8:7). As we learned in studying chapter 5, one's culture of origin has a huge influence on how one sees reality and we bring this cultural knowledge with us when we come into Christ.[14] Paul can empathize with these weak members of the Corinthian community. He does not agree theologically. But he appreciates their struggles and the risks they face. He will fight vehemently against legalists (as in Col 2). But here he is sensitive to the inner struggles of the new believers.

Paul clarifies that the specific substance has no moral weight. "Food does not bring us near to God; we are no worse if we do not eat, and no better if we do" (8:8). Here he defines clean versus unclean in a way that is consistent with Jesus' teachings, as for example Mark 7:18–23, where Jesus says,

> "Don't you see that nothing that enters a person from the outside can defile them? For it doesn't go into their heart but into their stomach, and then out of the body." (In saying this, Jesus declared all foods clean.) He went on: "What comes out of a person is what defiles them. For it is from within, out of a person's heart, that evil thoughts come—sexual immorality, theft, murder, adultery, greed, malice, deceit, lewdness, envy, slander, arrogance and folly. All these evils come from inside and defile a person."

According to Jesus, holiness is not about a substance. Uncleanness does not attach itself to material stuff. The actual meat, in the Corinthian case, falls into the category of *adiaphora* (a Greek word used by the church fathers to refer to "matters of indifference.")[15] Therefore, the knowledge these members have is correct, but . . .

---

14. In studying ch. 5, we considered how primary socialization instills in a person deep values that are difficult to change. See the study of sociology of knowledge in reference to ch. 5.

15. Alister McGrath defines *adiaphora* as "literally 'matters of indifference.' Beliefs or practices which the sixteenth-century Reformers regarded as being tolerable, in that they were neither explicitly rejected nor stipulated by Scripture" (*Christian Theology Reader*, 392). It means simply those things which are neither commanded by Scripture nor forbidden by Scripture. The idea of *adiaphora* is that these actions are neutral. They aren't sinful because they don't break any commandments, but—having no command from God to do them—there is no sin in abstaining from them.

8:9–11: "Be careful, however, that the exercise of your rights does not become a stumbling block to the weak."

Paul is zeroing in on the real moral issue in 8:9—holiness is about relationships. He explains the potential peril that might result from an insensitive expression of so-called freedom in 8:10–11. Here's how this might work: "For if someone with a weak conscience sees you, with all your knowledge, eating in an idol's temple, won't that person be emboldened to eat what is sacrificed to idols? So this weak brother or sister, for whom Christ died, is destroyed by your knowledge." Note carefully who it is that is seen as weak in this situation. A person is deemed weak in that this person cannot be true to his/her own inner convictions. Being weak has to do with being easily enticed or influenced; not able to stand firm. So this is the scenario that Paul says we must guard against if we have knowledge. Paul asks them to imagine a common scenario:

- I know that an idol is merely a block of wood (Isa 44).

- I accept an invitation to a business lunch which is held in the dining court of a pagan temple (as was so very common in Corinth).

- I know there is no reality to the idol or the shrine. Jesus is Lord! I am free.

- But a fellow Christ-follower, who has walked a different pathway and who is hyper-sensitive to the perils of idolatry (maybe a former priest or temple worker who has experienced the fear), sees me enjoying the meal within the shrine. That person is emboldened by my example to join a similar business engagement at a shrine, even though his inner voice is telling him this is defiling and unclean.

- The result is that this brother is destroyed (his conscience is contaminated)

The issue identified in 8:7 is the contaminated conscience. This contamination results from doing something which my own inner moral value system says is immoral. I am enticed by the example of a fellow believer to act in a way that I believe I must not act.

Why should I care if someone else has issues as a result of their limited theological understanding? Paul is aware (and apparently some Corinthians are not) of the infinite value of the sister or brother over whom I might have influence because of my choices. He refers to this fellow Christ-follower as a "brother or sister, for whom Christ died" (8:11). The Christian brother is dearly loved by Jesus, who shed his own blood for that person. In 6:19–20, we discovered that we are not our own, but that we have been "bought with a price." Therefore this weak brother is a person purchased and possessed by Jesus at infinite cost. Furthermore, we are members of one another because we are all in Christ, and together the risen Jesus is in us, and this mystical oneness defines our identity. Thus, a sin against a brother is to be understood as a sin against the Messiah himself. "When you sin against them in this way and wound their weak conscience, you sin against Christ" (8:12).

8:13: "Therefore, if what I eat causes my brother or sister to fall into sin, I will never eat meat again, so that I will not cause them to fall."

Paul builds to a crescendo in verse 13. Paul is free to give up rights in order to do what's best for the other person. This is the Jesus ethic of Phil 2 applied in this relational context. Paul is so free that he can relinquish his right to eat (it is not morally evil, nor is it unclean). What really matters is that "weak" friend. So here is the first application of the *great idea*: The greatest Christian exercise of freedom (and the greatest evidence of true divine *gnōsis*) is the free act of renouncing my rights for the sake of a Christian brother. Chapter 8 is a teaching about *agapē* even through the word is not found here in verse 13. *Agapē* is the core value of the community and the heart of new-creation lifestyle.

Paul continues his apostolic counsel by presenting (in what we refer to as ch. 9) a long personal testimony which gives an extensive illustration of how 8:13-type freedom works. Paul is redefining freedom based on Jesus. Learning to see freedom as voluntarily imposing constraints on my desires is really counterintuitive. But the ways of the new-creation lifestyle will always be counterintuitive. Our minds are being transformed.

CASE STUDY IN FREEDOM (1 COR 9)

So how does an effective leader go about resocializing a community into an alternative value system? In their wildly successful executive training program, *The Five Principles of Exemplary Leadership*, Kouzes and Posner affirm that exemplary behavior number one is for a leader to "model the way." It's what effective leaders do. They truly walk the talk. "Eloquent speeches about common values are not nearly enough. Exemplary leaders know that it's their behavior that earns them respect. The real test is whether they do what they say; whether their words and deeds are consistent."[16] About 2,000

16. Kouzes and Posner, *Five Principles of Exemplary Leadership*, 2.

years ago, a radically transformed Jew named Paul was already on to this. Since *agapē* is the counterintuitive core value of this new movement and the heart of new-creation lifestyle, Paul understands that it's up to him to be the model. At the end of this entire exploration of the idol-meat issue, Paul will write: "Follow my example, just as I follow the example of Christ."

9:1–14: Why an Apostle has a right to be compensated.

Chapter 9 is a case study in living the free life. Paul begins with a series of rhetorical questions to engage his readers. The answers to the four questions in verse 1 are obvious to all—"yes." "Yes, Paul, you are indeed free"; "Yes, Paul, you are a *bona fide* apostle"; "Yes, Paul, you have encountered the risen Lord Jesus in person"; and "Yes, Paul, our very existence as Christians is the result of your mission."

These friends know from experience that it was as a result of Paul's proclamation of the gospel about Jesus that they have been transformed and reconciled to God. The verification of the legitimacy of Paul's claim to the apostolic role is the impact that his life has had on these people.

Paul continues to guide this process by raising three more provocative questions in verses 3–6. Once again, we know the answers to the questions being raised. There is no dispute. "Yes, Paul, you certainly have a right to a living allowance for all your apostolic labor"; "Yes, Paul, it would be very legitimate for you to travel with a believing wife (just like other apostles do, e.g., Peter)[17]; and"No, Paul, you should not be required to do manual labor to fund your apostolic mission." This question about whether it is only Paul and his colleague Barnabas who have to pay their own way as they offer Christ to new regions is the link to the next segment of this case study.

Paul will craft a compelling argument in verses 6–14 which establishes his legitimate right to be compensated for his apostolic work. He builds his case on five pillars, and crowns the argument by referring to Jesus himself, who says that those who live to declare the gospel ought to be compensated for this work. Paul is not making a mockery of the principle of fairness in compensation and the need that a responsible worker be given what he is due. This is basic justice. But next Paul pulls the trigger rhetorically. He now stuns us by announcing that, although it is

17. Paul's rhetorical questions have sparked considerable debate, especially his reference to taking along a believing wife. Some scholars argue that it would be highly irregular for Paul to have achieved such prominence in Judaism in this time (see Phil 3) if he were not married. The rabbis expected a Jewish man to marry. Some speculate that Paul's wife's family forced her to desert Paul following his conversion. This is all speculation, with no historical data.

abundantly clear that he can legitimately make the claim to compensation, he will never cash in on that right.

9:15–17: Paul's joyful gospel freedom is expressed in his renouncing compensation.

By describing his own free choices, Paul is counseling the know-it-alls introduced in chapter 8 to set aside their legitimate rights and use their freedom to serve the weak brothers. Are they free to eat anything? Definitely. Is the right to eat anything I want evidence of a superior level of knowledge and spiritual prowess? Actually, no. Paul's case study seeks to redefine freedom, and Paul is daring to use his own choices as the model of this new-creation value. In verse 12, he says his reason for not claiming compensation is so that his motivation driving his gospel ministry cannot be called into question. In today's religious environment, this question concerning motivation has a huge impact on our credibility.

There is a widely held perception in many parts of the globe today that preachers are only in it for the money. We who are Christian leaders bear a big piece of the responsibility for this perception. We have all agonized through multiple scandals involving high-profile TV preachers exposed for living extravagant lifestyles at the expense of their faithful donors.[18] The apostle is very discerning and realizes that in the Corinthian cultural context it is highly probable that the economics of ministry will impact the credibility of the messenger and the perceived validity of the message.[19] Paul renounces all deceptions and money-making scams. Paul chooses a lifestyle that will reflect pure motives and not call into question the integrity of the gospel.

The climax of this case study is verses 14–15, in which Paul lays bare his inner motivations. He has just stated that the Lord Jesus himself has authorized compensation for apostolic work (v. 14). And immediately Paul declares: "But I have not used any of these rights." He clarifies that this case

18. The US news, not long ago, covered the scandal of TV evangelist Creflo Dollar's urgent campaign to raise enough money from "the faithful" to fund the purchase of his new private jet (Kuruvilla, "Televangelist Creflo Dollar Defends His Plans."). In Africa, hardly a week passes with yet another news article about a shepherd who is exposed as "fleecing his flock." See Njeru, "JTM."

19. Witherington, *Conflict and Community in Corinth,* 208, notes: "There were itinerant teachers throughout the Mediterranean region, some of whom accepted fees or patronage or like the Cynics begged for a living. Apparently Paul did not want to be identified with such people even in the least, especially where some might suspect that he was in the preaching business in order to bilk people. The Sophists were particularly noted for bilking patrons; the Cynics turned to work and begging as a protest against such greed."

study is not a veiled attempt to manipulate the Corinthian disciples into putting him on their payroll. He's not dumping guilt. "I am not writing this in the hope that you will do such things for me" (v. 15).[20]

He goes so far as to say that he would actually rather be dead than be deprived of his freedom to do God's work without receiving a paycheck from the recipients. This exercise of freedom means so much to Paul. He asserts that, by carrying out his God-given assignment, but doing this work free of charge, this expression of freedom to renounce rights is something that he celebrates since it is an evidence of cross power working through his own weakness.[21] "What then is my reward? Just this: that in preaching the gospel I may offer it free of charge, and so not make full use of my rights as a preacher of the gospel" (v. 17).

9:18–22: Paul's freedom is expressed in building gospel relationships with all kinds of people

Paul's joyful gospel freedom is expressed in other ways in addition to his renouncing compensation. Freedom is not just about finances (although freedom *vis a vis* money is certainly a huge achievement and blessing). He says he is free to move into multicultural contexts and freely adapt his ways to a variety of social and religious dynamics. Paul's freedom is expressed in building gospel relationships with all kinds of people (vv. 19–22). "I have voluntarily become a servant to any and all in order to reach a wide range of people: religious, nonreligious, meticulous moralists, loose-living immoralists, the defeated, the demoralized—whoever" (MSG). This is really very stunning for a man who was a very scrupulous and devout Jew. Recall Paul's testimony recorded in Phil 3, in which Paul boasts that he was an

20. Paul's refusal to accept gifts from Corinthians (especially the few wealthy members) seems to have been an ongoing source of conflict. Some proud, wealthy members were quite insulted, it seems, when Paul would not agree to become the client of a wealthy patron, as was common in Corinthian society. See Witherington, *Week in the Life of Corinth*, 58: "One of the most dangerous things a person could do was to refuse a gift from a social superior."

21. Paul talks a lot about boasting in his letters. There is a paradox in his boasting. When he boasts, it is not an arrogant expression of superior human achievement. Paul is continually conscious that God has called him to the apostolic work and that God's power at work in him is the source of all the good that Paul might accomplish. Paul's only contribution is his "weakness" (see 1:29). When he boasts, he is delighting in what cross-power is able to do through a sinful vessel. Paul sees preaching the gospel without financial compensation as another manifestation of his human weakness. See Fee, *First Epistle to the Corinthians*, 417–18. Also see Rom 15:17–18.

overachiever in all matters of his religion. Adherence to rigid cultural and religious boundaries would have been completely normal to Paul.

But Paul has been transformed. And Paul is given (by the Spirit of Jesus) deep insight into God's universal agenda. Paul becomes convinced by a direct revelation from the risen Jesus that this is truly the new-creation era which is now unfolding following the resurrection of Jesus. Israel's God is God of all people, not a tribal deity (as in 8:4–8, "one God of all creation"). Paul affirms: "God made peace with everything in heaven and on earth by means of Christ's blood on the cross . . . The good news has been preached all over the world, and I, Paul, have been appointed as God's servant to proclaim it" (Col 1:20, 23).

Paul has the courage to recognize that this global agenda means that the new movement cannot be captive to any one culture or religious tradition. So Paul, as an agent of the crucified and risen Lord of all, experiences wonderful freedom to build redemptive relationships with diverse cultural groups. "I have become all things to all people so that by all possible means I might save some" (1 Cor 9:22). Please note the clear motive and goal: so they will be saved. Paul is not an early crusader for some sort of relativistic, open-ended multiculturalism. "Though I am free and belong to no one, I have made myself a slave to everyone, to win as many as possible" (1 Cor 9:19). Ben Witherington III observes that:

> Paul believed that Christianity could not be an ethnically specific religion (9:20). If it was to be for everyone . . . accepting all as they were in their cultural orientations, it could not in its essence be about food, clothing, or other ethnic and culture-specific customs (such as circumcision). Why does Paul take this approach? . . . For Paul, the boundaries of the Christian community should be defined theologically (one God and one Lord with no participation in worship of false gods) and ethically (no sexual immorality), but *not* socially or ethnically. All social levels, all races, all ethnic groups, and both genders can be Christian just as they are.[22]

Paul's freedom presents a challenge to today's church to be continually reforming so as to be more missionally adaptable and intentional.[23]

---

22. Witherington, *Conflict and Community in Corinth*, 200–1 (italics original).

23 " . . . ecclesial conversion as openness to a constant self-renewal born of fidelity to Jesus Christ: Every renewal of the Church essentially consists in an increase of fidelity to her own calling . . . Christ summons the Church as she goes her pilgrim way . . . to that continual reformation of which she always has need, insofar as she is a human institution here on earth . . . There are ecclesial structures which can hamper efforts at evangelization . . . I dream of a 'missionary option,' that is, a missionary impulse capable

Paul is a wise spiritual director. He knows very well that this freedom can be abused. Paul is always the champion of freedom and he will not back down. The letter he wrote to the Galatian Christians is evidence of the extent of his conviction and his willingness to face severe suffering as a result of this radical teaching. "It is absolutely clear that God has called you to a free life. Just make sure that you don't use this freedom as an excuse to do whatever you want to do and destroy your freedom. Rather, use your freedom to serve one another in love; that's how freedom grows" (Gal 5:13).

The problem with embracing freedom is not that somebody might get away with something naughty. The deep concern is that people who might abuse his ideas may just self-destruct and miss the beauty of the new-creation life. Thus Paul issues a strong call to self-awareness and self-discipline in 9:24. Note again that, as a great leader, Paul is the model, and he is doing himself what he urges them to do. "Do you not know that in a race all the runners run, but only one gets the prize? Run in such a way as to get the prize. Everyone who competes in the games goes into strict training. . . I strike a blow to my body and make it my slave so that after I have preached to others, I myself will not be disqualified for the prize" (9:24–25, 27).

The emphasis on freedom can be misconstrued by persons who are not thoroughly resocialized into the new-creation narrative and values. Old ideas about what it means to be really free die hard. Freedom without the kingdom context can simply mean doing whatever I feel like doing, and this can lead to slavery to animal instincts or present-evil-age perversions. Therefore Paul ends the chapter 9 discussion with a brief testimony regarding his personal disciplines and how he trains himself to manage his animal impulses. He works out like an athlete. The sports metaphors are Paul's way of communicating that he makes strenuous efforts to be in control of his body. He controls his body so his body does not control him. Only the Holy Spirit can bring about the deep transformation of our hearts, but we can do our part by cultivating self-control in the physical dimension of ourselves.

---

of transforming everything, so that the Church's customs, ways of doing things, times and schedules, language and structures can be suitably channeled for the evangelization of today's world rather than for her self-preservation. The renewal of structures demanded by pastoral conversion can only be understood in this light: as part of an effort to make them more mission-oriented" (Pope Francis, "Evangelii Gaudium," 1.2.26–27).

10:1–14: The danger of spiritual arrogance: "if you think you are standing firm, be careful that you don't fall!"

As we begin reading the next part of this discussion (which we call chapter 10), Paul unleashes a direct exhortation to the know-it-alls, and a severe warning about the consequences of engaging in idol worship and immorality. The focus in the chapter 10 exhortation confirms that the serious peril under discussion in chapters 8–10 is participation in the banquets in Corinth's pagan shrines. The know-it-alls feel free to continue to participate in these common Corinthian social gatherings. It is part of doing business in Corinth and it is how the more well-to-do network and maintain their social standing.[24] They justify their participation on the truth that "an idol is nothing" and that there is only one true God. These are teachings that Paul brings to them and with which they agree.

But Paul issues a loving warning about how dangerous this participation is, basing his exhortation on the Old Testament. He urges us to learn the lessons from the spiritual ancestors. Paul's conviction about the relevance of the Old Testament narratives (his hermeneutic) is spelled out in verse 11: "These things happened to them as examples and were written down as warnings for us, on whom the culmination of the ages has come."

Paul believes that the Christian community is an eschatological community. We are the ones "on whom the culmination of the ages has come." But although this is our true identity, this does not mean that we are invincible or so spiritually advanced as to be exempt from danger and temptation. Gordon Fee explains the assumption of some members of the Corinthian community:

> They had a considerably "over-realized" eschatological view of their present existence. . . . Despite their continuing existence in the body, the Corinthians consider themselves to be the "spiritual ones," already as the angels . . . Being people of the Spirit, they imply, has moved them to a higher plane, the realm of the spirit, where they are unaffected by behavior that has merely to do with the body. . . . Their worldview was tainted (ingrained by a lifetime) by Hellenistic dualism.[25]

As a result of their exalted state of spirituality, some Corinthians believed nothing could harm them in the lower (and transient) realm of the flesh.

---

24. Witherington gives us a fictional, but historically grounded, description of what a typical banquet might have been like in Corinth at this time in *Week in the Life of Corinth*, 60–68.

25. Fee, *First Epistle to the Corinthians*, 11–12, 250.

It seems they concluded that it makes no difference what we do with our bodies.

Although we are part of the new creation, the experiences of our spiritual ancestors are still extremely relevant. Even if, in the new-creation community, we are established and sanctified by means of baptism and Holy Communion, our OT ancestors still had analogous privileges according to Paul. Paul senses such danger to his community in their distorted view of freedom that he issues the severest of warnings. Our elect ancestors (God's chosen holy people) were spiritually blessed and nurtured. But Yahweh judged and punished them when they disobeyed and deliberately engaged in idolatry and immorality. We too face such prospects if we push the limits and choose to participate in idol worship. This is a sobering warning about arrogance and the sense of spiritual invincibility (knowledge "puffs up," 8:1) that can infect a community. Paul disturbs this complacency in verse 12; "if you think you are standing firm, be careful that you don't fall!"

There is a promise grounded in God's character (10:13) which is be-loved by many who struggle with deep-rooted sin patterns. It is full of hope for us. But in this context it is not intended to make us comfortable, but rather to verify that we are actually able to turn away from evil. "No tempta-tion has overtaken you except what is common to mankind. And God is faithful; he will not let you be tempted beyond what you can bear. But when you are tempted, he will also provide a way out so that you can endure it." Paul's emphasis here is that you never need to go down the path to immoral-ity because there is always an escape route. Your challenges (temptations) are quite within normal range. You are not overpowered. Our faithful God has pledged to insure that you are not placed under such extraordinary cir-cumstances that a disastrous failure is inevitable. You are enabled by the Spirit to resist.

Do not miss the fact that the very next statement is a clear imperative: "therefore, flee idol worship!" God has made it possible for you to escape. So get out of there. Don't go testing the limits.

10:15–30: Apostolic guidance for real-life situations.

Beginning with 10:15, Paul at last provides specific guidance concerning the issue which surfaced in 8:1, "concerning meat offered to idols." Notice Paul's pastoral strategy. Before Paul gives this clear prohibition, he has of-fered the believers a probing analysis of the issues. He does not desire blind obedience to his apostolic commands or mere compliance with a new rule book. His goal is that every Christ-follower will grow toward maturity in decision-making. His priority is resocialization and he wants Christ-follow-ers to be transformed at a deep level. He reframes the issues so the Corinthi-ans can grasp this great idea: the greatest exercise of true freedom (and the greatest evidence of authentic divine wisdom) is the free act of renouncing my rights for the sake of a Christian brother.

10:15–22: First application for Corinthian situations.

A very specific application is given with regard to participation in a sacred banquet in a pagan shrine. Sharing meals in the community of those who are devoted to the service and worship of the god actually results in a "sacra-mental union."[26] Paul warns: "the sacrifices of pagans are offered to demons, not to God, and I do not want you to be participants with demons. You can-not drink the cup of the Lord and the cup of demons too; you cannot have a part in both the Lord's table and the table of demons" (1 Cor 10:19–22).

Paul teaches that there is a parallel between the pagan feasting in a Corinthian shrine and the Christian's Holy Communion meal. Paul's stern prohibition is based on the reality which takes place in Holy Communion when the Christian community gathers. He argues that at the Lord's Table we participate in (koinōnia) Jesus' body and blood. "Because there is one bread, we who are many are one body, for we all partake of the one bread" (v. 17). In our common sharing in the Lord's Table feast, there is a mystical uniting that actually happens.

Paul says (16–22) that while it is true that the big wooden carved statue that portrays the pagan god is definitely not real (that's not actually a "god," according to Isa 44:9–20), in fact there are demonic spirits which infest that environment. The demonic invades the sharing of the sacred meal, which is done in honor of the false god. It's not that the actual meat is tainted, but Paul is clear that a meal shared creates oneness and common participation.

Paul's point is that since you are bound in unity to the in-Christ family, it is inconceivable that you would now also share in becoming united to an alien community which has pledged itself to the worship of demons. It is idolatry. As Paul asserts, it is an arrogant affront to the Lord himself! "Are we trying to arouse the Lord's jealousy? Are we stronger than he?" (1 Cor 10:23).

26. I refer to this as a "sacramental union." The essence of a sacrament is that a physical substance or object or activity is potentially full of spiritual significance. Paul is clear that a meal shared creates oneness and common participation. Most cultures that are not thoroughly secularized appreciate that sharing a sacred meal creates a bond.

Again, Paul quotes the mantra of the arrogant know-it-alls: "'I have the right to do anything,' you say—but not everything is beneficial. 'I have the right to do anything'—but not everything is constructive" (v. 23). Paul confronts them with their own words to expose their arrogance and sense of spiritual invincibility. Paul has already challenged this thinking back in 6:12, where the same distorted idea was surfacing concerning sexual liberty. He offers the same critique.

Two alternative value statements are set side by side in sharp contrast in verses 23–24. These two affirmations represent two contrasting "wisdoms":

- Wisdom type A (v. 23)—"all things are permissible. . ."
- Wisdom type B (v. 24)—"let no one seek his own good, but the good of his neighbor"

Wisdom type B is the Jesus way. It is the core value of the new-creation lifestyle.

10:25: Second application for Corinthian situations.

Verse 25 concerns going to the local butcher shop. But before he gets to his summary, Paul offers additional counsel to guide the believer's discernment. He clarifies that there is no moral problem with eating meat no matter what its source. Paul says you are indeed free to buy and eat. The meat itself is not what is polluted or infested with spirits. Meat is meat. Paul inserts an Old Testament quotation from Ps 24:1 to validate his claim that everything in creation is the Lord's and thus nothing is inherently unclean. This is a radical idea for a pure-blooded Jew like Paul.[27] Paul has embraced the way of Jesus and he has absorbed the significance of Jesus' own words and example. Therefore, Paul says a Christ-follower is free to buy some meat at a local butcher shop and to roast it for dinner.

---

27. In fact Paul repeats this in 1 Tim 4:3–5, and even expresses it more forcefully. Witherington, *Conflict and Community in Corinth*, 200–1, says, "This chapter helps us realize that a large part of the Christian life is not regulated by New Testament rules. For instance, most choices of apparel, food, cars and the like are not dictated by pre-existing regulations. . . . Doubtless many Christians who have grown up in denominations with rules about dress, entertainment, drink, food, or Sabbath or Sunday observance might find the implications of what Paul says disturbing."

10:27–30: Third application for Corinthian situations.

There is one additional word of application that Paul offers to guide his friends. This concerns the choices faced in sharing a meal in a private home. Paul counsels the believers to use their best discernment and try to assess the impact of the significance of the meal for the unbelieving host. He urges that Christians express their freedom with discernment. Always the first concern of a Christ-follower is "What is best for this other person?"

10:31—11:1: Final summary—New-creation community core values

Paul brings to a climax the entire discussion which makes up chapters 8–10 by returning one more time to the new-creation community's core values (10:31—11:1.) These terse bullet points are the essence of this entire teaching and the key to truly being the free men and women of the new-creation:

> So whether you eat or drink or whatever you do, do it all for the glory of God. Do not cause anyone to stumble, whether Jews, Greeks or the church of God—even as I try to please everyone in every way. For I am not seeking my own good but the good of many, so that they may be saved. Be imitators of me, as I am of the Messiah

We display God's glory when we are a reflection of *YHWH*'s nature and character. The Triune God is a community of self-giving love and oneness. We "give him glory" when we make small strides in manifesting oneness and love. This emphasis in Paul on giving up rights for the good of others is not just a minor matter that helps make church life more pleasant and tolerable. Living in unity (and doing the work to build this, as explained in Eph 4:1–5) is essential to our truly being human beings and demonstrating what the image of God is all about. Martin Luther famously wrote: "A Christian is a perfectly free lord of all, subject to none. A Christian is a perfectly dutiful servant of all, subject of all, subject to all."[28]

For Paul, this is primarily an issue about being the new-creation community. Paul devotes a considerable amount of space (three chapters) and attention to this issue. As we have seen, he does not simply lay down the law by quoting the Jerusalem Council's letter which issued a prohibition of the matter under discussion. Instead, Paul takes the opportunity to probe below the surface of the presenting problem. He is concerned about a core issue

28. Luther, "Treatise On Christian Liberty," 251.

of the heart. Meat itself has no moral significance, but there are attitudes in play that can destroy community. The twisted notion of freedom discerned in the questions and affirmations of the know-it-alls is fundamentally opposed to the mind of Christ. The central value of Jesus becomes the community's core value.

LET'S OFFER TO TODAY'S CULTURE ONE BEING SHREDDED BY DISRESPECT, HATRED, AND VENOMOUS CONFLICTS: A WORKING MODEL OF HOW TO DISAGREE WITH OTHERS AND AT THE SAME TIME MAINTAIN UNITY AND MUTUAL RESPECT

In the United States in the 2020s, we are experiencing what is described by many as a breakdown in civility. Historically in US society, there have always been vigorous debates about all kinds of issues. In the political arena, there are widely divergent views on almost any issue you can bring to the table—foreign policy strategies, saving social security, creating jobs, who should pay taxes and how much, etc. But toward the end of the twentieth century, there began to emerge a degradation of the political discourse. No longer is the debate conducted over philosophy of the role of government or policy priorities for solving key national problems, like funding entitlements. To a greater and greater degree, everything is personal now. The 2020 presidential election campaign season may go down in history as a new low point. Today's political atmosphere is filled with venom and hate and lies and personal insults. What is particularly troubling and damaging to the fabric of this society is the extent to which it seems that a candidate's popularity is enhanced by his/her ability to eviscerate the opponent by the use of insults, early-adolescent profanity, lies, ridicule, etc. The more coarse the hate speech, the higher the candidate's standing in the polls.

I believe that this negative atmosphere in the political domain offers Christians a great opportunity to show "a more excellent way." Wouldn't it be powerful if Jesus' followers were increasingly known as those people who, on the one hand, stand up for truth and justice and who have strong convictions; and who also, on the other hand, demonstrate respect for others with whom they disagree and speak in a manner which is gracious and thoughtful? This kind of testimony could go a long way to commend the Christian movement in today's culture. In fact, pursuing reconciliation is close to the heart of what we do. As Richard Mouw writes, "We are supposed to be a model community in which other people can see how God intends diverse individuals and groups to get along."[29]

J. P. Lederach is one of the world's leading scholars/practitioners in the discipline of peace-building. From his decades of work around the world as a peace-builder, he knows firsthand the potential contained in the church. He writes:

> Jesus provides overall guidelines in his teaching. The church as envisioned here is not simply a glee club of harmonious voices. It is a place to interact with each other, express differences, and work through what may be painful theological and relational issues and concerns. The church is a forum for expressing and handling conflict. What is needed is both the vision of integrating conflict as a healthy part of our life and the skills to make it a constructive experience.[30]

Truth + love

In God's word, we are called to be people who express truth plus love. In the letter to the Ephesian Christians, Paul writes: "Instead, speaking the truth in love, we will grow to become in every respect the mature body of him who is the head, that is, Christ. From him the whole body, joined and held together by every supporting ligament, grows and builds itself up in love, as each part does its work" (Eph 4:15–16). Because God himself is the source of both truth and justice, we who are imitating God will be people who have strong convictions about what is true and right. But this same God is love and acts with love and mercy in all his ways. Thus as we become "conformed to his image," we too will be characterized by this seemingly counterintuitive combination of divine qualities.

GUIDANCE FOR DEALING WITH SENSITIVE MATTERS WHERE SINCERE BELIEVERS DISAGREE AND EACH SIDE HAS DEEPLY HELD CONVICTIONS

First, be clear about what behaviors are not acceptable. It is not acceptable to shut up and simply comply. It rarely helps to "stuff it." Issues are not resolved in a healthy way if we deny our honest convictions and stifle the conscience.

29. Mouw, *Uncommon Decency*, 48.

30. Lederach, *Reconcile*, 152.

It is also not acceptable to split up and go our separate ways. If we abandon the relationship, we abandon the possibility of agreement or cooperation. Of course, for Christ-followers, it is not acceptable to bully the opposition into submission and defeat. Our calling is to do the hard work of pursuing peace. We must commit ourselves to seeking peace as a priority in Christ. Paul exhorts us to strenuously exert ourselves in this holy effort. Writing to the Ephesian Christians, he says, "Make every effort to keep the unity of the Spirit through the bond of peace" (Eph 4:3).

Here are ten important actions we can take to be peace builders:

1. Be *ruthlessly honest with yourself.* Seek deeper self-awareness.

Dig deep into your heart to uncover motives. Ask yourself, "Why am I taking the position I am taking? What are my emotions signaling?" Pray Ps 139:23–24 and listen for the Spirit's voice: "Investigate my life, O God, find out everything about me; cross-examine and test me, get a clear picture of what I'm about; see for yourself whether I've done anything wrong—then guide me on the road to eternal life" (MSG). It's always personal!

2. *Repent (personally and corporately) for past failures.*

Jesus gave us a memorable parable which guides us in our efforts to sort out other people and their misguided thinking. Jesus talks about a well-intentioned counselor who sees a speck of sawdust in his adversary's eye. But Jesus satirizes the situation by reminding us that before I can assist the other person with his problem, I first need to get the log out of my own eye. Jesus calls us to abandon self-deception and to repent. Richard Mouw offers us his own commentary on Jesus' wisdom:

> Convicted Christians will often be tempted by the crusading spirit. So a rule of thumb is necessary: For starters, concentrate on your own sinfulness and on the other person's humanness.... We Christians seem to go through epidemics of serious moral amnesia. We argue about important issues with no memory of the past. . . . Christians should approach discussions . . . in a spirit of sorrow and repentance over our past behaviors and attitudes.... We know that God meets us in our helplessness and honors the sincere acknowledgement of our guilt.[31]

31. Mouw, *Uncommon Decency,* 52, 96.

3. See the other person with whom I may disagree as a beloved child of God for whom Jesus died.

When I encounter another Christian who sincerely holds a very different point of view from mine concerning an emotionally charged issue, what/who do I see? I am exhorted by the apostle to show respect and honor. In Rom 12:10, Paul says, "Honor one another above yourselves." We must cultivate the spiritual discipline of looking at that other through Jesus' eyes. We might also benefit from making a *list of all the things we do agree on* (see Eph 3:4–6).

4. Listen to the "adversary."

If we hope to be agents of reconciliation and to "make every effort" to create unity among sisters and brothers, we must cultivate the difficult discipline of active listening. This sounds so easy but it actually is extremely difficult. It is one thing to passively allow the sound waves projected by another to cause the membranes in your physical ears to vibrate. But that's not really listening. Real listening is rare. By this I mean that it requires skill and discipline to really, deeply listen to the ideas and emotions and authentic meaning of another person. Swiss psychiatrist Paul Tournier wrote, "Listen to all the conversations of our world, between nations as well as between individuals. They are, for the most part, dialogues of the deaf."[32] Prov 18:13 says, "Answering before listening is both stupid and rude" (MSG).

5. Assess the weightiness of this issue. Is it a core gospel belief? Is it *"adiaphora?"* Is it found in the universal church's creeds?

One clue that it's not a core issue is to determine whether there are sincere and respected Christ-followers on both sides of the question. The Bible's central ideas are taught unambiguously in multiple texts from beginning to end. I must be certain that the opinion I hold is strongly attested to throughout the word of God.[33]

---

32 Tournier, *To Understand Each Other*, 8.

33. Theologians often speak about the "analogy of faith." The analogy of faith was a key principle of interpretation taught by the Reformers, which teaches that Scripture should interpret Scripture. This principle is stated in the *Westminster Confession of Faith* (1.9) in this manner: "The infallible rule of interpretation of Scripture is the Scripture itself: and therefore, when there is a question about the true and full sense of any Scripture (which is not manifold, but one), it must be searched and known by other places that speak more clearly." There must be a consistency in all revealed truth because it represents absolute truth in the mind of God.

We would do well to adopt this ancient motto: *In necessariis unitas, in dubiis libertas, in omnibus caritas.* This is best translated as, "in necessary things unity; in uncertain things freedom; in everything compassion."

6. Really, seriously *study the Bible for yourself.*

Do your homework. Do not rely on social media posts or Tweets or religious broadcasting. Go to the Bible to seek understanding, not merely to find ammunition. Study all the Bible's teachings (not just the verses you agree with). Study all sides of a controversy by hearing different disciplined teachers of the Scriptures. Pray while you study and employ the commonly agreed upon principles for interpretation of the Bible.

7. *Speak truth (as you understand it) but without a "crusading" spirit.*

Reject labels, reject stereotyping, reject insults. Trust the motives of the "adversary" (at least at the start). "Crusaders are people who think the cause they are fighting for is so important that they must use all means at their disposal to win. . . . They don't appear to care whether they are fair in characterizing the views of their opponents."[34]

You might win an argument by "standing up for God's truth" and actually lose by damaging the other.[35] Peter the apostle exhorts us to always have an answer to defend faith and convictions, but to do so with respect: "in your hearts revere Christ as Lord. Always be prepared to give an answer to everyone who asks you to give the reason for the hope that you have. But do this with gentleness and respect" (1 Pet 3:15–16).

8. *Practice Christian civility.*

The former president of Fuller Seminary, Richard Mouw, has written a very timely and discerning book called *Uncommon Decency: Christian Civility in an Uncivil World.* Mouw offers counsel on "civility"—a model for engaging in disagreement without venom. It's about much, much more than playing nice. At its heart, Mouw's vision of civility involves noting the following

---

34 Mouw, *Uncommon Decency,* 50.

35. Francis Schaeffer wrote a small booklet in which he laments the impact of the prolonged conflicts within the reformed Presbyterian "family" in the first half of the twentieth century. He describes how arrogantly insisting on the purity of one's doctrinal formulations became ugly and failed to project to the "watching world" observable love and oneness (*Church before the Watching World,* 69).

truth: "Treating other people with the gentleness and reverence of Jesus requires that we be deeply sensitive to the pain and brokenness of a creation that has not yet been fully delivered from its cursedness."[36]

Mouw commends biblical attitudes and behaviors seen in Jesus—patience, flexibility, humility, awe, modesty, self-awareness, and respect for others as God's creation—but he clearly sees how challenging this is, especially when the differences between people's convictions are genuinely significant. He writes:

> Dealing with other human beings often means dealing with ideas and behaviors that we simply don't like—and as Christians, we ought not to like. Slipping into an anything-goes relativism, then, is no solution. Many of the barriers of behavior that separate us actually mark off boundaries of behavior and belief that signal very deep and important differences having to do with our competing understandings of the human condition. We have to recognize that, then. But we can't just leave it there. The biblical mandate is clear: we must strive to live at peace with all human beings. We must approach those with whom we disagree with gentleness and reverence; we must show honor to all of God's human creatures. . . . God created all human beings. Even the shattered and broken ones are still his original works of art.[37]

9. Pray for your "adversaries" and together with your "adversaries."

Jesus says, "Bless those who curse you; pray for those who mistreat you" (Luke 6:28). Whenever it's possible, sit together and listen for the Spirit's insights—humbly, not as an additional weapon.

10. Cultivate skills as a peacemaker.

Jesus says "you are blessed" if you are a "peacemaker." It is worth asking why we do not assign greater value to the art and skill of making peace. It seems in many churches that we equip members for many functions within the church. We typically have seminars and workshops to equip people to evangelize and to teach and perhaps to work with adolescents. We have training in how to manage money and how to have a happy marriage. I wonder why we do not invest more effort in equipping peacemakers?

36. Mouw, *Uncommon Decency*, 169.
37. Mouw, *Uncommon Decency*, 73.

Ken Sande has founded a strategic ministry called "Peacemakers." The mission of Peacemakers is to equip believers to be reconcilers and to experience the power of the gospel to heal conflict.[38] Let's nourish an army of well-equipped peacemakers. This is what we do if we trust Jesus. Imagine how powerful it might be if Jesus' followers were widely recognized as experts in mediating conflicts. Let's design intensive training seminars and workshops, and make such training mandatory for all church leaders. Study key books together, such as the enormously useful book by John Paul Lederach, *Reconcile: Conflict Transformation for Ordinary Christians*.

There can be a tendency to behave as if the priority of love only applies in selected noncritical missions. When great moral or doctrinal matters are on the line, we must win at all costs. In 1 Cor 13:2, the Spirit will challenge us by saying, "Without love, it's all worthless." May the Spirit of Jesus continually remind us of his words: "A new command I give you: Love one another. As I have loved you, so you must love one another. By this everyone will know that you are my disciples, if you love one another" (John 13:34–35).

38. The ministry now reaches internationally and is based on the model explained in Ken Sande's helpful book, *The Peacemaker*.

Chapter 8

Renewing the Role of Women

Gender and New Creation (Ch. 11)

"God envisioned his sons and daughters forging a Blessed Alliance that would become an unstoppable force for good in the world. . . . He created his image bearers male and female, blessed them, and spread before them the global mandate to build his kingdom . . . the Blessed Alliance calls for gospel living, which means putting the interests of others ahead of your own interests . . . the Blessed Alliance results in mutual flourishing."

CAROLYN JAMES[1]

READ: 1 COR 11:2-16

Why the early Church had a huge impact

Why did the early Christian movement flourish? The distinguished sociologist Rodney Stark focused his scholarly energies on the questions surrounding the remarkable success of the Jesus Movement in the context of

---

1. James, *Half the Church*, 137, 148.

the Roman Empire in the first 400 years. His book is called *The Rise of Christianity: How the Obscure, Marginal Jesus Movement Became the Dominant Religious Force in the Western World in a Few Centuries*.[2] Stark evaluates many crucial factors, using the tools of social science. One prominent feature of the movement in these early years was its posture toward women. He argues, based on his examination of the ancient sources, that "Christianity was unusually appealing to pagan women" because "within the Christian subculture women enjoyed far higher status than did women in the Greco-Roman world at large."[3] He presents abundant evidence that one central factor in the movement's success was that Christianity recognized women as equal to men, children of God with the same supernatural destiny. In addition to offering women a new Gospel-based identity, the movement's ethics transformed the situation of women. Christian ethical teachings rejected polygamy, divorce, birth control, abortion, infanticide, etc. The effects of this new morality contributed to a positive transformation of the well-being of women. In the Christian movement, women were no longer seen as powerless serfs in bondage to men. Instead, Christian teaching exalted women to the status of full personhood, with dignity and rights in both the Church and the State. "Women also filled leadership positions within the church."[4]

The same is true today in sub-Saharan Africa, where I have worked for the past twenty-five years. I have witnessed firsthand the impact of Christian faith on African women. There is a dramatic, observable, positive difference in the status of women in Christian contexts when compared with most Muslim women and women in traditional African cultures. Jesus makes life better for African women. The lives of the vast majority of African women and girls today continue to be excruciatingly difficult due to systemic poverty, deeply entrenched dehumanizing cultural traditions, and blatant injustice. But where there have been positive changes in the lot of women, it can consistently be traced to the impact of Christian faith and the gospel.[5]

2. Stark, *Rise of Christianity*, ch. 5.

3. Stark, *Rise of Christianity*, 95.

4. Stark, *Rise of Christianity*, 128. Also, Scott McKnight writes: "In the church, we discover a fresh empowerment of women to exercise what God calls and gifts them to do. I think of Priscilla, who taught Apollos; I think of Phoebe, who was a church leader and probably read the letter of Paul to the Romans, and who therefore had to answer questions about what Paul meant; I think of Junia, who is called a superlative apostle/missionary; I think of Euodia and Syntyche, who were 'co-workers' with Paul in his Gospel work; I think of the daughters of Phillip, who were prophets. Invisible women in the Roman empire become visible in Christ. Of the fellow missionary workers named alongside Paul, 20 percent were women—no small number in a male-oriented, hierarchical, women-can't-vote society" (McKnight, *Fellowship of Differents*, 90).

5. It would be foolish to deny that there are significant exceptions to this general

However, Evangelical Christ-followers are not typically perceived as being pro-woman in today's society. We in Jesus' church have a very serious image problem, especially in the West. (And the problem goes deeper than merely image.) N. T. Wright appeals to the church:

> I believe we have seriously misread the relevant passages in the New Testament, not least through a long process of assumption, tradition, and all kinds of post-biblical and sub-biblical attitudes have crept into Christianity. . . . We need to radically change our traditional pictures both of what men and women are and of how they relate to one another within the church, and indeed of what the Bible says on this subject.[6]

If we are dreaming of becoming a movement which transforms communities, cities, and nations through the power of the Spirit, then the wisdom, courage, charismata, love, leadership, and dreams of all women must be respected and fully embraced and unleashed. But Carolyn James questions whether we are actually standing on the side of women's emancipation and empowerment. She writes, "instead of casting a powerful gospel vision that both validates and mobilizes women, the church's message for women is mixed at best—guarded, negative, and small at worst. Everywhere we go, a line has been drawn establishing how much or how little we are permitted to do within the church."[7]

Why would we want to limit what the Spirit desires to do through women who are fully devoted followers of Jesus? In the bewildering multitude of confounding debates over the role of women, Paul's writings typically have a prominent place. I am certain that the way his words are used in many of these arguments is not at all what Paul would have wished. Paul's vision was clearly to see that the churches he helped to birth would be communities of shalom (Rom 15:5–7, 33).

Paul's vision for life in Christ for himself and for every believer is best captured in Phil 2. This text defines Paul's identity and behavior, and therefore it would be a travesty for him to hear that his writings provide fuel for battling believers. For Paul, maturity is "the mind of Christ," not staking claim to positions of power. When believers fight with one another and seek to dominate or win, it's a sign of immaturity (1 Cor 3:1–4). However, there

---

trend. There are places in which the church mirrors the local culture and perpetuates the oppression of women. A remarkable Congolese woman has done research on her home district in DRC, and her assessment is disturbing (Katho, "Rethinking Women's Dignity").

6. Wright, *Surprised by Scripture*, 82.

7. James, *Half the Church,* 48–49.

are three sentences found in Paul's Letters which feature prominently in the debates in churches concerning women's participation (1 Cor 11:3; 14:34; 1 Tim 2:12).[8] If all we had from Paul on the issues were these three statements, it would be fairly easy to confirm the accusations often leveled at Paul that he is a woman-hater. But, of course, we have much more from Paul's pen than these three sentences.

EXAMINING THE APOSTLE'S COUNSEL IN 1 COR 11

We must keep in mind that 1 Corinthians is a real letter set in a specific historical-cultural context. Paul responds to the issues as they surface in his interaction with the believers from Corinth. So this is not an exhaustive presentation of the theology of gender relationships or women in ministry. There is no such thing in the New Testament. To craft a complete doctrine, we as God's people must honestly wrestle with dozens of sections of Scripture which give us Spirit-inspired instruction on specific topics. In 1 Corinthians, we are watching a skilled pastor work to guide the community into a way of life that will have the greatest positive impact on those outsiders whom the church is seeking to evangelize. The 1 Cor 11 text is concerned with missional impact.

The great idea that is revealed in this unit is—*Women and men who are devoted to Jesus can express their freedom by choosing to restrict their God-given rights in order to do what is best for the other person–especially the pre-Christian whom we wish to see encounter Jesus through the community's witness.*

Commendation—11:2

Paul begins this new unit of pastoral counsel with a word of affirmation for the church.

> I praise you for remembering me in everything and for holding
> to the traditions just as I passed them on to you.

Is Paul sincere or is he trying to build rapport and encourage the members to make it a habit to follow the apostle's guidance? Remember that he says he never uses "flattery" in 1 Thess 2:5. So we must assume that at least a majority of the church is heeding his teaching. The church is anchored and

---

8. For a judicious overview of these controversial texts, I recommend Mathews, *Gender Roles and the People of God.*

sustained and given a foundation in truth by traditions handed down from the beginning of the Christian movement. Paul summarizes the core of the saving gospel tradition in 15:1–5.

Paul presents a teaching on headship and "hierarchy"—11:3

> But I want you to realize that the head of every man is Christ, and the head of the woman is man, and the head of Christ is God.

Paul talks about three parallel arrangements and they are all assumed to share the same kind of relationship. But Paul does not list them in top-down order. This statement of triple headship relationships raises questions, since this model of parallel headships seems to contradict other very fundamental biblical teachings. If we simply accept that the idea being presented is that of patriarchal hierarchy—man is head of woman—we could be in danger of distorting the essence of the Trinity, which affirms the complete equality of the three divine persons and the truth that Jesus is "very God of very God."

Some interpreters of verse 3 who stress that the verse is an affirmation of patriarchal hierarchy seem to corrupt the powerful gospel affirmation that "there is one God and one mediator between God and humans, the man Christ Jesus, who gave himself as a ransom for all" (1 Tim 2:5). Women answer directly to one Lord, Jesus. A woman is not required to seek her husband's approval in discerning the voice of God. It is "impossible to serve two masters," says Jesus. A believing woman is filled with the Spirit of God and hears directly from God. We must be sure to interpret all these ideas in a coherent manner.[9]

First Corinthians 11:3 raises the question: Does the Bible consistently teach a male is head over a female? The simple answer is "no."[10] To be clear about what we are looking for in reading Paul's words, the meaning we seek is the meaning that was in Paul's mind when he wrote *kephalē* in verse 3. *Kephalē* is the Greek word translated into English as "head." In verses 4 and 5, it refers quite literally to one's physical head. But in verse 3, the

---

9. Students of Scripture should also determine if we should translate *anēr* as "man" (i.e., all males) or as "husband." This helps us to know if Paul is referring to all women and all males, or if he speaks about relationships within marriage. The Greek word could refer to either. Here it seems to refer to a generic male person.

10. This text has been the basis of an enormous amount of debate throughout the centuries. I will not try to rehearse that debate here because there are a number of very responsible surveys. See especially Thiselton, *First Epistle to the Corinthians*, 812–22; Van Leuween, *After Eden*; Van Leuween, *Gender and Grace*.

word "head" is a metaphor. It says something about the three relationships noted in the sentence. Now we must be careful not to jump immediately on the meaning that first pops into our minds as English speakers in the twenty-first century. That's easy to do, but might be misleading. You read a statement and say to yourself, "I know what it means to be the 'head' of something." We all do. But what was Paul thinking? We might think it's obvious. Mary Teresa Barra is the head of GM. She's the Chief Executive Officer of the General Motors Company. That seems pretty clear in my society. I suppose there are a few outdoorsy folks for whom "head" means "source" or "starting point," as in head of a stream. Many scholars who resist the notion of patriarchal headship argue vehemently that for Paul, "head" means "source." This may be correct. If we go back to the hermeneutical principles that commonly guide our interpretation of texts, we might be given some direction.[11] Typically we accept that words have meaning in their original context and that an apostle like Paul is a coherent thinker and not a person who contradicts himself. So how does this guide us?

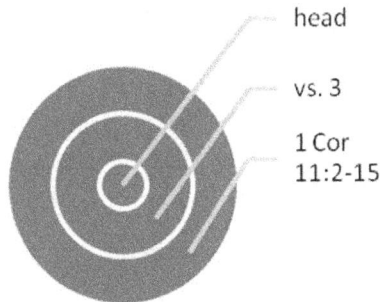

head

vs. 3

1 Cor 11:2-15

This illustrates the principle of context, although we actually need several more concentric circles surrounding these three in the inner circles above. The unit of thought in chapter 11 is contained in 1 Corinthians. First Corinthians is part of a collection of thirteen letters written by Paul. This is Paul's body of work, and taken together it is a good guide to how Paul thinks. But as Christians we also believe in the canon of Scripture. Christians confess that all sixty-six books found in our Bibles speak with a united voice. So all of these circles of meaning provide a context for understanding the metaphor of "head" in 1 Cor 11:3. And in light of this multi-dimensional context, I have concluded that "head" in verse 3 does *not* teach that the male has authority over the female. Here are the reasons:

11. For a discerning analysis of the hermeneutics that support interpretation, see Fee, "Great Watershed," 52–65.

First, the "whole counsel of God" does not support a view of the Trinity in which the Son is subordinate to God the Father. If we say males are inherently to be "in authority over" females, then the parallel needs to apply also to the God-Christ relationship. It does not. Miroslav Volf states it clearly, "within a community of perfect love between persons who share all the divine attributes, a notion of hierarchy and subordination is inconceivable."[12]

Secondly, in 11:4–5, women are said to be "prophesying." When we come to chapters 12–14 we will see that prophecy is a very important and authoritative charisma. A prophecy is a word from God given by the Spirit through a gifted member of the church. Paul makes prophecy the second-most important gift ahead of teaching (1 Cor 11:28). So the context rules out the understanding of *kephalē* in verse 3 as "person in authority over" because Paul immediately goes on to speak of men and women leading the congregation in prayer and prophecy in the Corinthian church. They are free to participate so long as they are differentiated by what they have or do not have on their head.[13] It seems to be a clash of authorities if God gives a prophetic utterance through a female. In addition, in the various Pauline texts which talk about charismata (which thus determine the basis for authority and leadership in the community) there is no mention of any gifts being gender-specific.

Thirdly, the Genesis narratives which teach us about the creation of male and female do not teach us about a male/female hierarchy (although Gen 1 is particularly concerned to spell out structures of authority in other domains of creation.) Elsewhere in Paul's writing, he speaks of mutual submission of every believer to every other believer. The man and the woman in Christ must pursue a lifestyle of cruciformity in every relationship. The narrative of Phil 2 directs our interactions in every dimension of life.

---

12. Volf, *After Our Likeness*, 217. He continues: "Salvation history allows us to infer the fundamental equality of the divine persons in their mutual determination and their mutual interpenetration; the Father . . . gives everything to the Son and glorifies him, just as the Son also glorifies the Father and gives the reign over to the Father (see Matt 28:18; John 13:31–32; 16:14; 17:1; 1 Cor 15:24). Moreover, within a community of perfect love between persons who share all the divine attributes, a notion of hierarchy and subordination is inconceivable. Within relations between the divine persons, the Father is for that reason not the one over against the others, nor 'the First,' but rather the *one among the others*" (217; italics original).

13. Paul expresses concern for the covering of heads or the failure to cover heads during prayer. This is what this unit is addressing. We must be careful not to extend the implications of the teaching.

Thus, I conclude that Paul is playing on the "multiple meanings"[14] of *kephalē* in 1 Cor 11:3–16, and in v. 3 it does not "denote a relation of subordination or authority over."[15]

Paul applies the concept from verse 3 to behavior and "heads" in a Christian assembly 11:4–6

> Every man who prays or prophesies with his head covered dishonors his head. But every woman who prays or prophesies with her head uncovered dishonors her head—it is the same as having her head shaved. For if a woman does not cover her head, she might as well have her hair cut off; but if it is a disgrace for a woman to have her hair cut off or her head shaved, then she should cover her head.

The application of the teaching that the "the head of the woman is man" is made in reference to a specific context. Paul applies the "head" teaching to the behaviors within the Christian assembly. It is not, in this particular text, given broad application such as directing a woman to obey her husband or demanding that a woman attend to household duties or care for children. Paul is concerned in 1 Cor 11 with propriety within the gathering and the missiological implications.

Verses 4–6 indicate that both males and females are praying and prophesying when the church gathers. The early "worship services" were highly interactive, as we will see in chapters 12–14. As the Spirit enabled, believers would articulate to the entire community the insights given to them. Women are not instructed to remain silent in verses 4–6, or anywhere in this unit of teaching.

Instead, Paul expresses concern for the covering of heads or the failure to cover heads during these prayers. We must be careful not to extend the implications of the teaching without a basis in the text, e.g., to mandate that women must only teach children. Paul says if a man prays with a covered head he has dishonored the Messiah. This brings shame on the head, who is Jesus. I do not know why this is so. Since it is not a teaching that is found elsewhere in the Bible, it seems that Paul is thinking of a cultural norm which was obvious in first-century Greco-Roman society.

---

14. Thistleton, *First Epistle to the Corinthians*, 811, and see the full discussion on 812–22.

15. Thistleton, *First Epistle to the Corinthians*, 816.

Paul then says if a woman prays without a covered head, she dishonors the male (or maybe her own husband). I also do not know why this is so, since like the issue of the man's head, this is not a teaching found elsewhere in the Bible. Every society has culturally derived expectations about what is proper for the female appearance.[16] Societies all regulate gender distinctions, and if we function within a specific society, we know instinctively what a woman is supposed to look like. Of course, if we shift to a different culture or a different time period, then the expectations about what is proper feminine fashion will probably be different.

Paul adds another subpoint to the directive in verse 6. He pushes this point even farther and says that if a woman fails to cover her head in the assembly, her uncovered head is the equivalent of a woman having all her hair shaved off. This Paul categorizes as a "disgrace." To get the interpretation of this right requires some exploration of Corinthian society and the symbolism which defines gender rules in that specific culture.[17]

It is difficult to see this as a significant *moral* issue, since the Bible seems to concern itself mostly with the issues of the heart or will, and the Bible often minimizes the significance of external trappings and clothing, etc. Yahweh rebukes his prophet Samuel with the well-known words: "Yahweh does not look at the things man looks at. Man looks at the outward appearance, but Yahweh looks at the heart" (1 Sam 16:7). The issue in the Corinthian community concerns shame and dishonor. What is considered shameful is relative to a specific culture and its norms. Cultural norms are not seen as moral absolutes in Scripture. In this case we are dealing with shame and dishonor.

The application of these instructions is complicated because shame is primarily a category that is a function of culture. Cultures establish norms (dress codes, standards of propriety, hair style expectations, gender relations rules, correct behaviors, etc.) and when a member of the society fails to comply, there is shame. Anthropologists have examined thousands of distinct societies and have described remarkable variety in terms of what is culturally proper. We do not know exactly what the hair styles, the hair lengths, or the covers being commended or rebuked were in Roman Corinth in AD 50. However, the meaning of all these words was well known to the Corinthians who received this letter. We must not insert our own mental pictures of what a proper hair style is for a male or a female (drawing from customs which seem so obvious in my own time).

16. See Cohick, *Women in the World of the Earliest Christians*.

17. Again, I recommend the comprehensive overview provided in Cohick, *Women in the World of the Earliest Christians*.

Is violating a cultural norm a sin against God? Is there a distinction between shame (disgrace) and moral evil in view of the fact that what is shameful is culturally defined? It is not a sin to violate a cultural "norm."[18] What matters is how my choices impact others. If my "shameful" actions disrespect another person or are lacking in *agapē* love, then my motivation might be wrong.

We very much want to obey God's word through Paul. We are not looking for a way to dodge uncomfortable instructions. But the cultural meaning of hair length and being covered or uncovered changes when we leave one culture and enter a new one. Hair length is *not* a moral absolute in the Bible. Long hair or short hair does not matter in God's eyes. What Paul is telling us is of importance is that we accept the customary norms of the culture in which we are living which define the differences between males and females. To apply and obey this Scripture today, we need to identify the dynamics which distinguish a man and a woman in our society. Then we can obey Paul's instructions by going along with these gender markers. This means that what obedience looks like will vary from place to place and time to time. But the intentions will be the same. This is not about teaching that there should be one hair length and hair style for every Christian woman everywhere on the planet.

Let me share an illustration of how the self-evident norms for masculinity vary from one culture to the next. In certain ethnic communities in south India, men just naturally grow substantial amounts of facial hair. It's in their genetic makeup. So in these communities, being a man means having a very bushy mustache. "Here in southern India, fabulous facial hair has long symbolized masculinity."[19] It is self-evident in that ethnic group that a man is marked by his big mustache.

18. "Norm, also called Social Norm, rule or standard of behaviour shared by members of a social group. Norms may be internalized—i.e., incorporated within the individual so that there is conformity without external rewards or punishments, or they may be enforced by positive or negative sanctions from without. The social unit sharing particular norms may be small (e.g., a clique of friends) or may include all adult members of a society. Norms are more specific than values or ideals." https://www.britannica.com/topic/norm-society.

19. Wax, "New Generation of Men," para. 2.

What a man looks like. What is shameful is culturally defined.

Now there are reports that some of the bright young men from this group are moving away from the village and finding good jobs in the megacities of India. They are getting education and getting high-tech jobs in urban areas. And since they are entering into a new cultural situation, apparently many of the young men are shaving off their substantial mustaches. In the cosmopolitan cultures of the high-tech industry, sporting a big bushy mustache is not seen as chic and sophisticated. Now the young up-and-coming entrepreneurs are not at first telling the village elders about this change in their appearance. But when the holidays come and the young men go home to their ancestral regions, there is a conflict. The village elders are shocked and the fathers of the sons are shamed. The young urbanites no longer look like men. Clean-shaven faces and naked upper lips look to the elders like the faces of women. Emily Wax, writing for *The Washington Post* Foreign Service, quotes one of the younger generation of Indian men, Nanda Kumar, 26, who are changing the definition of shame: "Our fathers thought they were not men without their mustaches. But 'hairy Hindustan' is over," said

Kumar, using a time-honored nickname for the subcontinent. "It's old India. The mustache is for my father, not for me."[20]

The point of this example is to illustrate that what is an obviously masculine appearance is determined by the specific culture. Had Paul been writing his Corinthian letter to the churches of south India ("hairy Hindustan") he most likely would have urged the men to sport their mustaches proudly and cautioned the young guys against having clean-shaven (feminine?) upper lips.

So our corporate challenge (we must do this together as a community) is to creatively contextualize. We must together arrive at some consensus regarding how to preserve male-versus-female gender distinctions as Christ-followers. What we embrace this year will need to be revisited in three to five years' time since the cultural symbols that express the difference are continuously changing in the modern Western world. But the shame that Paul wishes us to renounce as a community is the cultural disgrace of men expressing their freedom by wearing women's fashions and vice versa for women. We are to maintain and celebrate the wonderful creational distinction between males and females. The "mind of Christ" (Phil 2) is concerned about what is best for the other person—especially the pre-Christian whom we wish to see encounter Jesus through the community's witness.

Paul adds two more arguments to support his case (11:7–10).

First, Paul presents an interpretation of the creation story:

> A man ought not to cover his head, since he is the image and glory of God; but woman is the glory of man. For man did not come from woman, but woman from man; neither was man created for woman, but woman for man. It is for this reason that a woman ought to have authority over her own head, because of the angels.

Paul says in verse 7 that the male is the "image of God's glory." Thus, man should not cover up his head. He also states that the female is the "glory of the male." I do not know how to interpret this statement made by Paul since the Genesis text clearly says that both male and female persons are "created in the image of God" (Gen 1:26–28).

The second argument Paul presents (vv. 8–9) draws on the creation account found in Gen 2. Paul makes the point that the female was taken "out of" man. This is what the Genesis story says when it describes how God took a rib out of the sleeping Adam and from that rib formed a woman. Paul

---

20. Wax, "New Generation of Men in India Shaving Off Mustaches," para. 3.

goes further and says that the female was made "for the male." This is based on the Gen 2 text when it says God made a "helper" for the solitary Adam and gave her to him. However, the best exegesis of these Gen 1 and 2 texts does not affirm hierarchical headship or chronological weight based on this creation narrative.

Gen 1:26–28 is a foundational text for thinking about almost everything. This text has huge implications for our understanding of what it means to be a human person inhabiting God's good creation.

> Then God said, "Let us make mankind in our image, in our likeness, so that they may rule over the fish in the sea and the birds in the sky, over the livestock and all the wild animals, and over all the creatures that move along the ground." So God created mankind in his own image, *in the image of God he created them; male and female he created them.* God blessed them and said to them, "Be fruitful and increase in number; fill the earth and subdue it. Rule over the fish in the sea and the birds in the sky and over every living creature that moves on the ground."

In the text, we see that at this climactic point of day six of the creation account there is a "divine council" (v. 26) which determines to create a "man" (singular) which will be a being described as one in the image and likeness of God ("image and likeness" reflects Hebrew parallelism).[21] But when God creates this eminent "person" (v. 27), the outcome is not one creature, but two. "Man" inevitably came as male and female. Years ago, my Bible professor at Wheaton College was Gilbert Bilezikian. He taught us how to read Genesis. He explains this crucial text as follows:

> The male/female sexual differentiation reflects realities contained within the very being of God and derived from Him as His image. Femaleness pertains to the image of God as fully as maleness. God is neither male nor female. He transcends both genders since they are both comprehended within His being. . . . By virtue of the fact that they bear God's image, humans are delegated to exercise some of His authority over creation. They are authorized to act as God's commissioned agents[22]

---

21. Scott and Hays, *Grasping God's Word,* explains parallelism, saying: "two lines of Hebrew poetry are grouped together to express one thought. 'Parallelism' is the dominant characteristic of Old Testament poetry. Usually one thought will be expressed by two lines of text" (337–38). However, Waltke, *Genesis* argues that "likeness" does not represent synonymity of terms. "Likeness" serves to insure the distinctiveness of humanity from God. Also see Longman, *How to Read Genesis,* 105.

22 Bilezikian, *Beyond Sex Roles,* 23–24.

Now this has implications for the statement we are considering in 1 Cor 11:7. Paul says that "man is the image and glory of God." Paul is here reflecting a viewpoint that would have been common in his Jewish culture of origin. But he expresses it in order to transcend his Jewish upbringing. New creation has dawned. The Christ-followers are now in the Lord. Mutuality and reciprocity are now the new ideal in the Lord Jesus. When Paul seems to say that the male is the reflection of God's image and glory it is quite possible that Paul is reflecting the assumptions common in his cultural milieu. It is not uncommon for preachers, in seeking to build a case for a particular exhortation, to make use of well-known, culture-specific pieces of wisdom or proverbial beliefs. One way to explain this ambiguous statement is to propose that Paul is stating what might be commonly believed in his society, only to then affirm that in the Lord Christians transcend this old thinking.[23]

It is certainly possible that Paul employs this common cultural understanding as a starting point for his teaching. He wants the new believers to realize that new-creation values transcend common-sense thinking. I am presenting this interpretive approach to verse 7 in order to prevent us from drawing conclusions about verse 7 which are inconsistent with the tenor of Scripture.

Some have sought to construct a case for patriarchy based on the fact that in the Gen 2 narrative, it says that God made the male human first. Does this necessarily indicate that the male is placed in a position of authority over the late-arriving female? The fact that the male was created first according to Gen 2 does not indicate that the males are superior or that they are assigned a higher level of authority. Listen to Professor Bilezikian's analysis regarding why chronological priority does not imply authority and control:

> There is no evidence in the creation texts for the temporal primacy of Adam to be interpreted as supremacy or rulership. Such a concept is present neither in the Old Testament nor in the New. As a matter of fact, a close scrutiny of Genesis invalidates such a theory. As soon as primal origination becomes a norm that confers dominance to the first in line, both Adam and Eve fall under the rulership of animals. According to Genesis 1, animals were created before humans. . . . The absurdity of such a theory

---

23. An alternative approach to making sense of Paul's statement in verse 7 is to see the idea that "woman is the glory of man" as a reflection of the Prov 31 portrait of the "virtuous woman." Her extraordinary virtue, creativity, and entrepreneurial drive are said to bring great honor to her husband. According to the "wisdom" of Prov 31, because of the wife's noble achievements, "Her husband is respected at the city gate, where he takes his seat among the elders of the land."

is evident. Temporal primacy of itself does not confer superior
rank. . . . Maleness and femaleness are presented as divine gifts
reflecting diversity within the *imago Dei*. The text does not permit their exploitation to support hierarchical dichotomies that
might justify predetermined role distinctions.[24]

There is a statement in verse 10 which is almost impossible to interpret
with any confidence since we do not know what it means for a woman to
have "authority on her head," nor do we know how to interpret the remark
about angels. There is no other biblical teaching which gives us any decisive
evidence or help in understanding these arguments confidently.[25] Beware of
teachers who think they know exactly what these words mean.

"But in the Lord . . ."—Paul reverses course and presents alternative ways to see this issue (11:11–12)

Nevertheless, in the Lord, woman is not independent of man, nor
is man independent of woman. For as woman came from man,
so also man is born of woman. But everything comes from God.

Does Paul cancel out all earlier arguments by shifting in verse 11 to "in the
Lord" and teaching mutual dependence and equality? Yes, Paul does seem to
modify and even overturn some of the earlier arguments when he reaches this
point and talks about how "all things are made new" once we are "in the Lord."
Paul reminds the Corinthians that they are now a new-creation community.
Beginning with Christ, his death, and his resurrection, God established the
new creation. The new-creation way of seeing means there is no independence
of the genders (v. 11). Rather, we live with a joyful, mutual interdependence.
Male and female are once again aligned in proper relationship.

There is a significant shift in vantage point at the end of verse 10. Prior
to this, Paul has been appealing to the Corinthians using arguments based
on their shared Hellenistic cultural assumptions. But following the obscure
reference to "angels" in verse 10, Paul says, "However," or "nevertheless" (the

---

24. Bilezikian, *Beyond Sex Roles*, 30–31, 216.

25. John Stott wrote: "The 'perspicuity' of Scripture was much insisted on by the
Reformers. They meant that it has a 'per-spicuous,' 'see-through,' or transparent quality.
They did not mean by this that everything in Scripture is plain. How could they . . . when
Peter confessed that Paul's letters contained 'some things that are hard to understand' (2
Peter 3:16)? If one apostle could not always understand another apostle, it would hardly
be modest for us to claim that we can! No, the Reformers' insistence was that the essence
of the biblical message, the way of salvation in Christ by grace through faith, is simple
enough for even the uneducated to grasp" (Stott, *Evangelical Truth*, 71).

Greek *plēn*). This small word marks a transition to an alternative and more weighty aspect of the argument. Grammarians indicate that this word has "an adversative and modifying sense to conclude a discussion and emphasize what is essential."[26] Paul is moving beyond the issues deriving from culture.

The final phrase of verse 12, *ta panta ek tou theou*, which is translated as, "everything comes from God," sets all the gender competition and strife in a huge, transformational reality. Gordon Fee helps us begin to grasp the glory of this new-creation experience:

> Everything for Paul begins with Christ, his death and resurrection, whereby he established the new order, the new creation. In the new creation, two things happen: the relationship between man and woman in the first creation is restored, but that relationship must be lived out under the paradigm of the cross. In Christ Jesus there is neither male nor female, not meaning that differentiation has ceased, but that both alike enter the new creation on the same footing, and thus serve one another and the rest of the church in the same way their Lord did—by giving themselves to the other(s).[27]

This new emphasis on mutual dependence seems more consistent with most other biblical teaching. It also is more coherent as far as Paul's vision of life in the body of Christ and the vision of the new-creation community.

Paul adds final arguments based on what "nature" teaches concerning the proper length of hair for each gender (11:13–15)

> Judge for yourselves: Is it proper for a woman to pray to God with her head uncovered? Does not the very nature of things teach you that if a man has long hair, it is a disgrace to him, but that if a woman has long hair, it is her glory? For long hair is given to her as a covering.

Paul concludes this unit of teaching by appealing to the Corinthian believers to think this matter through as a community of Christ-followers. He is certain they will come to conclusions similar to his own. Note that Paul continues to affirm that women will be participating in the assembly. They will be praying.

26. Blass and Debrunner, *Greek Grammar of the News Testament*, 234 explains that *plēn* is an adversative conjunction often meaning, "nevertheless." In Paul's writing it is used to conclude a discussion and emphasize what is essential.

27 Fee, *Listening to the Spirit in the Text*, 76.

In verse 14, Paul makes an appeal to a concept he calls *phusis,* which we usually translate as "nature." This seems to be a reference to the commonly agreed upon cultural gender markers. In Roman Corinth, it was apparently self-evident that men did not have long hair. In that society, it was shameful for a male to let his hair grow out. In a similar fashion, it was expected in the culture that a woman's hair would be allowed to grow long but apparently braided in a customary manner and fastened tightly on the top of the head.

"Nature," in the sense of the physical world, does not consistently teach us about cultural mores. But although a culture's perception of the significance of hair length is not grounded in the natural world, to those of us who are indigenous and thus enculturated within the society, these customs seem to us to be a given, intrinsic to the nature of things. We are socialized in the earliest period of life and we embrace these prereflective assumptions without question or analysis.[28] But once we move beyond the boundaries of our culture of origin, we discover there's wild variety.

What does "nature" tell us about hair? That is totally determined by the culture which is doing the teaching. There is an iconic east African ethnic group known as the Masai. In this community, it would be entirely expected to see a dignified, feminine Masai women with a totally shaved head. There is no shame in this in her culture.

Final appeal: this is the common practice in all his churches (11:16)

> If anyone wants to be contentious about this, we have no other practice—nor do the churches of God.

It should be noted that Paul does not use the more weighty word from verse 2 (and 1 Cor 15) for "sacred tradition," *paradosis*. Instead he refers to this practice as *sunetheian*. It seems that this represents a less weighty category of church policy.

---

28. Recall the discussion in ch. 5 concerning "primary socialization." See Berger and Luckmann, *Social Construction of Reality*.

The great idea found in the 1 Cor 11 teaching: *Women and men who are devoted to Jesus can express their freedom by choosing to restrict their God-given rights in order to do what is best for the other person—especially the pre-Christian whom we wish to see encounter Jesus through the community's witness.* We celebrate the wonderful creational distinction between males and females in respectable, culturally appropriate ways.

The heart of Paul's concern is that in the community's worship men should follow the dress and hair codes that proclaim them to be male, and women the codes that proclaim them to be female. This counsel is driven by Paul's passion to reach lost people. Christ-followers are free to adapt to cultural norms if doing so will reduce the obstacles facing a pagan in receiving the gospel. This is the same missiological principle Paul taught in 1 Cor 9:19, 22–23: "Though I am free and belong to no one, I have made myself a slave to everyone, to win as many as possible. . . . I have become all things to all people so that by all possible means I might save some. I do all this for the sake of the gospel."

I have urged that the interpretation of these verses must be grounded in the experience of the first Corinthian believers. Paul's message was consistently a message of freedom.[29] The gospel is a declaration that God's new creation has begun in Jesus' death and resurrection. For women enslaved in oppressive and dehumanizing societies, the gospel was truly good news. Gordon Fee helps us begin to grasp the glory of this new creation experience:

> The atonement of Christ has overturned all the effects of the Fall, including the blighting curse on both men and women pronounced in Genesis 3. This does not mean a denying of male and female distinctiveness—that is a part of creation and the image of God—but it does mean a restoration of their lost joint mandate both to image God (now in a fallen world) and to serve together in having dominion over the earth.[30]

In Corinth, the firstfruit of the new-creation life, the Holy Spirit, was often experienced as a powerful rush of ecstasy. The sense of being possessed by Jesus' Spirit, overwhelmed by his love, and energized by his power was genuinely *awe*-some. Women who were formerly disrespected, discriminated against, dehumanized, and marginalized found a new freedom which was exuberantly expressed. They were no longer a lower caste, but

---

29. Paul's message was about freedom. See Gal 5:1; Bruce, *Paul*. Professor Bruce understood Paul and got it right. Paul's ministry and message was a message of freedom. It announces freedom from death, freedom from guilt, freedom from law, and freedom from bondage to forces of the "present evil age." See also Longenecker, *Paul*.

30. Fee, *Gospel and Spirit*, 64.

had direct communication with the Most High God. Paul was a champion of this gospel.

It seems plausible, in light of what we know about Corinth and about revival movements, that some women who were overcome by the Spirit may understandably have gone to extremes in behavior.[31] N. T. Wright helps us appreciate these dynamics:

> In Paul's day (as, in many ways, in ours) gender was marked by hair and clothing styles. We can tell from statues, vase paintings and other artwork of the period how this worked out in practice. . . . perhaps some of the Corinthian women had been taking Paul literally [in his teaching that there is "No male and female: you are all one in the Messiah," Gal 3:28] so that when they prayed or prophesied aloud in church meetings (which Paul assumes they would do regularly) they had decided to remove their normal head coverings, perhaps also unbraiding their hair, to show that in the Messiah they were free from the normal social conventions by which men and women were distinguished. . . . If the watching world discovered that the Christians were having meetings where women "let their hair down" in this fashion, it could have the same effect on their reputation as it would in the modern West if someone looked into a church and found the women all wearing bikinis.[32]

Because these women were relatively new to the Christian experience, they were not yet sufficiently mature or resocialized into the ways of Jesus to be able to discern or exercise the Spirit's fruit, which includes self-control. It is plausible that some of their expressions of freedom involved rejection of the constraints and injustices of the present evil age's cultural roles for women. They knew that the old self had died in baptism. A new person had been born—a person unrestrained and alive to God. Paul's concern is that some of these ecstatic expressions of joy may have had the potential to bring shame on the new Jesus movement.

Paul appeals to his "sisters" (the females in Corinth) to express their freedom in Christ as he himself does (as he testified in ch. 9) by choosing

---

31. See the detailed discussion of ecstasy in Dunn, *Jesus and the Spirit*, ch. 7. "The enthusiast is an unpopular figure in Christian history and theology. He believes he has been specially favored by God, that the Spirit of God has been given to him in a fuller way than to other believers. He claims to experience God more directly and in more evident manner than others . . . Christianity began as an enthusiastic sect within first-century Judaism" (Dunn, *Jesus and the Spirit*, 157). See also the classic study Knox, *Enthusiasm*.

32. Wright, *Surprised by Scripture*, 74.

to restrict their God-given rights. Paul does not in any way seek to quench this or restrict women's voice. Instead, Paul asks the women to cover their heads during the gathering of the Christians in Corinth. He urges them not to abandon the gender-specific style that sets them apart as women in Graeco-Roman Corinth. Paul is thinking missiologically.

The Jesus movement faced many challenges and was frequently misunderstood in the larger society.[33] Women in the Christian community should agree to accommodate the culturally sanctioned gender markers in order to refrain from placing any additional obstacles to persons who need to receive Christ. There are two crucial issues which are decisive in my thinking:

1. UNDERSTANDING THE TRINITY

In verse 11:3, Paul puts three relationships side by side as parallel:"the head of every man is Christ, and the head of the woman is man, and the head of Christ is God." The meaning of "head" in verse 3 must be determined by the core Christian teaching about the equality of the three persons of the Trinity, since Paul sets the three relationships in this parallel framework. The weight of church tradition[34] supports the perspective on the Trinity which views Father, Son, and Holy Spirit as equal members in value and authority while doing different tasks, with no member eternally subordinate to another. To do less would take us down a dangerous path to reducing members of the Trinity to less than fully God. Professor Millard Erickson explains:

> The Trinity is a communion of three persons, three centers of consciousness, who exist and always have existed in union with one another and in dependence on one another. . . . Each is essential to the life of the others, and to the life of the Trinity. They are bound to one another in love, *agape* love, which therefore unites them in the closest and most intimate of relationships. This unselfish, agape love makes each more concerned for the other than for himself. There is therefore a mutual submission

---

33. The early church was viewed with suspicion and contempt in Roman society. Some examples of scandals that the early Christians were accused of include: cannibalism, atheism, gross immorality (especially incest), lack of patriotism, disruption of business, antisocial behavior, causing disasters, encouraging poverty. See Guy, *Introducing Early Christianity*, ch. 3 for a carefully assessment.

34. See Giles, *Trinity and Subordinationism*, for an extensive review of historical theology.

of each to each of the others and a mutual glorifying of one another. There is complete equality of the three."[35]

It is particularly important that our doctrine of the Trinity is more than an abstract shelf document. Our life together must reflect the character and presence of the Trinity. We must wrestle with how our doctrine of God shapes our lives. I agree with Giles's conclusions concerning how this lofty doctrine impacts our view of human relationships:

> Because virtually all theologians agree that the doctrine of the Trinity should inform human relationships correctly, enunciating the historically developed doctrine of the Trinity is of great practical consequence. If in the Trinity all have the same authority, "none are before or after," all are "co-equal" (the Athanasian Creed), then the doctrine of the Trinity calls into question all forms of human domination. . . . This then is our model for what being created in the image of God looks like as we try to relate in a holy and perfect way to each other.[36]

Because the nature of the Trinitarian relationship is revealed throughout the Bible, it seems to me that we must interpret that word "head" in verse 3 in a nonhierarchical manner, and thus I conclude that the concept of "head" as source or origin is to be preferred.

2. THE NATURE OF "DISGRACE"

Paul makes an appeal to the believers based on what would be considered "shameful" in the Corinthian context. He does so in verses 6 and 14. He does not refer to the behavior as sinful. Paul uses the social pressure conveyed by the concept of shame or disgrace to try to persuade the Corinthian Christians. He urges women to comply with the socially prescribed hairstyle/hair coverings which distinguish them as respectable women within the Hellenistic culture in which they live. The concern is that the fashion statement made by Christians does not bring disgrace on the Jesus movement, because it blurs or obliterates the cultural markers which distinguish males from females.

How important is disgrace? It's a morally ambiguous concept, not an absolute. In some cultures honor and shame are of paramount importance.[37]

---

35. Erickson, *God in Three Persons*, 331.

36. Giles, "Doctrine of the Trinity and Subordination," para. 42.

37. To understand how an "honor/shame" culture functions, see deSilva, *Honor, Patronage, Kinship, and Purity*; Witherington, *Conflict and Community in Corinth*, 154–55. Also Malina, *New Testament World*.

These societies believe that there is no greater transgression than to act in a way which brings shame on one's self or one's family (even if some issues of truth or justice are ignored). But not all socially sanctioned values concern matters of moral significance. Most cultures have dress codes which signal propriety. Many of the behaviors associated with shame/disgrace function to sustain sexual mores and closely related activities. Shame can also be attached to behaviors which support social stratification/status. We learn how to behave in the presence of VIPs.

So must we abide by all these social expectations and avoid bringing disgrace at all costs? Sometimes. In determining the moral weight associated with shame we must understand and evaluate the cultural value being protected, plus the motivation for transgressing, plus the harm done as a result of an act that brings shame to me and to others. Shame can often have moral implications because it has an impact on relationships and because the symbolic behaviors are a form of powerful communication.

The most compelling reason to avoid actions which bring disgrace is that every single person you encounter is worthy of respect by virtue of her/his being God's creation. C. S. Lewis has given us a memorable affirmation regarding the stunning holiness of a person in his great essay, the "Weight of Glory":

> Remember that the dullest most uninteresting person you can talk to may one day be a creature which, if you saw it now, you would be strongly tempted to worship, or else a horror and a corruption such as you now meet, if at all, only in a nightmare . . . . It is with the awe and the circumspection proper to them, that we should conduct all of our dealings with one another, all friendships, all loves, all play, all politics. . . . There are no ordinary people. You have never talked to a mere mortal."[38]

Your wife, friend, neighbor, brother-in-law, boss, and co-worker, even your enemy is worthy of respect—not disgrace.

Alternatively, there are times (as Jesus' example shows) that we must take action to protect, heal, love, or embrace a social outcast who is being abused by the culture's shaming system. In all cultures, there are socially sanctioned systems which exclude some. We must endure society's shame as we protect the oppressed and the poor. Jesus' example may in certain situations lead us to actions which offend certain cultural sensibilities. We must be prepared to follow our "shameful God!"[39]

38. Lewis, *Weight of Glory and Other Addresses*, 15.

39. The example of Jesus shows that honor/shame dynamics are not absolute or strictly ethical. Jesus is frequently seen transgressing some of the honor/shame norms

OBEYING THE TEACHING OF 1 COR 11
IN THE TWENTY-FIRST CENTURY

Avoid scandal for missional reasons

Think with me about a frontier missions situation. If the gospel begins to take root in a traditionally Muslim culture and people are being saved, what would be the prudent approach to the issue of women being covered with the hijab? In Christ, a woman is free and no longer obligated to wear the Islamic symbols of woman's submission.

But thinking missionally, a Christian community in a predominantly Muslim environment might well discern that it would be a prudent expression of gospel freedom for female followers of Jesus to set aside their rights to self-expression and to continue to cover themselves in public so that the Muslim society would not be scandalized by the disgraceful appearance of uncovered women. The gospel message concerning a God who was crucified is scandalous in and of itself (see 1 Cor 1). We might prayerfully agree

---

of first-century Judaism (see John 4 and Luke 7:36–50; 10:38–42). One of his most beloved parables, that of the prodigal son, is remarkable for the way Jesus upends honor/shame dynamics.

that we should seek to reduce certain other elements which might be seen as offensive in a certain social setting. This does not represent the continuing oppression of women, but rather it represents an opportunity for female Christ-followers to live the freedom principles which Paul articulates (and lives) in 1 Cor 9: "Though I am free and belong to no one . . . I have become all things to all people so that by all possible means I might save some."

Paul believes that women of dignity and competence can have a strong impact on the society in the Hellenistic context in which the Jesus movement is taking root. I believe the ideal of a godly woman's character is a deeply held Pauline conviction. Robert Wall explains the driving motivation in Paul's apostolic counsel:

> Paul envisions a community whose participants are modest and restrained in their behaviors, rather than ostentatious or provocative. . . . Do not give unnecessary offense, but behave in ways that are modest. Both men and women in the Christian community, and its worship, are to exhibit good judgment, prudence, and modesty. The world is watching. Worship is mission. . . . Good manners lend integrity to the gospel's truth claims.[40]

Let the church rise up and lead the global movement for justice and equality in Jesus' name

In much of the world, pursuing justice and dignity for women is an urgent issue (actually, it's literally a life-and-death matter). William Kristoff and Sheryl WuDunn are journalists who write for *The New York Times*. This wife-and-husband team is working to be a catalyst to a global movement focusing on justice which is surfacing everywhere imaginable according to their evidence. Their must–read book is titled *Half the Sky: Turning Oppression into Opportunity for Women Worldwide*. The authors are forthright about their goal. "So let's be clear about this up front: We hope to recruit you to join an incipient movement to emancipate women and fight global poverty by unlocking women's power as economic catalysts."[41]

Kristoff and WuDunn have chronicled hundreds of stories from all around the planet. Many of the accounts they have researched will break your heart. They give factual accounts of women who are dehumanized in a dizzying assortment of ways. They report stories of girls being sold as sex slaves. They report accounts of systemic injustices in nation after nation.

40. Robinson and Wall, *Called to Lead*, 56, 63.

41. Kristoff and WuDunn, *Half the Sky*, xxii.

There are reports of rape, discrimination, infanticide involving girl babies, and the common practice of denying girls the opportunity to receive an education. This is not easy reading at points, but it is necessary that we become aware. Jesus is very aware—and he weeps.

Kristoff and WuDunn make a compelling case that the issue of ensuring justice and dignity for all women is *the paramount moral issue* of our time.[42] The urgency is grounded in tragic facts:

> The global statistics regarding the abuse of girls are numbing. It appears that more girls have been killed in the last 50 years, precisely because they were girls, than men were killed in all the battles of the twentieth century. More girls are killed in this routine "gendercide" in any one decade than people were slaughtered in all the genocides of the twentieth century. . . . Our own estimate is that there are 3 million women and girls worldwide who can fairly be termed enslaved in the sex trade.[43]

Wouldn't it be a powerful witness to Jesus and his reign if these *New York Times* reporters were able to report that over and over, in a thousand different contexts, it was followers of Jesus who are giving their lives in bold, creative initiatives which are transforming the lives of oppressed women? There are bold Christ-followers doing amazing things, but I fear that justice for women in today's world is not high on our priority list. In fact, in many situations there is evidence that distorted versions of church teachings are being used to provide sacred legitimation for worldviews and cultural traditions which inflict abuse and injustice on women.[44]

42. Kristof and WuDunn, *Half the Sky*, xvii: "In the nineteenth century, the central moral challenge was slavery. In the twentieth century, it was the battle against totalitarianism. We believe that in this century the paramount moral challenge will be the struggle for gender equality around the world."

43. Kristof and WuDunn, *Half the Sky*, xvii.

44. One example of this sacred legitimation for systemic abuse of women is the significance of the word translated as "helper" in Gen 2:18. This word was often used to suggest that a woman/wife is a kind of personal assistant to the dominant male. It is actually a word which assigns her a significantly high-status relationship. The Hebrew word for "helper" in Gen 2:18 and 20 (*ezer*) appears about twenty times in the Old Testament (e.g., Exod 18:4; Deut 33:7, 26, 29; Ps 33:20; etc.). In most cases *ezer* refers to God. Bilezikian explains, "There was a time when uninformed teachers of the Bible seized upon the word *helper* to draw inferences of authority/subjection distinctions between men and women. According to them, *helper* meant that man was boss and woman his domestic. Fortunately, the study of the use of the word *helper* in the Old Testament has dispelled such misconceptions. It is now a matter of general knowledge that this Hebrew word for 'helper' is not used in the Bible with reference to a subordinate person such as a servant or an underling. It is generally attributed to God when He is engaged in activities of relief or rescue among His people" (Bilezikian, *Beyond Sex Roles*, 28; italics original).

The church-at-large is not seen as bringing courageous prophetic rebukes to the perpetrators of this tragic moral evil of our day, nor are we identified in the society as the champions who offer hope and empowerment to abused girls. "Americans of faith should try as hard to save the lives of African women as the lives of unborn fetuses."[45] This is a kingdom issue.

When the Holy Spirit is moving to revitalize and reform the church, Jesus' followers will be compelled by his Spirit to actively pursue shalom for women everywhere. The Jesus movement grasps the real truth about time. God has begun his new-creation agenda in the death and resurrection of Jesus. As followers of the risen Lord, who is making all things new, we must learn together to live into this alternative view of how life is unfolding. The full gospel must transform our thinking about everything.

> The good news is that the *one true God has now taken charge of the world, in and through Jesus and his death and resurrection. . . .* God's plan to put the world right has finally been launched. He has grasped the world in a new way, to sort it out and fill it with his glory and justice, as he always promised. But he has done so in a way beyond the wildest dreams of prophecy. The ancient sickness that had crippled the whole world, and humans with it, has been cured at last, so that new life can rise up in its place. Life has come to life and is pouring out like a mighty river into the world, in the form of a new power, the power of love. The good news was, and is, that all this has happened in and through Jesus; that one day it will happen, completely and utterly, to all creation; and that *we humans, every single one of us, whoever we are, can be caught up in that transformation here and now.* This is the Christian gospel.[46]

This gospel changes everything for women. In Christ we are not slaves to the present evil age and its heritage of degradation of the dignity of women. In Christ, women discover that they have a vital and essential purpose as partners with the Trinity in transforming planet earth. As *Half the Sky* vividly explains, women are "not the problem but the solution."[47] Together we must become agents through whom God answers the prayer that his kingdom may come and his will be done "on earth as it is in heaven" (Matt 6:10). Carolyn James catches this empowering new reality when she writes to the daughters of God:

---

45. Kristof and WuDunn, *Half the Sky*, 244.

46. Wright, *Simply Good News*, 55 (italics original).

47. Kristof and WuDunn, *Half the Sky*, xviii.

We are his image bearers—welcomed into the inner circle to know the God who created the universe. We represent him in the world—speaking and acting on his behalf. He is counting on his daughters along with his sons to be guardians of the whole earth and to rule it as he himself would. . . . Following Jesus' example, today's image bearers—both halves of the church—have kingdom work to do.[48]

If we were to give Paul the last word, what do you suppose he would say to us? I think he would pray: "May the God who gives endurance and encouragement give you a spirit of unity among yourselves as you follow Christ Jesus, so that with one heart and mouth you may glorify the God and Father of our Lord Jesus Christ. Accept one another, then, just as Christ accepted you, in order to bring praise to God" (Rom 15:5–7).

48. James, *Half the Church*, 60–61.

Chapter 9

Renewing Worship

Celebrating the New Creation (Ch. 11:17–34)

When Jesus himself wanted to explain to his disciples what his forthcoming death was all about, he didn't give them a theory, he gave them a meal.[1]

—N. T. WRIGHT

READ: 1 COR 11:17–34

There is close to a consensus among scholars that going to church in the first Christian communities involved coming together with other Christ-followers and with Jesus himself (present through the Holy Spirit) to eat a common meal together.[2] Having church meant eating and drinking with

---

1. Wright, *Day the Revolution Began*, 182.

2. Richard Hays expresses the conclusion of most scholars: "Christians accustomed to experiencing the Lord's Supper only as a ritual 'in church,' removed from a meal setting, will need to discipline their imaginations to keep this original setting in mind . . . when Paul refers to the Lord's Supper at Corinth, he is not talking about a liturgical ritual celebrated in a church building. At this early date, there were no separate church buildings for worship. The Lord's Supper was an actual meal eaten by the community in a private home" (Hays, *First Corinthians*, 193). Also, Ben Witherington writes: "It

Jesus and with all those who were united with you by the grace of God in Christ. Thus, Robert Banks writes, "The most visible and profound way in which the community gives physical expression to its fellowship is the common meal."[3] Is this a matter of mere historical curiosity, or might it have something to do with the authenticity of community? Can you be the body of Christ and share *koinōnia* without eating together?

In this radical guidance regarding Holy Communion we encounter this great idea: *Celebrating the community's common meal with Jesus and his friends can be a profound and formative experience which the Spirit can use to shape and revive the community's identity, values, and vitality.*

Everybody's got liturgy.[4] It is what groups of humans do (religious and secular). All sorts of communities create various kinds of rituals, and by repeating those patterned group behaviors we are actually defining, clarifying, and reinforcing our self-understanding. In Holy Communion, Jesus gives us a simple ritual by means of which *gospel* values will be enacted over and over, and through this process we will define our community.

FOUR DIFFERENT WAYS OF CELEBRATING

What kind of community is being shaped by the forms we embrace for the celebration of Holy Communion?[5] Here are brief descriptions of four different ways (out of thousands) of experiencing Holy Communion:

A 1950s Baptist in USA

Growing up in a fundamentalist Baptist church setting, I knew that this memorial was to be referred to as an ordinance (never as a sacrament). Jesus commanded us to do this in remembrance, and thus it was ordained. As a kid, I knew that Jesus thought this ordained remembering was best done once a month—a good balance since "familiarity breeds contempt," as the

---

appears clear from the outset that the context in which the Lord's Supper happened was in a home and in the social setting of a meal, perhaps a love feast that was part of an act of worship in the home" (Witherington, *Making a Meal of It*, 48).

3 Banks, *Paul's Idea of Community*, 80.

4. When I speak of liturgy, I am referring to a pattern which organizes a group's public worship assembly. It arranges the various elements (prayers, songs, Scripture readings, rituals, creeds, sacred actions, etc.) of the group's gathering before God. It may be ancient or modern, formalized or simply the structure that emerges from repetition.

5. I choose to refer to this as "Holy Communion," but it can also be called the Lord's Table, Lord's Supper, and Eucharist. See the discussion in Marshall, *Last Supper and Lord's Supper*, 15.

old saying goes. On the first Sunday, there was an appendix added to the morning service during which the pastor came down from the pulpit to floor level. He stood behind a communion table which was set with silver plates covered in white linen napkins and two stacks of silver communion cup dispensers. The tiny cups were filled with grape juice. The silver plates held pinky-finger sized bits of crackers. Eight men in dark suits marched down the aisle and stood by the pastor in a straight row. Strict protocol was observed—words and actions were the same each time. (Although we denied we were liturgical in any sense. As a child, I understood that people who followed liturgy out of a book were clearly insincere.) It was very somber since we all had to quietly interrogate our souls and search out hidden sins. No outsiders were invited to this ordinance—only members. After reflecting on the state of our wretched souls for two to three minutes, the men in black distributed the trays with the small chips of crackers. We sat and waited until all members were served and ate the tiny morsel on command. This was how we remembered that Jesus died for our sins. We partook of the small cup of juice in the same manner. The juice was red because it recalled Jesus' blood. Soft music played on a piano. No one seemed in the least bit happy at being told that their sins were forgiven. It felt to me as a child like a pretty sad time. We had zero connection with other people in the congregation during this solemn seven minutes. This was between you and God. We did not allow Jesus to join in since this was about recalling his death. (And we were 100 percent opposed to the Catholics and their superstitious heresy that Jesus was really present on the altar when the priest said the magic words.)

An Anglican Tradition—The Great Easter Vigil

The Great Easter Vigil is an ancient Christian tradition that begins at sundown on Saturday night.[6] The three-hour festival would be a collage of color, sound, smells, music, shouting, bell-ringing, and tasting (full of "bells and smells"). The evening began in darkness and an atmosphere of mourning. It was still Good Friday. The drama of God's redemptive work throughout the Old Testament was read and affirmed. Suddenly the lights were turned up and the celebrant shouted the news, "Christ is risen." This triggered not only a verbal response from the assembly, but a riot of

6. Actually, the Great Easter Vigil is part three of the Triduum which begins on Maundy Thursday and continues to Good Friday. The three parts are one experience. The vigil begins at sundown on Saturday since in Jewish tradition the new day starts in the evening.

exuberant sound—shouts and a tsunami of elegant organ sounds. There was deafening "tintinnabulation,"[7] following another ancient tradition, and the clergy and choir processed through the sanctuary while we sang songs that celebrated Jesus' conquest of death.

Then it came time for the Eucharist, and the cohort of priests behind the altar (far above us) reenacted an ancient ritual with incense and bells and lots of bowing and making the sign of the cross. The congregation was thundering back our responses according to ancient liturgical words. With one voice we prayed the "prayer of humble access" after the celebrant said the words of consecration. You could hear the wafer crack as Jesus' body was broken. Then we were all welcomed to walk up to the altar rail. "The gifts of God for the people of God. Take and eat in remembrance that Christ died for you." For the next twenty minutes, row after row streamed to the front and kneeled at the altar rail. The army of priests served each person who knelt with open hands. To each one the priest would say, "The body of Christ, broken for you." A second clergy person offered a sip of sweet wine from the common cup. "The blood of Christ; cup of salvation." I recall thinking that there is something impressive about hundreds of people—old, young, black, white, wealthy, poor—all kneeling side by side. There was a youth with a purple mohawk next to the CEO of a local bank. Here we were, all on our knees, waiting for signs of grace.

An Early Christian Gathering—From Justin, "First Apology"[8] (AD 150)

> . . . on the day called Sunday, all who live in cities or in the coun-
> try gather together to one place, and the memoirs of the apostles
> or the writings of the prophets are read, as long as time permits;
> then, when the reader has ceased, the president verbally in-
> structs, and exhorts to the imitation of these good things. Then
> we all rise together and pray, and, as we before said, when our
> prayer is ended, bread and wine and water are brought, and the
> president in like manner offers prayers and thanksgivings, ac-
> cording to his ability, and the people assent, saying Amen; and
> there is a distribution to each, and a participation of that over
> which thanks have been given, and to those who are absent a
> portion is sent by the deacons. And they who are well to do,
> and willing, give what each thinks fit; and what is collected is

7. "Tintinnabulation" is bell-ringing by members of the worshipping community as an expression of joy.

8. Justin Martyr, "First Apology," 1:186.

deposited with the president, who succours the orphans and widows and those who, through sickness or any other cause, are in want, and those who are in bonds and the strangers sojourning among us, and in a word takes care of all who are in need. . . . And this food is called among us *Eukaristia* [the Eucharist], of which no one is allowed to partake but the man who believes that the things which we teach are true, and who has been washed with the washing that is for the remission of sins, and unto regeneration, and who is so living as Christ has enjoined.

A traditional East African tribe becoming Christian—The Masai[9]

So the first Masses in the new Masai communities were simplicity itself. I would take bread and wine, without any preceding or following ritual, and say to the people: "This is the way it was passed on to me, and I pass on to you that on the night before he died, Jesus took bread and wine into his hands, blessed them and said, 'This is my body. This is the cup of my blood of the new covenant, poured out for the forgiveness of sins. Do this in my memory.'"

The people took it from there. . . . Masai men had never eaten in the presence of Masai women. In their minds, the status and condition of women were such that the very presence of women at the time of eating was enough to pollute any food that was present. Hence, men could never eat with women. How then was eucharist possible? In their minds it was not. If ever there was a need for eucharist as a salvific sign of unity, it was here. I reminded them that besides the law of love which I had preached to them and they had accepted, I never tried to interpret for them how they must work out this law in their homes. . . . But here, in the eucharist, we were at the heart of the unchanging gospel that I was passing on to them. They were free to accept that gospel or reject it, but if they accepted it, they were accepting the truth that in the eucharist, which is to say "in Christ, there is neither slave nor free, neither Jew nor Greek, neither male nor female."

They did accept it, but it was surely a traumatic moment for them, as individuals and as a people, that first time when I blessed the cup, or gourd in this case, and passed it on to the

9. The Masai tribe is a Nilotic pastoralist ethnic group in east Africa, living mostly in Kenya and Tanzania.

woman sitting closest to me, told her to drink from it, and then pass it on to the man sitting next to her. I don't remember any other pastoral experience in which the "sign of unity" was so real for me . . .

Mass in the Masai communities took on an open and free form, as open and free as the life the people lived. As the Mass began, I picked up a tuft of grass and passed it on to the first elder who met me, and greeted him with "the peace of Christ." He accepted it and passed it on to his family, and they passed it on to neighboring elders and families. It had to pass all through the village. [Grass was another sacred sign among the Masai. Since their cattle, and they themselves, lived off grass, it was a vital and holy sign to them, a sign of peace and happiness and well-being.] If the life in the village had been less than human or holy—if there had been selfishness and forgetfulness and hate-fulness and lack of forgiveness . . . in the life that had been led here—then there was no eucharist.[10]

There are, no doubt, thousands of other liturgies which diverse groups of Christians have followed in celebrating Holy Communion. I share these four sketches as illustrations of such diversity. None can be said to be the only right way to obey Jesus' word, "Do this in remembrance of me." But every liturgy tells a story and every liturgy shapes a community's identity and values.

It is imperative, according to Paul's teaching, that our Holy Communion actions manifest that we are a community of justice and equality in Christ. Our celebrations must be inclusive across social and economic lines. Because we are all "sinners saved by grace," we must demonstrate mutual respect and Jesus-style love (Phil 2:1–8, once again). Holy Communion tells us who we are.

HOLY COMMUNION IN CORINTH
IN AD 55 — 1 COR 11:17

As we saw elsewhere in this letter to the church in Corinth, Paul is respond-ing and his apostolic guidance reflects a skilled pastor working to reframe the particular issues and thus guide the community through a step-by-step resocialization process. In this second half of chapter 11, the presenting issue is *schismata*, meaning "divisions," or "a relational breakdown of community

---

10. This account comes from Donovan, *Christianity Rediscovered*, 121–25.

based on differences in social status." Paul writes in 11:18, "when you come together as a church, I hear that there are divisions among you."

Paul's passion in this unit of teaching is to stress that when this new-creation community assembles to share their common meal and to worship Jesus, the risen Lord, there must be a manifestation of the oneness of the body of Christ. Since the shared meal is so central and formative, it is no place for the prejudices and arrogance of the present evil age to be dominating relationships. "Paul's understanding of community is nothing less than the gospel itself in corporate form."[11] Mutual respect, resulting in reconciliation and oneness, is an urgent aspect of living together under Jesus' values.

What went on in a Corinthian assembly?

The Holy Spirit chose not to give us a standard order of service or liturgy for early Christian worship gatherings. He could have provided a one-size-fits-all rubric for all Christian assemblies forever, since such documents did exist in the ancient world. Scholars found a rather detailed liturgy among the famous Dead Sea Scrolls.[12] But such a source does not exist in our Bibles, and thus we can conclude that the Spirit wanted the church to be free to listen for his voice in a wide variety of diverse cultures. We are given freedom by the Spirit to organize our gathering as the Spirit directs, in ways that are meaningful in a particular community.

Professor Ben Witherington III's wonderful little book, *A Week in the Life of Corinth*, presents a fictional reconstruction of what might have been taking place in an early Christian gathering: "The worship service itself would take some three or four hours, what with the meal, the Lord's Supper taken in the context of that meal, the discourse of Paulos, the time of witnessing, the singing, the prayers, and the prophesying and speaking in tongues."[13]

Since the Christian movement was taking shape in the social milieu of Hellenism, it should not surprise us that the Christian gatherings took some of its forms from the cultural environment.[14] If we look more closely at the

---

11. Banks, *Paul's Idea of Community*, 190.

12. Among the documents sometimes referred to as the Dead Sea Scrolls there is a scroll referred to as the "Manual of Discipline." It gives precise details for the celebration of a sacred meal by the Jewish sectarians of Qumran. It is a liturgical framework. For an English translation of the Qumran "Manual of Discipline," see Dupont-Sommer, *Essene Writings from Qumran*. If we look for the earliest source which contains a Christian liturgy, most scholars turn to Hypolitus (fourth century).

13 Witherington, *Week in the Life of Corinth*, 126. See also Banks's similar fictional reconstruction, *Going to Church in the First Century*.

14. Crowe, *From Jerusalem to Antioch*, is a perceptive study of several NT

cultural dynamics of an ancient Roman colony like Corinth, the situation becomes even more understandable.[15] Professor Wayne Meeks explains how the dynamics of a typical Hellenistic dinner party might have shaped the gatherings of the Corinthian community:

> If a person like Gaius, who opened his house for gatherings of the whole *ekklēsia* of Corinthian Christians, regarded himself very much in the way that a wealthy patron of a private association or a pagan cultic society might do, that would not be surprising. If at the common meals of the Christian community, held in his dining room, he moreover made distinctions in the food he provided for those on his own social level and those who were of lower rank, that would not have been at all out of the ordinary. . . . The divisions in the group (11:18,22) are primarily between rich and poor. The wealthier members of the church are hosts of the gatherings and probably provide all the food for all. It was apparently not uncommon for these to become occasions for conspicuous displays of social distance and even for humiliation of the clients by the rich, by means of the quality and quantity of food provided to different tables.[16]

Remember that the Corinthian community is a group that is relatively new to the Christian faith. These believers are largely a group of former pagans who were socialized by Hellenistic society. To engage in social interactions in patterns organized by the caste system seemed to be just the way life is. This highlights again the urgency of Paul's agenda of resocialization into a new narrative which will give shape to new values which will result in

---

communities which were emerging. We discover amazing diversity already in the first fifty years. The new creation movement was taking root in a variety of ancient cultures. The apostles and the sisters and brothers took the gospel everywhere and they were brilliant contextualizers (no doubt because of a remarkable degree of openness to the Spirit.) Gatherings in the early church were not monolithic experiences.

15. A Roman governor posted to an office in Asia Minor writes a description of the normal dinner party. Pliny's letter is giving advice to a young friend. The governor advises: "I happened to be dining with a man—though no particular friend—whose elegant economy, as he called it, seemed to me a sort of stingy extravagance. The best dishes were set in front of himself and a select few, and the cheap scraps of food before the rest of the company. He had even put the wine into tiny little flasks, divided into three categories, not with the idea of giving his guests the opportunity of choosing, but to make it impossible for them to refuse what they were given. One lot was intended for himself and for us, another for his lesser friends (all his friends are graded), and the third for his and our freedmen." (Ep. 2.6; quoted in Meeks, *First Urban Christians*, 68). Pliny, early in the second century in Bithynia, forbade such meals, in accordance with Trajan's ban against clubs (Ep. 10.97.7).

16. Meeks, *First Urban Christians*, 68.

social transformation in relationships. But until the new normal is socially legitimated, old systems still seem obvious, and their legitimacy was never questioned or thought to be morally objectionable.

11:17–19—Paul rebukes the community because they are divided when they assemble.

Paul begins with a touch of satirical rebuke. He tells the Corinthians that he has gotten a report that there are divisions within the community. With a bit of sarcasm, he writes that he "can hardly believe this news." He continues to prod them saying their coming together is not beneficial, but actually makes things worse (vv. 18–19).

Paul offers an interesting bit of discernment in saying that divisions serve some purpose within a community. They disclose authenticity and uncover true motivations. I think he is suggesting that when we see a person's actual behavior (in this case some wealthy persons humiliating the poorer members), we are given an accurate reading on the condition of the heart. It seems likely that Paul has in mind Jesus' words, "By their fruit you will recognize them. . . . Every good tree bears good fruit, but a bad tree bears bad fruit."[17]

11:20–21—The specific problem described.

In any group situation, we tend to fall into patterned behaviors. This is human nature. Corinthian assemblies had become predictable. But what seemed normal was totally contrary to the values of Jesus. Paul exposes the fact that the wealthy arrive early for the Christian assembly and eat without waiting for others. Eventually they even get drunk, as was customary at Roman feasts. But the poorer members of the community arrive later since they are not free to abandon their jobs, and by the time they arrive, there is nothing remaining. They go hungry.

When Corinthian social dynamics reveal a pattern of prejudice and disrespect for the lower-class sisters and brothers, this unmasking exposes the true condition of others' hearts and becomes a judgment of *grace*. It offers an opportunity for the hypocrites who say "Lord, Lord," to repent and allow the Spirit to transform their inner attitudes of prejudice. It is urgent that this repentance take place, since a final unmasking of the truth will

---

17. Matt 7:17–18.

surely take place and all secrets will be revealed on the day of the Lord. Today's divisions could be a preview of coming judgment if not corrected.

So in 1 Cor 11, Paul says that these relatively new followers of the way of Jesus are not experiencing the Lord's Supper. They are meeting and eating and praying and prophesying, but the dynamics of their gathering are negating the gospel and its values: "Your meeting does not amount to an eating of the Lord's Supper. . . . For in eating, each one goes ahead with his own meal. One goes hungry, another gets drunk. What! Do you not have houses to eat and drink in? Or do you despise the church of God and humiliate those who have nothing?" (1 Cor 11: 20–22).

The seriousness of these relational dynamics is evident from Paul's rebukes. In 11:22, Paul seeks to show them the unthinkable character of their behavior. He stresses that "You are not actually eating the Lord's Supper." He characterizes the social prejudices of the wealthy as "despis[ing] God's church." Then he leads them to recognize the terrible implication of this deeply entrenched pattern: "You are guilty of the body and blood of Christ" (1 Cor 11:27).

11:23–26—The bedrock tradition concerning Jesus' words of institution.

In correcting this serious offense against the Lord and his community, Paul reminds them of a teaching which he has already passed on to them during his earlier teaching ministry. He takes them back to Jesus himself. Paul clarifies that these exact words come from Jesus:[18]

> For I received from the Lord what I also delivered to you, that the Lord Jesus on the night when he was betrayed took bread, and when he had given thanks, he broke it, and said, "This is my body which is for you. Do this in remembrance of me." In the same way also he took the cup, after supper, saying, "This cup is the new covenant in my blood. Do this, as often as you drink it, in remembrance of me." For as often as you eat this bread and drink the cup, you proclaim the Lord's death until he comes.

The sacred words that Paul says he received directly from Jesus (not as an ecstatic revelation, but through the teachings of the Twelve in the Jerusalem Church) are some of the words that Jesus spoke at the Last Supper with the

---

18. The two verbs that Paul uses in verse 23 were words that the original readers would have recognized as referring to the process of passing along sacred traditions of high value to a religious community. They are technical rabbinical terms for sacred tradition. See Bruce, *Tradition*, 30, and Jeremias, *Eucharistic Words of Jesus*.

Twelve disciples. What Jesus said to his disciples on the night before he was executed is the foundation of the Lord's Supper. It is this event which the churches have remembered, and the memory of which has been passed from church to church during the thirty years since the crucifixion and resurrection.

The churches remember some very specific ritual actions accompanying the words, which are what Jesus did as he hosted the Passover meal as described in the Synoptic Gospels. They are not a magical performance, nor are the words any sort of incantation.[19] The actions are what a host/father does in every Jewish family as the Passover Haggadah[20] unfolds and the Exodus narrative is retold. We, as his followers, remember that as he anticipated offering himself as a sacrifice to fulfill his messianic destiny, Jesus *took* bread, *gave thanks, broke* it, and *gave* it to his friends.

The words which Jesus spoke when sharing the Passover feast that night are forever remembered and passed on from generation to generation. "This is my body on behalf of you. Do this in remembrance" (1 Cor 11:24). However, we face a challenge in seeking to determine the precise meaning that Paul intended to communicate in passing on these eight Greek words.[21] The Corinthian believers were familiar with these words. Paul had passed along this core tradition during his earlier eighteen months of teaching ministry in Corinth (see Acts 18). Here in chapter 11, he simply reminds them of what they already know. We are wishing he gave them (us!) more exposition in this letter. We also are the beneficiaries of 2,000 years of meditation and theological clarification. This is an invaluable treasure trove of insight. But this wealth of reflection can make it very difficult to actually determine what is in Paul's mind as he guides this new community.

We can be certain that Paul understands *Jesus' death as substitutionary.* The words come from "the night he was delivered up (or betrayed)" (1 Cor 11:23). Jesus was executed the following day. The meaning of "my body on behalf of you" (1 Cor 11:24) certainly must be interpreted as a statement

19. An incantation in animistic religions is a very specific verbal formula which, if spoken or sung exactly, is believed to release magical powers.

20. Passover Haggadah is the order of worship for the Passover Seder. It has developed over 3 millennia and is shared by most Jews even today. The traditional Jewish Passover involved a leisurely family meal during which the story of God's redemption of the Hebrews was retold and various elements of the supper were interpreted and held up as symbols of significant dimensions of the community's story. Bitter herbs, unleavened bread, and several cups of wine were elements which traditionally called for commentary. The Haggadah is the script. Jesus used the traditions of the Haggadah to give a new community a new identity.

21. They are eight in Greek text—"*touto mou estin to sōma to uper humōn.*" On the quest for *ipsissima verba,* see the classic study Jeremias, *Eucharistic Words of Jesus,* chs. 3 and 4.

referring to Jesus' death as substitutionary. He gives up his body in death on behalf of his follower-friends.[22] In 1 Cor 1, Paul has used another expression which refers to the same reality—"the message of the cross" (1:18). The words remembered from Jesus immediately prior to his death ("my body on behalf of you") have the same meaning as Paul's expression, "we preach Christ crucified" (1 Cor 1:23). In the briefest possible form, these expressions call to mind a supremely powerful act of the Trinity. Jesus, the Lord of the community, is fulfilling the destiny of Israel's Messiah. Jesus freely offers his life ("my body") as the most stunningly profound expression of love for his own friends (see John 15:13). Jesus chooses to be "obedient to death, even death on the cross!" (Phil 2:8). And every person who is in Christ experiences the impact of Jesus' death on the cross. As Paul explains the implications of this act of substitution in chapter 1, he repeatedly explains Jesus' death as God's counterintuitive power. "Christ, the power of God and the wisdom of God" (1:24–25).

Remembering Jesus

Paul's version of the words of institution, which he passed down, are the earliest record we possess of these from Jesus' at the Last Supper.[23] In Paul's version, we twice find the phrase "Do this in remembrance of me" (vv. 24 and 25). In Corinthian society, it was common for people to conduct memorial meals in honor of the departed. The Lord's Table was not this kind of funerary event, although a few of the more recent converts might have seen it as such. But as Witherington says, "in the Lord's Supper one does not merely celebrate the life of the deceased Jesus; *one communes with the living Christ,* and one also proclaims his death until he comes again, by having this meal and by other means."[24] So what exactly does Paul mean when he instructs us to share this meal "in remembrance?" Here again we need to get some

---

22. See Rutledge, *Crucifixion,* ch. 11 for a probing and at times inspiring analysis of the theology of substitution. The substitutionary atonement theme is expressed in fuller form in many of Paul's letters. For example: "You see, at just the right time, when we were still powerless, Christ died for the ungodly. Very rarely will anyone die for a righteous person, though for a good person someone might possibly dare to die. But God demonstrates his own love for us in this: While we were still sinners, Christ died for us [on behalf of us]. . . . For if, while we were God's enemies, we were reconciled to him through the death of his Son, how much more, having been reconciled, shall we be saved through his life!" (Rom 5)

23. The Corinthian letters were written at an earlier date than the Synoptic Gospels. On the date of this letter, see Thistleton, *First Epistle to the Corinthians,* 29–32.

24. Witherington, *Making a Meal of It,* 56 (italics ours).

interpretive keys from the context. This was more significant than merely a pleasant mental exercise, such as we might engage in if we as a family sat around the dinner table on Thanksgiving Day and told stories about good old Uncle Harry, who passed away in 1985. In a Jewish cultural context, memory was a key theme in Jewish Passover feasts. As the community of Yahweh, we are invited to enter into the narrative events which make up our people's history. We saw in 1 Cor 10 that Paul was clear that eating the bread entails a deep spiritual transaction. He used the word *koinōnia*, meaning "a participation in or a sharing of something in common." "Is not the bread which we break a sharing in the body of Christ? Since there is one bread, we who are many are one body; for we all partake of the one bread" (10:17).

This surely indicates that our participation involves more than calling up a mental picture of Jesus dying on the cross. Professor Ralph Martin explains, "'In remembrance of me,' then is no bare historical reflection of the Cross, but a recalling of the crucified and living Christ in such a way that He is personally present in all the fullness and reality of His saving power, and is appropriated by the believer's faith."[25] Eating the bread is *koinōnia*. We are bonding spiritually with Jesus, his death, and his family. "Remembrance" as it is used here, entails this ontological spiritual connectivity. This is a transaction engaged in by faith, and it is empowered by the Spirit of Jesus who is present at the Table. There's real grace available because there's really Jesus in our midst.

11:25—Embracing God's new covenant

In verse 25 we find the second of the words of institution: "In the same way He took the cup also after supper, saying, 'This cup is the new covenant in my blood; do this, as often as you drink it, in remembrance of Me.'" Jesus' words, which Paul passed along to give us the significance of the cup of Passover wine, tell us that the cup is the means by which we enact a covenant. Paul does not teach that the cup contains Jesus' blood in a symbolic or real form. The Christian community is not said to drink the blood of Jesus. This, of course, would have been a horrific thought for every Jew, and for most pagans. (Although, 150 years later, there were rumors circulating in various Roman towns that the Christian movement engaged in all sorts of disgusting and immoral activities in their secret meetings, including drinking blood. The slander was based on a misunderstanding of the Lord's Table experience.)

The cup is the sign of the new covenant which is enacted on the basis of Jesus' blood, which means his death. In the Exodus narrative, the covenant

25. Martin, *Worship in the Early Church*, 126.

which Yahweh graciously offers to his redeemed children at the base of Sinai is put into effect and sealed with blood. The Exodus 24 accounts states, "Moses then took the blood, sprinkled it on the people and said, 'This is the blood of the covenant that the Lord has made with you in accordance with all these words'" (v. 8). Our eternal, unshakeable covenant relationship with God has been put into effect and sealed with blood. This is for every Christ-follower a source of unimaginable joy and deep assurance. As we drink the cup we are assured that "neither death nor life, neither angels nor demons, neither the present nor the future, nor any powers . . . nor anything else in all creation, will be able to separate us from the love of God that is in Christ Jesus our Lord" (Rom 8:38–39).

When we as a community pass this cup around and take a drink from it, one by one, we are renewing the covenant bonds and reaffirming our identity and calling to be the new-creation community. New-covenant language requires a narrative to be meaningful. The narrative is Yahweh's love story with his son, Israel. Remembering the promise of the new covenant (Jer 31:31–34) means we enter this story and make it our own. God has kept his promise. Through Jesus, Yahweh has fulfilled his ancient promises and come in person to "make all things new" (Rev 21:5, echoing Isa 65:17). Drinking the cup says we believe "God has already begun the ultimate, final work of new creation."[26] Together we lift the cup in faith and we say "yes" to all that God has done, is doing, and will do in the future.

In verse 26, Paul adds his own comment to the tradition that he is passing on. He reminds us, "For as often as you eat this bread and drink the cup, you proclaim the Lord's death until He comes." This striking note makes us aware of all the diverse ways in which God communicates. Some of the most powerful communication is nonverbal, according to communication theorists. Personal experience verifies this. Paul declares that the eating and drinking is a proclamation of the cross. He calls the sharing of the Lord's Table *katangelete*, a word which elsewhere refers to his own apostolic evangelistic ministry (as in 2:1). It is preaching which has power!

11:26—The supper anticipates the return of Jesus!

The final three words of verse 26 shift our focus to the future. They tell us what time it is. "You proclaim the Lord's death until He comes." We know we are participants in the new-creation age of fulfillment because the same Jesus who died on our behalf was also raised from death by the power of God's Spirit. But there's more to come. We have been arguing that one of Paul's

26. Wright, *Surprised by Scripture*, 94.

big challenges in resocializing the Corinthians is to guide them into an accurate eschatological perspective. The Corinthians lost sight of the future dimension of the narrative. They were so captivated by ecstatic experiences, they assumed the day of fulfillment was now. But the return of the Lord and the comprehensive completion of God's promises is "not yet." When the new-creation community shares the Lord's Table, it is with this hope in view. N. T. Wright captures our real situation, which is what we affirm in Holy Communion:

> One day, God—the God now made known in Jesus—would come back to finish the task, to be all in all, to fill the whole world with his glory and love, to transform everything, to rectify everything, to heal everything with his powerful love. . . . That was the good news, according to the Bible and according to Paul. Something *had* happened. Something *would* happen. And in between, something powerful and mysterious *was happening* in the lives of all those who found themselves caught up in it.[27]

Paul regards the sharing of the common meal and the remembrance of the Lord's death as absolutely central and formative to the community's life. Therefore he urges the church to grasp that the values of Jesus the Lord (who is present at the Table) must be in evidence in the relationships among the community's members. "The complete obliteration of social and cultural distinctions as a basis for life under God was clearly understood by Paul as essential to the presence of Jesus in his people . . . Paul's policy with regard to the redemptive community simply followed the gospel of the Beatitudes [of Jesus]."[28] We can never preach one gospel and live another which is in sharp contrast. Continuing to allow society's system of social stratification to create division and prejudice in church gatherings is unthinkable in light of Jesus' words and sacrifice and presence. The teachings of Jesus must be followed over and over in each assembly, because reconciliation is at the core of the new-creation community's life. Jesus taught, "If you are offering your gift at the altar and there remember that your brother or sister has something against you, leave your gift there in front of the altar. First go and be reconciled to them; then come and offer your gift" (Matt 5:23).

---

27. Wright, *Simply Good News*, 34 (italics original).

28. Willard, *Divine Conspiracy*, 125.

11:27–32—God sends judgment on all who participate in the "meal" in ways which do not recognize the significance of that participation.

> Whoever, therefore, eats the bread or drinks the cup of the Lord in an unworthy manner will be guilty of profaning the body and blood of the Lord. Let a person examine himself, then, and so eat of the bread and drink of the cup. For anyone who eats and drinks without discerning the body eats and drinks judgment on himself. That is why many of you are weak and ill, and some have died. But if we judged ourselves truly, we would not be judged. But when we are judged by the Lord, we are disciplined so that we may not be condemned along with the world.

There's a shocking teaching in verses 27–32: to eat and drink in an "unworthy" manner is to be guilty of the death of Jesus (v. 27). It is important in Bible interpretation that we define a word or concept from within the context. Thus, the meaning of "unworthy" in verse 27 is explained by verse 29 and in the context of the community divisions. There has been much teaching and theological reflection on this matter of worthiness and unworthiness over the centuries. Some of it has caused unimaginable torture to sensitive souls. I have many friends who worship and serve in the Africa Inland Church of Kenya. They report to me that in many rural congregations, there are very few AIC members who will receive Holy Communion when the opportunity is given.

Why such a low percentage? The pastors indicate that the first generation of members was severely warned about receiving communion in an unworthy manner. They were terrified by the 1 Cor 11 warnings about Corinthians who had died as a result of unworthy communing. These warnings make good sense in the African context in which ritual taboos are held to have dire consequences for those who trespass. The distorted interpretation of chapter 11 has held a generation of Christians in bondage to fear. Unworthiness is thought to have wide-ranging implications. A few unscrupulous pastors have stressed that one's worthiness for communion may be correlated with one's faithfulness in giving tithes and offerings. The body is fractured and corrupted by false teaching. Sensitive Christians are deprived of the grace of hearing again and again about the love of God expressed through Jesus' death and the free forgiveness of sins.

Ben Witherington's assuring words are correct, "I have had church members who would not participate because they did not think they were worthy of doing so. I have had to remind them that it's not about *their* being worthy—*Christ is the only worthy one*; it's about them willingly participating in a way that honors Christ. That implies repentance of sins and a willingness to be forgiven and to forgive."[29]

Paul says judgment results from failure to "distinguish to body" (*diakrinōn to sōma*) (v. 29). If we keep in mind the urgent concerns on Paul's heart beginning in verse 17, we must agree that "body" here is talking about the community. "Discerning the body" does not have in view some requirement that we grasp fine theological nuances regarding "Eucharistic theology."[30] Paul's focus is the ethical imperatives that flow out of the Jesus story. He points to the "body" of 10:17: "Because there is one loaf, we, who are many, are one body, for we all share the one loaf" In 10:16–17, he teaches that eating the sacred meal with the community binds the members together, since all are united to one Jesus (by the one Spirit). The relationship goes beyond sociology and *esprit de corps*. This is an ontological reality. We should also recall that in chapter 8, Paul is clear that to do damage to a weaker member of the community is to sin against Jesus himself. So the specific behavior which is being rebuked in 11:29 is despising others (the poor) in the Christian family—dehumanizing a sister or disrespecting a brother. Paul has already taught that to divide the community is a terrible evil (see 3:16). The nature of God's loving discipline and judgment is that some in the community are suffering illness and some have even died (v. 30). How do we understand this?

When the community assembles, the risen Christ is a participant—indeed Jesus is *the* dominant participant. (Recall the exhortation in 5:4.) Jesus' presence means we are on holy ground. Since he is the God of ineffable love (see Eph 3:16–19), as we draw near to him, any habits, behaviors, and attitudes that are the antithesis of his holy love are liable to incur consequences. Witherington communicates well the nature of this holy atmosphere:

---

29. Witherington, *Making a Meal of It*, 135 (italics ours).

30. The church's quest to probe the depth of meaning in the Lord's Supper has produced an abundance of eucharistic theology. I do not disparage this heritage, but we must recognize that the literary deposit is highly contextual and often adversarial. Martin Marty once wrote: "What do we mean by the presence of Christ in this Supper? . . . Whoever studies this history of dispute over the sacrament or listens to present day theological debate might conclude that it is the number one issue. Why? Because it provides grist for intellectual debate and becomes a kind of text for people who like to sharpen their philosophical tools on things sacred. Being a historian of Christianity, I find it hard to look at the record without adding that if there is any feature of the Lord's Supper that brings out the meanest growls from partisan Christians, this is it. . . . The special problem with the presence of Christ in the Lord's Supper grows from the fact that the Scriptures are so nearly silent about it" (Marty, *Lord's Supper*, 127).

The Lord's Supper should be seen as a chance for a close encounter with Jesus, a chance for a moment of clarity and recognition in one's life that Christ comes to meet us, bless us, forgive us, over and over again, and that we can and must actively participate in this joyful event. It is not about magical rituals or medicinal elements; it's about the living presence of Christ, which can either be honored or dishonored by how we partake of the Meal. Yes, indeed, a spiritual transaction happens at the meal, and it can be positive, and it can be negative. The real spiritual presence of Christ meets us at and in the Meal if we receive him by faith.[31]

The assembling of Christ-followers embodies a community saturated with numinous[32] reality. When we meet, we are a holy temple in which God lives by means of his Spirit (Eph 2:22). In this situation, to flaunt disobedience and to disrespect the risen Christ by dehumanizing one of his own daughters or sons is to invite a response of holy judgment. Therefore, Paul is challenging every Christ-follower to use the meal shared by the community as a catalyst to sober-minded self-assessment. We will always have a tendency to fall back into familiar patterns of behavior, especially those which are normal in our society. The sharing around Jesus' Table can be an encouragement to a believer to "put off the old . . ." Paul exhorts each member of the community to judge himself/herself (v. 28) and thus to avoid God's punishment and even ultimate condemnation (vv. 28, 31, 32).

11:33–34—Final instructions: "Wait for one another."

This entire unit of counsel from the apostle regarding the community meal contains four imperative verbs. Twice we are exhorted in the words of institution to "do this . . ." The other two imperatives are "examine" in verse 28, and "wait" in verse 33. So when we ask ourselves what it is that Paul wants us to do in response, we observe that the exhortations concern relationships. In some ways, the climax might seem rather disappointing. The counsel ends with a call for common courtesy and mutual respect. This is, in reality, "the mind of Christ." Paul's solution is extremely practical. This is the same principle as enunciated in 10:24, 33.

31. Witherington, *Making a Meal of It*, 134.

32. The concept of the numinous is a way scholars speak of the experiential awareness of supernatural powers, or a visceral sense of the divine presence. The specific use is derived from Otto, *Idea of the Holy*.

While the final exhortation to "wait for" or "welcome"[33] one another might seem a bit of a letdown, if we see it in its social context it is actually quite radical. For those of us in America, an analogy might help us appreciate the significance. What Paul commends here is like exhorting a community of white slave owners in 1850s Mississippi to eat together with the black members of their household. Or, in African contexts in which men do not traditionally eat with women, imagine Paul saying, "Brothers, wait. We will take our food as soon as the women and children join us and are served along with us."[34] Not a big deal, you say? Truly, it *is* a big deal. Paul's simple words represent a strong assault on cultural assumptions that oppress sisters and brothers in many social situations.

Paul's conclusion regarding the matter does not call for us to engage in the speculations of later eucharistic theology. The community of Christ-followers is the temple in which the Father, Son, and Spirit are now manifesting their divine presence on earth. The life of the community must resemble the life of the Trinity. Love is the essence. This is not trivial, but rather is the application of the new commandment given by the Lord of the community. We do not have church unless we engage in loving relationships with sisters and brothers in Christ.

By setting 1 Cor 11 in its historical context, we discover that the real cause of the divisions is the severe social stratification of Roman society. In his teaching regarding the Lord's Supper, Paul is promoting a radically egalitarian vision of community in Christ. Paul is appealing for countercultural oneness because of the cross and resurrection of Jesus. When this new-creation community assembles to share their common meal and to worship Jesus the risen Lord, there must be a manifestation of *agapē*, which is the fundamental ethical value and dynamic in the community. "Here there is no gentile or Jew, circumcised or uncircumcised, barbarian, Scythian, slave or free, but Christ is all, and is in all" (Col 3:11).

The *great idea* we are discovering is that *celebrating the community's common meal with Jesus and his friends can be a profound and formative*

33. The verb Paul uses in 11:33 is the Greek word *ekdechesthe*. One cannot help but wonder if this calls to mind the description of the countercultural ways of Jesus. In Luke 15:1–2, we are told that Jesus "welcomes sinners." The word there, *prosdechetai*, is built from the same root word.

34. One of my friends, Titus Kivunzi, a distinguished African bishop, has over the years created quite a scandal in the church by insisting that his wife and daughter be treated equally. In African tradition, the males and the elders and the clergy are given prominence and always receive food first. Leftovers may be given to women and girls, if available. Males eat separately from women and women serve the men. Bishop Kivunzi's daughter, Mueni, shared with me how honored she felt by her dad's controversial and tradition-defying stance.

experience which the Spirit can use to shape and revive a Jesus-centered community's identity, values, and vitality. In chapter 11, Paul corrects the Corinthians' practice of sharing Holy Communion because he knows that the ritual that was developing in Corinth was not forming a Jesus-centered fellowship of mutual respect and Jesus-style love.

Philosopher James K. A. Smith, in his book *You Are What You Love*, explores the nature of persons and describes how liturgies (sacred and secular alike) shape our desires and our selves. Smith's plea to those who long to know Christ intimately is that we must embrace the reality that "worship is the heart of discipleship."[35] He demonstrates that we are shaped and transformed by the habits we intentionally cultivate, and that in order to know God we must devote ourselves to the habit of worship which "is a repertoire of Spirit-endued practices that grab hold of your gut, recalibrate your *kardia*, and capture your imagination."[36] Smith writes:

> Because we are liturgical animals, we need to recognize the rival liturgies that vie for our hearts and then commit ourselves to the rightly ordered liturgy of Christian worship as a recalibration and "rehabituation" project. . . . You won't be liberated from deformation by new information. . . . If we want to be people oriented by a biblical worldview and guided by biblical wisdom, one of the best spiritual investments we can make is to mine the riches of historic Christian worship, which is rooted in the conviction that the Word is caught more than it is taught. . . . The Scriptures seep into us in a unique way in the intentional, communal rituals of worship.[37]

Since liturgy is a primary means the Spirit uses to shape and revive the community, I am appealing to today's churches all around the world to reimagine Holy Communion. Let's make a meal of it. I propose that we outsource Holy Communion to small house church groupings. In these more human-scale units, relationships can flourish. I propose that churches prioritize personal interaction and sharing the new-creation life. I propose that we craft new indigenous liturgies which celebrate our master narrative. Here are two reasons why this might be a catalyst to renewal through the Spirit's influence.

Making Holy Communion a central experience in church life (regularly sharing a meal with Jesus and his family) is *missionally strategic*. When the Christian community enjoys a shared meal as the focus of their

35. Smith, *You Are What You Love*, 25.
36. Smith, *You Are What You Love*, 83.
37. Smith, *You Are What You Love*, 83–84.

gathering, then the dynamics of doing church correspond to the deep longing for belonging and community which is widespread in today's Western societies, and in African urban environments which are being transformed by globalization.

We are experiencing an epidemic of loneliness. Sociologists and cultural analysts[38] are nearly unanimous in saying that our modern affluent lifestyles are destroying one of the most fundamental dynamics of being human—belonging to an authentic community. The tragic statistics recording the number of suicides in American society testifies concerning the depth of human despair in our culture. The beloved Mother Teresa insightfully names this as deep poverty: "The most terrible poverty is loneliness, and the feeling of being unloved."[39] Kurt Vonnegut referred to "the terrible disease of loneliness."[40] Recovering the early Church's Holy Communion meal practices can shape a more relationally intense community life.

Typical Western going-to-church experiences do little to quench the thirst for significant relationships and a sense of true community. Have you observed how many megachurches in North America are equipping their massive facilities with sophisticated and appealing food service capacities— delis, bistros, etc.? The discerning leaders recognize a need and an opportunity. Their members want to share food together after the service. Their members long for space and time to nourish relationships. The auditorium-based assembly is not the right environment for relationships. The audience was passive and anonymous, but after church, over a veggie pizza or a fresh garden salad, some really important connections are now taking place.[41]

---

38 There are many sociological works which seek to understand the roots and impact of our lonely society. The classic is David Riesman's *The Lonely Crowd: A Study of the Changing American Character*. This was followed by popular works such as Bellah et al., *Habits of the Heart*. Of course, the Beatles were also doing social analysis when they wrote and sang "Eleanor Rigby."

39. Mother Teresa, *Simple Path*, 79. She also refers to loneliness as the leprosy of the modern world.

40. Vonnegut, *Palm Sunday*, 73.

41. In churches around the world today it would be wise to engage in serious conversation around the issue of virtual community. We must discern together ways to understand how worship through the medium of digital communication forms an identity among members. What is the identity being shaped when I fellowship with other believers all alone through the medium of a hand-held digital device? Justin Wise has offered us some cautionary guidance in his book *The Social Church: A Theology of Digital Communication*. Wise observes: "The danger behind technology—specifically behind technology related to digital communication—is when we become unaware (or, rather remain unaware) of how a medium affects us" (114). He warns that online campuses (for churches) that exist solely to increase the convenience quotient in one's life are detrimental and to be avoided at all costs. Wise suggests that online campuses

In light of the cultural epidemic of loneliness in our culture today, why would we *not* embrace the missional relevance of sharing Holy Communion in the framework of a common meal? Instead, it seems we are fleeing from this biblical model in our attempts to accommodate the comfort zones of our fragmented, social media-driven culture, with its obsession with speed and efficiency and convenience. Methodist bishop Will Willimon protests:

> Over the years both the glasses and the wafers got smaller until the church seemed to have a make-believe meal without food. . . . I finally said "enough is enough" a couple of years ago when I read of a man in the West, who, believing that the Lord's Supper is time consuming and cumbersome because of the individual cups involved, has begun marketing a product for those in a hurry. He produces airtight packets which contain a crackerlike pellet in one compartment and two grams of grape juice in another compartment—a disposable, self-contained, eat-on-the-run Lord's Supper—sort of "This is my body packaged for you." There you have it. The last hindrance to totally self-contained, self-centered religion is removed. . . . Now thanks to this unit packaging, we need never come into contact with or be touched by another human being again. Just when you thought modern life had depersonalized the gospel to the uttermost, we have another breakthrough—Communion without communion.[42]

The really central question is: What kind of community are we seeking to become?[43]

The second reason for urging that we reimagine Holy Communion recognizes that sharing the meal with Jesus and our brothers and sisters is eloquent communication. To make a difference in our lives and in our world, our communities' forms and dynamics must *communicate with impact in a word-resistant culture*. When going to church is primarily associated with

---

are intended to facilitate connection to the church community, not to replace it. I would agree with Wise that we need to be honest with the reality that online community has limitations. Wise argues, "For example you cannot hug somebody via Twitter; you cannot break bread in a Facebook group. Further we cannot truly share in one's sorrow or suffering in an online environment" (155). To engage in what the NT calls *koinōnia* requires physical presence. Having said that, Wise also says online community is definitely preferable to no community. He accepts that the church gains whatever lives have been changed, saved, and redeemed all because gospel-centered online communities have outreached (155). Let the conversation continue.

42. Willimon, *Sunday Dinner*, 103–4.

43 During the COVID-19 pandemic in 2020, many congregations began using small, plastic-enclosed packets containing grape juice and a wafer. This, in fact, was seen as an act of love for fellow believers since it observed pandemic safety guidelines.

anonymous and passive attendance at a one-hour lecture/performance, we will not meet the needs of our society. Millennials and Gen Zers are not interested. In large group settings, we achieve only minimal formation results.

Our master narrative is acted out again and again in Holy Communion and this nonverbal speech tells us who we are and reminds us what time it is. Any person who observes or participates in our corporate meal will get a really powerful "sermon."[44] As we participate together, we are a living demonstration that Jesus has power to reconcile "all things through his Cross" (Col 1:19). The truth about the God who revealed himself in Jesus is acted out again and again. It announces really revolutionary news—Jesus eats with sinners!

If someone were to transcribe the libretto for the nonverbal sermon which is Holy Communion, it would read like this thoughtful summary from Professor Gregory Jones:

> The eucharist is an eschatological meal that recalls the past, anticipates the future, and sustains the present. It recalls the past of Jesus' table fellowship with tax collectors and sinners, enacting the forgiveness of communion in concrete situations and lives, even as it also anticipates the messianic banquet in God's kingdom, to which all are invited and in which no one will be hungry. . . . It recalls the saving sacrifice of Christ's death and resurrection. . . . In the eucharistic meal, Christ grants communion with himself through his presence and, in doing so, transforms our communion with one another.[45]

Paul's expression for all this is simplicity itself, "as often as you eat this bread and drink the cup, you proclaim the Lord's death until he comes" (1 Cor 11:26).

---

44. George Mallone wrote: "The evangelical church has not listened to this Reformed emphasis [on unity of word and sacrament] and has comforted itself with the exclusive use of the audible sacrament—sitting and listening to the Word of God. Praise God that his word is being taught! But an overemphasis on preaching and the neglect of worship in the Lord's Supper is like an overweight kite tail: though given for stability, it ends up as an accomplice in the destruction. God's people need, want, and are commanded to worship. Preaching is to give guidance to that worship so that it is worship 'in truth.' But the exclusive use of a one-dimensional preaching sacrament, God speaking to his people through his Word and servant, is a denial of true worship . . . Christ is to be perceived everywhere, in our ears, in our eyes, minds, hearts, hands, and mouths. C. S. Lewis once commented that 'a man cannot always be defending the truth; there must be a time to feed on it'" (Mallone, *Furnace of Renewal*, 69–70).

45. Jones, *Embodying Forgiveness*, 175–76.

Chapter 10

Gifts That Renew

Body Life in the New Creation
(Chapters 12 and 14)

May the grace shown by the Lord Jesus Christ be with you all.
May the love that God has given us be with you.
And may the sharing of life brought about by the Holy Spirit
be with you all.

2 COR 13:14 NIRV

READ: 1 COR 12-14

The draconian tyrant Idi Amin unleashed an horrific reign of terror on the beautiful African nation of Uganda during the mid-1970s. In the midst of the suffering, a young professor of art history at Makerere University became caught up in a fresh work of the Holy Spirit. The professor's name was Kefa Sempangi, and he was a reluctant pastoral leader, preferring the sanity of the university lecture hall to the call to preach the word of God in the midst of the tsunami of indescribable atrocities overtaking his nation. But as conditions in Kampala became more and more dangerous, Jesus unleashed his Spirit in a surprising counterterrorism initiative. King Jesus was reclaiming enemy-occupied territory, and Sempangi humbly and sometimes tentatively submitted to the lordship of Christ. He discovered that the Spirit of Jesus was empowering him to do things he never imagined he would do. Sempangi was existentially aware of the truth of theologian Richard Purves's declaration that "It is not our ministries that make Christ present and possible; it is the present, living Christ who makes our ministries possible."[1]

In his gripping autobiographical book, *A Distant Grief*, Kefa writes:

> The triumph of evil overwhelmed me. I felt a deep fear. . . . Who was I to feed God's children in this most desperate hour? What words could I speak? . . . They needed strength to sustain them in suffering. They did not need my sermon. . . . As I prayed for strength and wisdom, the words of Matthew 14:19 came to my mind: "And taking the five loaves and the two fishes he looked up to heaven, and blessed, and broke and gave the loaves to his disciples, and the disciples gave them to the crowds." . . . With this verse, I heard the convicting voice of the Holy Spirit. It was Jesus who provided bread for the crowds. . . . It was God who sustained his people. . . . It was He who had provided the vision and it was He who would provide the ability. From the beginning to the end it was His work.[2]

It is difficult to humbly accept that we don't engineer an authentic work of God. I find this especially hard to assimilate as a well-educated American, skilled in the craft of casting vision, setting goals and objectives, and drafting strategic plans. God's ways typically are radically counterintuitive. While it seems that we might be able to make some choices that could help in positioning ourselves to partner in God's new-creation movement, we need to get one thing clear: it's God's project.

The teaching on charismata (usually translated as "spiritual gifts")[3] in 1 Cor 12–14 is essential to grasping how God carries out his mission of

---

1. Purves, *Resurrection of Ministry*, 79.

2. Sempangi, *Distant Grief*, 117, 52.

3. The Greek word *charismata* is the plural form of the word "charisma." It is often translated into English as "spiritual gift." It comes from the root word *charis*, which means "grace." The English word "charismatic" has several commonly understood meanings. In popular usage, we sometimes refer to a great leader such as Nelson Mandela as a charismatic personality. In addition, in the discipline of sociology you will often see reference to a charismatic leader. This refers to a specific type of leadership in sociological theory. In modern evangelicalism we often refer to the charismatic movement. This refers to a mid-twentieth-century revival movement which emphasized tongues, healing, and prophecy. The fourth meaning is the one intended by the apostle Paul in 1 Cor. It strongly emphasizes that capacities given to believers by the Holy Spirit

"making all things new." The counsel Paul gives his "children in the Lord" is not a detour from the main theological road, pulling off into an exotic alley of mysterious spiritual phenomena. These teachings regarding charismata are actually intended to present to those of us in Christ what is to be the standard operating procedure in the new-creation community. This is the way Jesus ministers today.

To think sanely about how the church functions and shifts to become a movement and how God carries out his mission in our world, we must begin with a clear-eyed awareness that we live in a new time zone. Andrew Purves skillfully articulates this sanity-sustaining worldview.

> Jesus is alive—this surely is the central Christian affirmation. . . .
> New Testament faith is Easter faith, faith in the living Lord Jesus.
> Jesus, living, reigning and acting is the issue. . . . He who was
> dead is now alive in a new way. He is alive, never to die again. He
> is alive, Lord over all time and space. He is alive, to come again
> to bring all things to the Father. This means that his ministry that
> was ended is, with the resurrection and ascension, continuing,
> though now through the Holy Spirit. From Pentecost onward,
> the community of the Lord of Easter Day and Ascension Day is
> empowered in the grace and freedom of the Holy Spirit. Without
> being gripped by these truths, there really is no Christian faith in
> the New Testament sense.[4]

EXAMINING 1 COR 12–14

We have earlier reminded ourselves that 1 Corinthians is a real letter to a group of relatively new Christ-followers. Persons new to the faith bring along with them the worldview and culture in which they were formed during their pre-Christian experience. Slowly and steadily, they are being "transformed by the renewing of [their minds]" (Rom 12:2). But deep change does not happen in a flash.

In 1 Cor 12, Paul again takes a presenting problem (sent to him in a letter from Corinthian believers, as we saw in chapters 7 and 8) and reframes the questions so it becomes a discussion of the priority of love, the passion for unity, and a rebuke to arrogance and pride. The process we described as resocialization is continuing. Paul skillfully provides pastoral guidance for

---

are all of grace. It will be discussed in this chapter.

4. Purves, *Resurrection of Ministry*, 86–87.

young believers to show them how to "practice resurrection life."[5] Also, keep in mind that chapters 12–14 are one continuous discussion, so we must read all three together to get the real context of any particular verse.

The great idea revealed in chapters 12–14 is: *All ministry, work, and service that results in transformation of persons and societies is the activity of the risen Lord through the Holy Spirit. In every believer (no exceptions), God manifests his indwelling presence in some way for the good of the whole body.* Reliance on grace given through the Spirit is the dynamic of the new-creation community.

In order to get inside the early church's experience and properly interpret chapter 12, we must take into consideration one aspect of Corinthian culture that scholars have labeled "ecstasy." This English word has a variety of associations.[6] If we follow the popular usage, we might imagine that ecstasy refers to "unbridled delight," such as the emotion experienced by the young bride-to-be when her lover proposes marriage to her. But ecstasy has a technical meaning when used by scholars who study religious behaviors.[7] Ecstasy refers to a range of spiritual experiences in which a person has a sense of being possessed by a powerful spiritual force or being. The force overwhelms the devotee, and there is an often delightful sense of being lifted out of the normal state of consciousness and transferred into an exalted sphere of experience. The often dramatic responses to being "under the power" are diverse. They might include singing in free form, laughing, shouting, dancing, *glossolalia* (speaking in tongues), falling into a trancelike state, or a sense of being out of the body, among other things.

Ecstatic experience is a dimension of Christian experience for many Christ-followers. However, ecstasy is not something unique in Christian

---

5. The phrase comes from Peterson, *Living the Resurrection,* 114.

6. The English word "ecstasy" has many definitions. *Merriam-Webster* provides the following:

1. A state of being beyond reason and self-control; may apply to any strong emotion;

2. A state of overwhelming emotion; especially: rapturous delight, intense bliss or beatitude;

3. Trance; especially: a mystic or prophetic trance; near immobility produced by an overpowering emotion;

4. A synthetic amphetamine used illicitly for its mood-enhancing and hallucinogenic properties

7. A useful, more technical definition of ecstasy in the study of religion is given by James D. G. Dunn. "By 'ecstasy' I mean here an unusually exalted state of feeling, a condition of such total absorption or concentration that the individual becomes oblivious to all attendant circumstances and other stimuli, an experience of intense rapture or a trance-like state in which normal faculties are suspended for a shorter or longer period and the subject sees visions or experiences 'automatic speech' as in some forms of glossolalia" (Dunn, *Jesus and the Spirit,* 84).

spiritual experience. In Paul's day in ancient Corinth, a number of the ancient religions in a city like Corinth marketed ecstasy as a benefit of participating in that religious community's worship.[8] Some Corinthian converts enjoyed experiences of ecstasy when they encountered Jesus. Coming into Christ in baptism was often a visceral experience accompanied by an overwhelming awareness that the Holy Spirit had taken possession of the new convert. This should not surprise us since the Holy Spirit is the agent of God's grace who applies the salvific benefits of Jesus' "finished work" to an individual's life (6:11). And the Spirit is God himself. He is the force who raised Jesus from the dead. When he takes possession of a person, something awesome is taking place. In many situations, that encounter shows itself in various expressions that we can categorize as ecstasy.

In Corinth, some new believers were particularly fascinated by *glossolalia*, and some Corinthians might have experienced ecstatic power encounters during their pre-Christian religious journey. Some brought that old pre- and anti-Christian behavior along with them when they became believers. Paul rejects these alien spiritual phenomena.

It also seems to be the case that some subset of the Corinthian community was imposing a spiritual caste system on the church. The text suggests that fellow believers were being categorized as more or less spiritual based on the frequency and vociferousness of their ecstatic expressions. Those possessing the most glamorous powers were assumed to be the more mature and angelic among the church members. Those lacking ecstatic capacities were judged to be substandard in spirituality.

When you confess true faith in the risen Lord, that faith is the outcome of an inner work done by the Spirit of Jesus (12:1–3).

How does Paul counsel the young community in Corinth in chapter 12? Paul begins his teaching by insisting in 12:1–3 that the fact that an individual is able authentically to confess the lordship of Christ is evidence that a person is under the influence of the Holy Spirit. Paul emphasizes that every believer is possessed by the Holy Spirit. "Jesus is Lord" was the basic Christian confession of faith in the early church (see Rom 10:9–10). When you confess true faith in the risen Lord, that faith is the outcome of an inner work done by the Spirit of Jesus. No person in Christ lacks this personal divine

---

8. To explore the prevalence of ecstatic phenomena in ancient Corinth context, see Aune, *Prophecy in Early Christianity and the Ancient Mediterranean World*. Witherington also gives a useful overview of the religious scene in his *Conflict and Community in Corinth*, 276–81.

presence as Paul explains in Eph 1:13–14: "And you also were included in Christ when you heard the message of truth, the gospel of your salvation. When you believed, you were marked in him with a seal, the promised Holy Spirit, who is a deposit guaranteeing our inheritance until the redemption of those who are God's possession—to the praise of his glory." Pastor A. W. Tozer expresses this grace this way:

> The primary work of the Holy Spirit is to restore the lost soul to intimate fellowship with God through the washing of regeneration. To accomplish this, He first reveals Christ to the penitent heart (1 Cor 12:3). He then goes on to illumine the newborn soul with brighter rays from the face of Christ (John 14:26) and leads the willing heart into depths and heights of divine knowledge and communion. Remember, we know Christ only as the Spirit enables us and we have only as much of him as the Holy Spirit imparts.[9]

Paul is beginning to lay the foundation from which he will dismantle any sort of elitist spiritual caste system that might have been set up based on comparative levels of ecstasy.

The rest of chapter 12 explains how church functions. A movement being transformed by Jesus in order to transform the world must embrace this radical vision of community. In chapter 12, Paul explains that all ministry, work, and service that results in transformation of persons and societies is the activity of the risen Lord through the Holy Spirit. Jesus engages in his mission in his own way. As an eschatological community, we are enabled by the firstfruit of the new creation—the Spirit who raised up Jesus (Rom 8:23)—to play our Spirit-determined parts in God's new-creation agenda.

The same Triune God manifests his indwelling presence in an infinite variety of ways (12:4–6).

In 1 Cor 12:4–6, the apostle shows us that the same Triune God manifests his indwelling presence in an infinite variety of ways. Paul can very naturally refer to Father, Son, and Holy Spirit in making his point about the equivalency of the diverse ways in which divine power is manifest. Do not miss what Paul is doing here. In verses 4–6 we find these pairings:

charismata	←→	Spirit
service	←→	Lord
workings	←→	God

9. Tozer, *That Incredible Christian*, 36.

Paul's purpose is to teach that these three ways of identifying a divine activity are all equivalent. He is stressing by the repetition of the same words in the three sentences that whatever you call these expressions of divine presence, they are not to be set in opposition to one another or into some type of hierarchy. In some instances, we might best describe the experience as an empowerment that enables one to effectuate (in Greek, "work") the diverse works of God. At another moment, we may describe the experience as a gracious enabling or charisma from the Holy Spirit. Alternatively, some Christ-followers may use the language of rendering service to their Lord. Right from the start, Paul takes aim at spiritual arrogance and elitism. God's ways of working in and through us are diverse, but God is one.

In every believer (no exceptions), God manifests his indwelling presence in some way for the good of the whole body (12:7–12).

The phrase "the body of Christ" has become such a familiar expression in our Christian movement that we might be in danger of missing its pointed emphasis or brilliance. Paul here introduces a metaphor (its use seems to begin here in verse 12) in order to help us grasp the nature of the relationships among fellow believers. We interact in ways that are similar to the dynamics at work within a human body. Notice that the body metaphor refers to the local assembly in Corinth.[10] The point Paul is trying to drive home is that the Christian movement is made up of many diverse parts, but we are one unit.

We can summarize the dynamic of becoming a radical community taught in 12:7–12 by saying: in every believer (no exceptions), God manifests his indwelling presence in some way for the good of the whole body. The expression "manifestation of the Spirit" in verse 7 is a good definition of charisma. "What is my spiritual gift?" we often ask. But it is not mine at all if it is genuine. It is a manifestation of the indwelling presence of the Holy Spirit. The Spirit of God invades the personality of the believer at conversion and takes up residence. When God's presence is dwelling within, that Spirit will make his presence known in some way. The Spirit manifests his life-giving power in a thousand different ways.

There is a dominant stress in verses 7–12 on *each* believer being Spirit-endowed (7, 11). There are no exceptions for those in Christ. Paul also

10. The metaphor of the body here refers to one local church, not to a mysterious global phenomenon. As Dunn notes in *Jesus and the Spirit,* 262: "Paul is here describing the local church at Corinth. When he says 'you are Christ's body' (12:27) he is not thinking of 'the universal church' nor does he mean 'you at Corinth are part of the international fellowship of Christians.' His thought is rather that the Corinthian believers are the body of Christ at Corinth."

emphasizes the variety of manifestations. Throughout this teaching, we will see Paul repeatedly place emphasis on "one and the same Spirit" and a variety of manifestations. Every individual Christ-follower is a unique work of God.

Paul includes a listing of nine possible manifestations (*phanerōsis*).[11] The list is representative, not exhaustive. So we are not expected to examine the list and see how we can find a way to express one of these nine. The really important affirmation in verse 11 is that the Spirit is sovereign. It is the Spirit who determines how his presence will be manifest in each person. We are not to anticipate uniformity. There is not one charisma in this list that can be singled out as the inevitable, fool-proof indicator of the Spirit's work. We can see that Paul, once again, is building his case to say that so far as charismata are concerned, there is no basis for pride, superiority, preference, judgment, or competition among believers. The Spirit decides who gets what grace.

The indwelling presence of the Spirit is the common experience of every Christ-follower. This same Spirit connects us to Jesus' community (12:13).

Paul's teaching in verse 13 affirms that all Christians are baptized by[12] one Holy Spirit into one body. Paul speaks of baptism here as the public expression of saving faith in Christ. In the early Christian movement, getting saved involved the public initiation ritual of water baptism.[13] The water had no saving power. But the Spirit of God showed up in the moment because of the faith of the convert and the grace of the risen Lord. So baptism here refers to one's initial incorporation into Christ (see Rom 6). And notice that being united with Christ necessarily includes incorporation into community. The Holy Spirit is the one who regenerates us and applies to us the redemption won by Jesus through his death. This same Spirit, as part of the salvation

11. See Dunn, *Jesus and the Spirit*, 209–56 for a thorough discussion of each "manifestation" mentioned by Paul.

12. In verse 13, the text says we have all been baptized *en eni pneumati,* and this phrase (using the Greek dative case) can either be translated baptized "by" one Spirit, or baptized "in" one Spirit. Over the years, there has been debate on the best way to understand the use of the Greek preposition *en* with the dative case of *pneuma*. Are we to understand that the Spirit is the agent who does the baptizing? Or is Paul considering "Spirit" as a gift (living water) which is poured down upon the believer by Jesus? See the classic discussion in Stott, *Baptism and Fullness,* 39. He concludes: "He is underlining our common experience as Christian believers of the Holy Spirit."

13. There is a classic New Testament study of baptism which is still the standard: Beasley-Murray, *Baptism in the New Testament.*

experience, connects us to Jesus' community—the one body. Observe that Paul says that every Christian enjoys this benefit regardless of race, social status, ethnicity, or gender. Being united to Jesus' body is true of all of us. All of our human hierarchies and social status categories are irrelevant when it comes to God's grace. The final phrase in verse 13 reinforces this core value of the movement. "We have all been given a drink of the one Spirit." This again emphasizes that the indwelling presence of the Spirit is the common experience of every Christ-follower. Paul uses the metaphor of drinking the Spirit because over and over in Scripture,[14] the powerful presence of the Spirit of God is described as coming like water or a stream or a river.

Many parts = one body (12:14–17).

Paul next unpacks some of the implications for community life that follow from his metaphor of the body. He continues to drive home his central theme, which is many parts = one body. He illustrates that all charismata are not identical. He even gives us the absurd, humorous mental picture of a body that is nothing but one big ear! The point is well made. We cannot expect every Christ-follower to be the same as far as how the Spirit makes His presence obvious. Paul further emphasizes that no charisma is useless. The body illustration teaches that there is no basis for the denigration of self or others. As we all can verify from actual life experience, all parts of one's physical anatomy are needed for proper functioning.

God is responsible for giving charismata (12:18).

The climax of this unit of the teaching is surely verse 18: "But in fact God has placed the parts in the body, every one of them, just as he wanted them to be." Repeating the truth from verse 11, Paul makes clear that we are not the ones who determine who has what Spirit-given capacity. God is responsible for giving charismata. He arranges the parts according to his inscrutable wisdom. Equal respect for all charismata demonstrates appreciation for God's sovereignty. This truth must impact our perception of other believers and the community. It also calls us to worship.

---

14. See the wonderful discussion in Bruner, *Gospel of John*, on the biblical use of living water as a metaphor for God's salvation through his Spirit. Bruner says, "The Hebrew Scriptures are full of promises of the 'day' when the Lord will climactically satisfy his thirsty people with fresh, living water, and then bless the world through these refreshed people" (489).

To be Christian is to be charismatic; no member lacks a
manifestation of grace. Every charism is indispensable (12:27–31).

Verses 27–31 are a summary of these themes from the apostle. He makes a
very direct affirmation: "You *are* Christ's body" (*humeis este sōma Christou*).
Being connected to other Christ-followers through our shared experience
of the Spirit is the reality in which we "live and move and have our being"
(Acts 17:28). He is saying this to the relatively small gathering of Christ-followers in Corinth. Each believer is a part of that community of Jesus. There
are no exceptions. Once more we hear him emphasize that God sovereignly
determines the distribution of charismata. All Christians do not enjoy identical charismata. God did not want it that way. But as the body metaphor
illustrates so beautifully, we are all bound together and interconnected. This
is ontologically true. It's not just a sociological group-dynamics feeling. We
actually are united in Christ.

No scholar I know has captured this radical teaching on how Jesus'
community functions better than James Dunn:

> The shared experience of the Spirit was fundamental to the unity
> of the early Christian communities. . . . To be Christian is to be
> charismatic; one cannot be a member of the body without shar-
> ing the charismatic Spirit. . . . The many members who make
> up one body are not simply individual believers, but individual
> believers as charismatics—that is, believers through whom
> the Spirit of grace may manifest himself in diverse ways at any
> time. . . . No member lacks a manifestation of grace. . . . Every
> charisma, every manifestation of grace is indispensable, for the
> Spirit's gifts are the living movements of Christ's body. . . . Not all
> of course "have" the same charisma; and no individual manifests
> all the charismata. . . . The idea of mono-ministry, of all the most
> important gifts concentrated in one man (even an apostle), is
> foolish nonsense to Paul. . . . Christian community exists only
> in the living interplay of charismatic ministry, in the concrete
> realizations of grace, in the actual being and doing for others
> (not simply for oneself) in word and deed. . . . Only a charis-
> matic community functioning as such could hope to manifest
> adequately the same grace that God manifested in the one man
> Jesus.[15]

First Cor 12:31 is a transition statement in the teaching on charismata (which runs from chapter 12 through chapter 14). Paul continues to
develop his response to the Corinthians' specific inquiry by stressing two

---

15. Dunn, *Jesus and the Spirit*, 260–65, 297–300.

additional important themes. First, he alerts us to the central thrust of his upcoming instructions on charisma and community worship that will make up what we call chapter 14. When he presents his very practical direction for the church, he, in fact, explains that there are "greater" gifts. Thus his encouragement in verse 31: "Be zealous for greater gifts." How can he refer to certain expressions of the Spirit as "greater" than others in light of chapter 12? We will see that the idea of greater is not about experiences that appear more ecstatically glamorous or dazzling. The value Paul assigns to the "greater" charismata in chapter 14 is the fact that prophecy has a more positive impact on the gathered community because it edifies others. We are to desire to have the Spirit manifest his amazing grace through our lives in ways that serve and build up other Christians. It seems that his assessment is quite the opposite of the Corinthians—and of ours. Greatness must be defined here based on the example and teaching of Jesus. Paul will pick up this theme in 14:1.

Our all-encompassing priority—love (12:31—13:13).

But first he will shine a brilliant light on the core value of the community of the risen Lord Jesus. We aspire to serve and edify others because of our all-encompassing priority—love. The second theme mentioned in 12:31 is the connecting link to the magnificent hymn to *agapē* in chapter 13. "But now I want to lay out a far better way for you" (MSG).

Chapter 13 fits here as the centerpiece of this extended discussion which includes chapters 12–14. If we read it the way Paul wrote it, we recognize that the memorable teaching on *agapē* is for the community and is fundamental to their experience of the Spirit's enabling presence. I am giving it a chapter on its own in this book (see ch. 10). Make no mistake, it belongs here. Since the Spirit who is making his presence known through us is the Spirit of Jesus, when this Spirit reveals his empowering presence, the manifestation will reflect Jesus' character. The way of Jesus is the way of *agapē*. Never forget that the first application of this much-loved chapter is to the issue of relationship in community.

FUNCTIONING AS A COMMUNITY OF
SPIRIT-ENABLED LOVE—CHAPTER 14

14:1–25 is a unit of teaching that builds on the themes of chapters 12 and 13 and makes a specific application to an issue emerging from the Corinthian community. Some members were particularly fascinated by *glossolalia* and valued this charisma as a higher expression of spirituality. Paul needs to correct them and help them reprioritize their behaviors. This chapter contains apostolic correction. As Bishop Stephen Neill observed some years back, "Paul's handling of the situation in Corinth is strictly practical, but, as in so many other cases, he uses practical problems as the occasion for some of his profoundest theological affirmations."[16] Gordon Fee helps us understand the Corinthian situation when he writes:

> The crucial issue is their decided position over against Paul's as to what it means to be *pneumatikos* (spiritual). Their view apparently not only denied the material/physical side of Christian existence (as we mentioned earlier in ch. 5–7), but had an element of "spiritualized (or over-realized) eschatology" as well. . . . The Corinthians seem to have considered themselves to be already like the angels, thus truly "spiritual," needing neither sex in the present (7:1–7) nor a body in the future (15:1–58). Speaking angelic dialects by the Spirit was evidence enough for them of their participation in the new spirituality, hence their singular enthusiasm for this charisma.[17]

Tongues and prophecy compared (14:1–25).

Paul provides an extended comparative analysis in order to guide the church. He contrasts tongues and prophecy. Paul has already tipped his hand in 14:1 that he thinks prophecy is more beneficial in the context of the gathered community. Paul stresses the priority of intelligibility in the assembly. This is because the purpose of the Spirit's empowering is to build up the community (12:7).

"Prophecy" can be defined as "spontaneous, understandable messages, orally delivered in the gathered assembly, intended for the edification or encouragement of the people."[18] Paul insists that when a believer is enabled to "manifest the indwelling Spirit" through tongues, that person speaks to God, not other believers. The benefit of the experience is primarily for the tongues-speaker himself. In contrast, Paul teaches when a believer is enabled to manifest the indwelling Spirit through prophecy, that expression of grace has the benefit of speaking to others in intelligible words in order to

---

16. Neill, *Jesus through Many Eyes*, 49.

17. Fee, *First Epistle to the Corinthians*, 573.

18. Fee, *Paul, the Spirit, and the People of God*, 171.

strengthen and encourage brothers and sisters (see Acts 15:32). That's really the basis of his stated preference for prophecy.

Paul affirms the value of *glossolalia*. In verse 5, Paul says he wants everyone to speak in tongues. "Paul does not damn tongues with faint praise, as some have argued, nor does he stand in awe of the gift. . . . Paul held it in high regard in its proper place."[19] But Paul's focus is on life together as a gathered community and therefore he prioritizes prophecy because of its ability to edify others in the assembly. We can summarize the counsel Paul gives in 14:6–19 as follows: Tongues are not helpful in the assembly since others do not understand the meaning of what is being said. Paul prefers intelligible speech when the believers assemble together.

Paul advances a missional argument in verses 20–25 by provoking us to think carefully about the contrasting impact of these two charismata on unbelievers. He argues that *glossolalia* will not be beneficial in bringing nonbelievers to faith in Christ. But prophecy, although primarily for the community, might have a stunning impact on a non-Christian who might be present in the assembly. The impact of the charisma of prophecy on unbelievers could be that the unbeliever is led to repentance. Paul proposes that there will be times in which the Spirit, through a gifted prophet, will reveal some deep secrets of the heart of the not-yet-Christian, and that this moment of exposure might lead to repentance (vv. 24–25). Paul believes that when the Spirit is being manifested through prophecy, there may be a moment when the pagan comes to recognize that God is present within the Christian community. So Paul lines up various strands of argument to insist that when the community gathers, the charisma with greater value is prophecy.

Bringing order to participatory charismatic assemblies (14:25–40).

This treasure trove of pastoral guidance to young believers finishes in verses 26–40 with some down-to-earth guidance for bringing order to their somewhat chaotic assemblies. We get a very valuable look at the dynamics of the Christian gathering in Corinth in verse 26. It is clear that it was a highly participatory experience. Paul expects that each person will be enabled by the Spirit to contribute some manifestation of the Spirit. All believers are charismatic. In Corinth, church happens when all come together to share a charisma in order to strengthen others in community. Again, we find the emphasis on building up (*oikodomē*).

19. Fee, *Paul, the Spirit, and the People of God*, 169.

We can turn to James Dunn again for a summary based on his remarkably comprehensive study of the early Christian assembly's dynamics. He explains:

> Every charisma, every manifestation of grace is indispensable, for the Spirit's gifts are the living movements of Christ's body. . . . To say that for Paul the church is a charismatic community means that the body of Christ in Corinth or Rome or Thessalonika or wherever is Christ's Spirit binding believers together and building them up through the wide range of his manifestations of grace. It means that each member of the community of faith has a function within the life of that community, a contribution necessary to the well-being of the whole.[20]

This emerging Jesus movement does not have centuries of tradition and well-crafted liturgies and familiar worship frameworks. This is still frontier missions in a new culture. So Paul wants to guide the community as it develops patterns for meeting together in God's presence. He offers some very specific direction on the expression of *glossolalia* in a worship gathering. He limits the number of utterances to two or three at most, and insists that the *glossolalia* must be interpreted so that the others can understand the message. He also directs that these utterances be presented one at a time. If there's no one enabled by the Spirit to render the tongues' utterance into the language of the people, the tongues' utterance should not be spoken.

While Paul has presented a high view of prophecy and its benefit for God's people, he also needs to guide the Corinthians in discernment. He knows very well that not every pronouncement which alleges to be from the Spirit of the Lord is actually a communication enabled by Jesus—the church's head. There was plenty of spirit-enabled prophecy in Corinth. But most of these ecstatic utterances were announced while the speaker was possessed by a demonic spirit. The young Christians had to develop discernment to recognize the voice of Jesus. A few years later he would write to Timothy, his protégé, "the Spirit clearly says that in later times some will abandon the faith and follow deceiving spirits and things taught by demons" (1 Tim 4:1). Paul's fellow apostle, John, issued a similar warning: "Dear friends, do not believe every spirit, but test the spirits to see whether they are from God, because many false prophets have gone out into the world" (1 John 4:1).

Paul directs the community to develop a practice for regulating and discerning prophetic words. He urges that there be only two or three prophetic words in a meeting. He exhorts the prophets to be in control of herself/himself (v. 32), not shouting out in an ecstatic frenzy. Prophets are to

20 Dunn, *Jesus and the Spirit*, 265.

be courteous and give way to other prophets. This will manifest the mind of Christ. Paul definitely wants the Christian assembly to have a different atmosphere than the boisterous spiritual frenzy of some of the local cults in the city. He uses a bit of theology to undergird his instruction. The God who is present when Christians gather is not a god of chaos and disorder, but God is a God of peace (v. 33).

Paul institutes a procedure for corporate discernment (14:29–38).

The members of this charismatic community must seek the guidance of the Spirit in order to recognize a word that is truly from Jesus. A genuine Holy Spirit-inspired prophet will gladly submit his insight to the recognized circle of prophets within the community. The Corinthians know from experience who is able to exercise the charisma of discernment. So before one speaks— allegedly in the Lord's name—the substance of the utterance must be vetted by the community-authorized panel of discerners. This counsel is the same as that which Paul gave to another young church. To the Thessalonians, he wrote, "Do not quench the Spirit. Do not treat prophecies with contempt, but test them all; hold on to what is good, reject every kind of evil" (5:19). And Paul reminds them of the purpose of these guidelines and, indeed, of prophecy in verse 31: "that everyone may be instructed and encouraged." Once again, he brings us back to the God-given purpose for "manifestations of the Spirit" for the community.

The guidance to the Corinthians in verses 34–35 has been the source of endless arguments and much misunderstanding. In order to understand these statements correctly, we must recognize where we are in the flow of the argument of chapter 14. Paul is talking about discernment of prophetic utterances in this paragraph. He is guiding the new believers in this church to establish procedures so that the community can truly be edified by genuine words from the risen Lord and protected from false prophecies that might confuse or damage the faith of the community's members. In establishing the procedure for regulating prophetic utterances, Paul instructs the Corinthians that women members should not be involved in this process of testing the spirits. It is not entirely clear why women are not to be involved in the work of evaluatng true prophecy. It is plausible that there are circumstances rooted in first-century Corinthian culture which are driving Paul's prohibition in verse 34.[21] For certain, the guidance here cannot be understood to cancel out the teaching from Paul in chapter 11. In that discussion, women

21. For a comprehensive analysis of the situation of women first-century Hellenistic culture, I recommend Cohick, *Women in the World of the Earliest Christians*.

are said to be praying and prophesying in the assembly. But when it comes to vetting the utterances, Paul tells the women of Corinth not to participate.

Paul draws this section of his apostolic counsel to a close by highlighting three key ideas: 1) Be eager to prophesy; 2) Do not forbid tongues; and 3) Keep the assembly orderly. In calling for order, he certainly cannot be interpreted to teach that the community's worship should be fundamentally transformed into a structured, highly regulated liturgical pattern, nor would he object to that pattern. He clearly prefers that prophecy be given pride of place. But tongues are not to be renounced. The imperative of this exhortation is definite. Given the considerations that Paul has laid down for use in the assembly, tongues are to be embraced with thanksgiving.

Overall, there is to be an orderly and respectful mutual concern in the gathering. We are certainly still a far cry from a framework in which the order is dictated by a fixed liturgical rubric or a minute-by-minute, highly coordinated script for the performance. But in our era of increasing sophistication in the management of worship assemblies and our overwhelming dependence on technology to produce an excellent and engaging performance, we would do well to remember the caution from A. W. Tozer:

> Now I freely admit that it is impossible to hold a Christian service without an agenda. If order is to be maintained, an order of service must exist somewhere. If two songs are to be sung, someone must know which one is to be sung first, and whether this knowledge is only in someone's head or has been reduced to paper, there is indeed a "program," however we may dislike to call it that. The point we make here is that in our times the program has been substituted for the Presence. The program, rather than the Lord of glory is the center of attraction. . . . We'll do our churches a lot of good if we each seek to cultivate the blessed Presence in our services. If we make Christ the supreme and constant object of devotion, the program will take its place as a gentle aid to order in the public worship of God.[22]

In light of 1 Cor 12–14, the much more urgent priority must be the nourishing of deep, loving relationships among brothers and sisters who come together in the presence of the risen Lord Jesus. We can welcome the wise counsel of Bishop Neill, who echoes Paul's teaching, and we must let this become the standard of excellence in our assemblies:

> What matters far more than anything else is the love that binds Christians to their Lord and to one another. If love is present, the self-giving love of which alone the term *agape* is used in the

22. Tozer, *Root of the Righteous*, 92–95.

New Testament, we may infer the presence of the Spirit; if it is absent, whatever pretensions may be put forward on behalf of those who claim to be spiritual, the spirit that is in them is not the spirit of the risen Jesus.[23]

HARVESTING SOME OF THE
TEACHINGS OF 1 COR 12–14

Let us now attempt to harvest some of the teachings of 1 Cor 12–14 and consider how Paul's themes drive a Jesus movement. The Scriptures are clear that without the life-giving presence of the Spirit of God, nothing real happens. In the 1970s and 1980s, there was a remarkable rediscovery of the power of the Holy Spirit in many parts of the Western church. In the decades leading up to this outbreak of joy, the Holy Spirit was often either reduced to a doctrinal affirmation to be tacitly acknowledged or ignored completely as an embarrassing casualty of the triumph of secular culture. As the charismatic movement swept like fresh fire through dozens of historic denominations, millions of believers were overwhelmed by a wave of love which was the experiential impact of their encounter with Jesus' Spirit.[24] Canon David Watson was a leader in this charismatic renewal movement that swept through many of the British Anglican churches in the 1970s. He would be the first to affirm that the movement was a Holy Spirit-driven movement. Watson wrote:

> In sharp contrast to the proud self-confidence of modern man in this machine age, the first Christians knew that without the Spirit's power they could not begin to turn man from darkness to God's marvelous light. . . . The Holy Spirit is the distributor of various gifts to the Church, the guarantee of our inheritance, the means of access to the Father, the bringer of God's love to our hearts, the means of sanctification, the ground of unity, and the producer of love, joy, peace, patience, kindness, goodness, faithfulness, gentleness and self-control.[25]

The Spirit is the personal presence of the Triune God. When we say that the Spirit is the indispensable well-spring of renewal, we are simply restating what was affirmed at the outset: "It is not our ministries that make

23. Neill, *Jesus through Many Eyes*, 49.

24. To understand the charismatic movement, see the thoughtful assessment by Hummel, *Fire in the Fireplace*.

25. Watson, *I Believe in Evangelism*, 174.

Christ present and possible; it is the present, living Christ who makes our ministries possible."[26] Therefore, we reaffirm the great idea from chapters 12–14: *All ministry, work, and service that results in transformation of persons and societies is the activity of the risen Lord through the Holy Spirit. In every believer (no exceptions), God manifests his indwelling presence in some way for the good of the whole body.* Reliance on grace given through the Spirit is the dynamic of the new-creation community.

If our twenty-first century churches are to be transformed into movements that have a radical impact on our world, we must pursue a new reformation in which we recover a genuinely biblical understanding of how the church functions in God's plan. We cannot live as God's chosen people if we allow business as usual to constrict our dreams. *Charismata* are given to each one of us as capacities to enable us to join Jesus in his present ministry as he completes the mission of God. All charismata are valued and expressed. In a movement, the Holy Spirit leads and we contribute as *he* enables. Reliance on grace given through the Spirit is the dynamic of the new-creation community.

By his use of the metaphor of a human body, the apostle Paul teaches that the beauty and power of a movement which manifests Jesus' presence and love in the world requires that "each part does its work." Paul writes: "From him the whole body, joined and held together by every supporting ligament, grows and builds itself up in love, as each part does its work" (Eph 4:16). The growth to maturity imagined by Paul is dependent on each contribution being expressed and embraced. N. T. Wright explains, "the Spirit is given so that we ordinary mortals can become, in a measure, what Jesus was: part of God's future arriving in the present; a place where heaven and earth meet; the means of God's kingdom going ahead. The Spirit is given, in fact, so that the church can share in the life and continuing work of Jesus himself."[27]

The path to oneness: opening our hearts to the Spirit's presence and power

The body of Christ metaphor also demands that we make the nurturing of authentic oneness a pursuit of the highest priority. Paul exhorts us to, "Make every effort to keep the unity of the Spirit through the bond of peace" (Eph 4:3). The oneness of the Christian movement must become our passion since the Lord of the church told us that the unity of his disciples is his

---

26. Purves, *Resurrection of Ministry*, 79.

27. Wright, *Simply Christian*, 124.

priority: "Father, I pray they will be one, just as you are in me and I am in you. I want them also to be in us. Then the world will believe that you have sent me" (John 17:21). The pathway to renewal must begin with repentance for our blatant disregard for Jesus' desire. The fragmented state of Christ's church seriously undermines Jesus' credibility.

The journey toward oneness must begin within me. I must repent of my spiritual arrogance and ecclesiastical tribalism. Then at the local church level we must make every effort to overcome barriers to oneness. Finally, we must seek fresh ways to manifest oneness at the level of denominations and neodenominational alliances.[28]

On the personal level

Each Christ-follower must undertake a searching self-assessment. Unity begins with identifying heart-issues and my own complicity in the fractured state of the body. "Don't be proud at all. Be completely gentle. Be patient. Put up with one another in love" (Eph 4:2). I must repent of my spiritual pride (rooted in insecurity) which tends to view other believers and their weird churches as defective or substandard. We seem wired to criticize Christians from other tribes for their worship style, dress codes, questionable teachings, idiosyncratic evangelistic methods, or preferred celebrity preachers. These judgmental attitudes are sinful and devastate the impact of the church's mission.

James, the Lord's brother, gives me the counsel needed in his challenge to seek authentic wisdom from God.

> Live well, live wisely, live humbly. . . . Mean-spirited ambition isn't wisdom. Boasting that you are wise isn't wisdom. Twisting the truth to make yourselves sound wise isn't wisdom. It's the furthest thing from wisdom—it's animal cunning, devilish conniving. Whenever you're trying to look better than others or get the better of others, things fall apart and everyone ends up at the others' throats.
>
> Real wisdom, God's wisdom, begins with a holy life and is characterized by getting along with others. It is gentle and

28. During the past two decades, traditional denominational organizational structures have become less significant for many churches. In the place of these old forms, many churches today identify with and are nurtured by neodenominational alliances. Examples of such alliances might include: The Gospel Coalition, Willow Creek Association, Good News Movement among United Methodists, the Global Fellowship of Confessing Anglicans, the Purpose-Driven Church Movement, and the Christian Coalition of America.

reasonable, overflowing with mercy and blessings, not hot one
day and cold the next, not two-faced. You can develop a healthy,
robust community that lives right with God and enjoy its results
only if you do the hard work of getting along with each other,
treating each other with dignity and honor. (Jas 3:13–18 MSG)

May the indwelling Spirit of Jesus enable each one of us to walk this pathway
of growth in authentic divine wisdom.

Local church implications: Word and Spirit churches

I served as pastor of a local Baptist congregation during the decade when
the Charismatic Renewal movement was flourishing. The exuberance of the
charismatics in our city was intimidating. They were enjoying, in fresh and
visceral ways, the "joy that comes from the Holy Spirit" (1 Thess 1:6). Our
tribal ethos was all about teaching the word of God. We stood firm on the
truth that, "All Scripture is God-breathed and is useful for teaching, rebuk-
ing, correcting and training in righteousness, so that the servant of God
may be thoroughly equipped for every good work" (2 Tim 3:16–17). Our
mandate was the charge given to Timothy, "Guard the good deposit that
was entrusted to you" (2 Tim 1:14). These charismatics, who seemed so bold
in their witness to God's presence and power, were certainly not our kind
of people. There was plenty of pride, mutual suspicion, and criticism to go
around. As a young pastor, my eyes were opened to my own urgent need
for a fuller engagement with the Holy Spirit. I recall being stunned when
reading some words attributed to A. W. Tozer (though they never appear
in any of his published works), "If the Holy Spirit was withdrawn from the
church today, 95 percent of what we do would go on and no one would
know the difference. If the Holy Spirit had been withdrawn from the New
Testament church, 95 percent of what they did would stop, and everybody
would know the difference."[29] I engaged in rigorous and extensive study of
the Holy Spirit texts in the New Testament. Together with the church's leaders we determined to become a "Word and Spirit" church. Understanding
and obeying God's written word would always be at the center of our ethos.
But we longed for a greater awareness of Jesus' presence and power. We
opened our hearts and minds and arms to charismatic friends. We told the
church's head that we would pursue oneness and seek to overcome polariza-
tion that so frequently characterizes relationships between neo-Pentecostals
and Scripture-centered congregations. Pastor Doug Banister wrote a book

29. Jones, "In His Absence," para. 1.

a few years later which chronicled his own journey in seeking to overcome the division and hostility between charismatics and evangelicals. Doug's story reflected my own journey and articulated my passion. He wrote:

> I had a foot in both camps. As an evangelical, I loved the Word but longed for more of the Spirit. As someone who had begun to drink from the water of charismatic renewal, I loved the emphasis on the Spirit's power, but saw that this power needed to be wedded with stronger rooting in the Word. I saw strengths and weaknesses in both traditions. Both camps hold a piece of the puzzle the other needs. . . . Think of the charismatic and evangelical traditions as two mighty spiritual rivers flowing through our century. Today the two rivers are merging into one mighty flood of spiritual power. God is blending the strengths of both . . . together in churches across America. I call these *word and power churches*."[30]

May the Spirit who speaks through the word and showers on us God's multidimensional grace bring this vision to greater and greater realization globally. May we hear what the Spirit is saying to the churches: "Accept one another, then, just as Christ accepted you, in order to bring praise to God" (Rom 15:7).

At the level of the regional, national, and global church: Accept one another

There is a movement which I believe has great potential to be a catalyst to the pursuit of oneness. The global church urgently needs *renovaré*. *Renovaré* is a Latin word meaning "to renew." Renovaré is the name of a most unusual Christian ministry founded by *Celebration of Discipline* author Richard J. Foster. It's a low-key ministry whose vision is expressed as, "We imagine a world in which people's lives flourish as they increasingly become like Jesus."[31] Renovaré team members together developed a "balanced vision of life in Christ and a practical strategy for spiritual formation"[32] that they teach in various venues all over the world. Participants in a Renovaré experience are invited to enter a covenant which states: "In utter dependence upon Jesus Christ as my ever-living Savior, Teacher, Lord, and Friend, I will

---

30 Banister, *Word and Power Church*, 19–21 (italics original).

31. https://renovare.org/about/overview, line 1.

32. https://renovare.org/about/ideas/the-six-streams, line 11.

seek continual renewal through spiritual exercises, spiritual gifts, and acts of service."[33]

The Renovaré vision celebrates the fact that for 2,000 years God's people have flourished in diverse contexts and there have been a wonderful variety of ways of expressing love for Jesus and the desire to walk with him. Each of the diverse traditions of spiritual life has a particular and necessary insight or focus that is needed by all of us. Instead of being suspicious of the other tribe and their strange piety, Renovaré says, "Let's determine to respect these alternative ways and study their traditions and passions." Doing so might just add richness to my own journey with Jesus.

Building on Richard Foster's *Streams of Living Water*,[34] Renovaré presents a model which urges every believer to "taste and see" (Ps 34:8) by exploring some of the pathways to spiritual life that these other Christ-followers treasure. Foster has distilled the wonderful variety of the Christian movement into six traditions or "streams." Renovaré says, "Taken together, these traditions help us envision a balanced spiritual life. They serve as a guide to help us take on the life of Jesus—to become like Jesus ourselves— and as a result to be transformed from the inside out."[35] The six streams are:

- *The Contemplative Tradition:* A Prayer-Filled Life: It stresses the value of silence, solitude, and prayer as ways we engage with God's presence. Put simply, the contemplative life is the steady gaze of the soul on the Father, Son, and Holy Spirit.

- *The Holiness Tradition:* A Virtuous Life: Responding with integrity: It emphasizes reformation of our hearts so that we are able to respond appropriately to the challenges of life. It pursues purity of heart.

- *The Charismatic Tradition:* A Spirit-Empowered Life: It focuses on the power of God's Spirit moving in and through us, fueling our lives from the presence and power of God.

- *The Social Justice Tradition:* A Compassionate Life: It expresses the themes of justice, compassion, and peace. It emphasizes wisdom and loving-kindness to bring relationships into harmony, unity, and balance. . .Love of God requires love of neighbor.

- *The Evangelical Tradition:* A Word-Centered Life: It emphasizes living the life-giving message. The "good news" is God's great message

33. https://www.renovare.org/about/overview, line 15.

34. Foster, *Streams of Living Water.*

35. For an overview of the Renovaré vision, see https://renovare.org/about/ideas/the-six-streams, line 11.

to humanity: that all can be redeemed and restored to its intended design. This faith stream addresses the crying need for people to see the good news lived and hear the good news proclaimed.

• *The Incarnational Tradition:* A Sacramental Life: This focuses on the relationship between the invisible Spirit and physical reality, helping us to see God's divine presence in the material world in which we live.[36]

Foster freely acknowledges that the six streams in his model are not comprehensive in scope, nor are they air-tight classifications. But the model helps us see a way toward overcoming our current state of fragmentation, personally and corporately. Most of us will identify a home tradition among the six. For some, the tradition that has been shaping us is comfortable and nurturing. For some others, we are grateful for what we have received but sense there might be alternative pathways to grow in our love. It is likely that each of us might be strengthened if we were to embrace a more balanced diet of spiritual disciplines. Most importantly, may the Spirit help us to learn to respect and treasure other people's ways of loving God.

I pray that this vision will infect Jesus' movement like a benevolent virus. I pray for community transmission that will spread this vision far and wide. The global church is severely fractured and there is a need for a practical strategy for pursuing oneness. For Jesus' sake, let us renew our commitment to: "Make every effort to keep the unity of the Spirit through the bond of peace" (Eph 4:3). The truth is, we are actually one. As Paul taught us: "Just as a body, though one, has many parts, but all its many parts form one body, so it is with Christ. For we were all baptized by one Spirit so as to form one body—whether Jews or gentiles, slave or free—and we were all given the one Spirit to drink" (1 Cor 12:12–13).

> Father, I pray they will be one, just as you are in me and I am in you. I want them also to be in us. Then the world will believe that you have sent me. (John 17:21)

---

36. https://renovare.org/about/ideas/the-six-streams.

Chapter 11

Renewing Love

The Currency of the New Creation (Ch. 13)

You, Lord Jesus, are love. Make me to be more like you.
Grant that your love may be my word and my wisdom,
my great offering and my one accomplishment.
For of all things, love is the greatest and it never comes to an end.

FROM A PRAYER OF ST. AUGUSTINE[1]

READ: 1 COR 13

Leadership guru Stephen Covey counsels us that for a leader, "The main thing is to keep the main thing the main thing." His *First Things First* has been a huge help to many of us. An uncluttered reading of the New Testament reveals that the CEO of the Christian movement was unequivocal about "the main thing."[2]

---

1. The Rev. Randolph Hollerith prayed this prayer during A Service of Morning Prayer and Reflection at the Washington National Cathedral on December 2, 2020. Washington National Cathedral, "December 2, 2020," 3:00–3:19.

2 Covey et al., *First Things First*, 75.

Jesus got this about two millennia before Covey discovered this wisdom. On his final night prior to his voluntary self-sacrifice and submission to the Roman execution, Jesus spoke plainly to the nucleus of the leadership of his new-creation community.

> A new command I give you: Love one another. As I have loved you, so you must love one another. By this everyone will know that you are my disciples, if you love one another. . . . My command is this: Love each other as I have loved you. Greater love has no one than this: to lay down one's life for one's friends. You are my friends if you do what I command.[3]

Paul's teaching in chapter 13 is leading the Corinthian believers to center on this main thing. One thing above all else must define our "brand" and shape our identity. For some folks, this talk of an *agapē*-centered[4] movement sounds hopelessly naive and idealistic—like so much silliness in our modern era. Maybe Jesus' love-ethic can have some limited relevance in our private lives. We should indeed try to be kind and generous people. But there's no relevance in a world of Islamic terrorism, multinational corporations, scientific advancement, and market forces. Often we assume Jesus' love-centered movement is out of touch with the concerns of the real world. Jesus is frequently relegated to the domain of "spiritual" matters. He's quite an expert in matters of sin and forgiveness, but in the real world, a love-centered movement seems out of touch.

Jesus' words are not mysterious or confusing. Nor is 1 Cor 13 a one-off statement. It really is a pervasive theme in the New Testament. Why is it so very rare that our churches embrace this value as the center of their identity and mission? Maybe the main reason we often react with skepticism is that we instinctively sense it is too hard, too extreme, too demanding. What British journalist G. K. Chesterton once said about Christianity is certainly true of embracing the centrality of the way of love. "The Christian ideal has not been tried and found wanting. It has been found difficult; and left untried."[5] But Jesus actually knows how life works. And Paul's teaching in chapter 13 affirms his solidarity with his Lord.

---

3. John 13:34–35; 15:12–13.

4. New Testament writers use the Koine Greek word *agapē* when speaking of God's love. The English language's semantic sign "love" is so thoroughly devalued that it is almost useless today. It can refer to a dramatic range of behaviors, experiences, and feelings. Thus, we will frequently use the Greek word for love which Paul used in his writing. That word is *agapē*.

5. Chesterton, *What's Wrong with the World*, 25.

Can you imagine a movement in which *agapē* was the main thing, and in which the main thing remained the main thing? Dream with me. Imagine that we are sharing together our regular *agapē* meal. We connect with one another at a variety of levels as we take this leisurely meal. We have time to nurture real friendships and grow transparency. The gathering moves into an experience of Holy Communion and we listen again to our identity-defining narrative. Phil 2 is recited and reflected on by all. We genuinely experience the love of God in fresh ways as we eat the bread which tells us about Jesus' body. We say "yes" again to the new covenant and recommit to the movement Jesus heads up which is making all things new. During this leisurely time set apart to connect with Jesus and our sisters and brothers, there are moments set aside for confession of sin and assurance of total forgiveness.

- Two men who had a business deal go sour are reconciled. One confesses to deception and is forgiven.

- A husband shares about his addiction to porn and asks for help to overcome. Two guys from the community come alongside him to support and walk with him.

- A wife confesses that the 24/7 care of her elderly husband is pushing her to the breaking point. The entire group mobilizes to help carry the load.

- A mother shares that her son has become addicted to opioids. Three men volunteer to come alongside the young man.

- A young woman discloses her recent breast cancer diagnosis. The church responds with prayer and the laying on of hands and anointing with oil.

- Parents weep and disclose that their son has been expelled from school for bringing a weapon. They are hopeless because he is a loner and depressed and seems friendless. The websites he frequently visits are evil. One of the house church groups adopts this family.

- A man who lost his job fifteen months ago tells us that he is still unemployed and giving up. He confesses that he is drunk more often, struggles with uncontrolled anger, and has bought a gun. He stopped going to church on a regular basis. A business owner in the church offers him a job and personal mentoring.

- Four families of Syrian refugees have been resettled in the apartment next door to one member. The church prays for wisdom and discernment on how to express God's love to these strangers in our midst.

- A church family gradually realizes that one family of kids in their daughter's second-grade class never has breakfast or dinner. They discover that there is no food in the house because the dad was in an accident and had a leg amputated. He can't work. Another of the house church groups adopts this family.

- A friend sees the tell-tale signs of bruises on one of her female friends and discovers she is being beaten. The church provides safe living space and three brothers go to confront the abuser.

- We mobilize for a three-month-long "Habitat-type" initiative to re-build an African-American church building in town which has been burned by white supremacists. Three couples decide to purchase Corollas instead of BMWs or Lexuses and donate the difference to the project. They give $90,000 and discover that Corollas are actually safe and comfortable. The members ask the African-American church members to spend the next six Tuesday nights leading workshops for us on the experience of being Black in America in 2021. We will share meals together as we meet. We send a delegation of five to meet our mayor and police chief to brainstorm on concerns about racism in the city.

Imagine what we who love Jesus might be able to set in motion through the power of the Holy Spirit. A global movement of Jesus' disciples, among whom love is actually lived out as the main thing, can have great impact in our word-resistant era.

The great idea which shines forth so brightly in chapter 13 is: *Other-centered agapē is the heart of new-creation living because it is the quality which defines the life of God. The Spirit has poured agapē into our lives through cross power. Agapē is the one thing which must define our brand and shape our identity.*

EXPLORING THE TEXT OF 1 COR 13

Like all of 1 Corinthians, chapter 13 is part of Paul's pastoral strategy of resocialization. With these memorable and poetic words, the apostle is shaping a community and guiding them into the radically alternative identity-defining narrative. What Paul is doing in chapter 13 is to redirect the Corinthians' focus to the main thing according to the teaching and example of the church's Lord. Let's examine this beloved chapter more closely.

"Be zealous for 'greater' gifts—and I will show you the more excellent way." First Cor 12:31 is a transition statement in the teaching on charismata which runs from chapter 12 through chapter 14. He has presented his essential apostolic counsel on the way the Holy Spirit graciously manifests His presence in the community in chapter 12. But before he addresses the specific issues that relate to Corinthian worship gatherings in chapter 14, he will first shine a brilliant light on the core value of the community of the risen Lord Jesus. Paul seeks to convince these young believers that we aspire to express charismata to serve and edify others because of our deep and pervasive core value—love. The second theme mentioned in 12:31 is the connecting link[6] to the magnificent hymn to agapē in chapter 13. "But now I want to lay out a far better way for you" (MSG).

All biblical truth has very down-to-earth implications for life. Paul here moves seamlessly from things of the Spirit to the nonnegotiable core value that must permeate every dimension of Christian life and thought— agapē. Note that Paul says it is a way, not a charisma. A particular charisma is a manifestation of the Spirit's indwelling presence. And the Spirit who is making his presence known through us is the Spirit of Jesus. Thus, when this Spirit reveals his empowering presence, the manifestation will reflect Jesus' character. The way of Jesus is the way of agapē. But please be sure to remember that chapter 13 fits as the centerpiece of this extended discussion, which includes chapters 12–14. If we read it the way Paul wrote it, we recognize that the memorable teaching on agapē is for the community and is fundamental to their experience of the Spirit's enabling presence. Go ahead and read it at the weddings, but never forget that its first application is to the issues of relationship in community.

In Corinth, it seems that for many the main thing was the delight and exalted state that resulted from the experience of ecstasy. Many in Corinth felt that they were an eschatological community because they experienced the Spirit who had, in their view, elevated the privileged to new heights of knowledge and power. This was most prominently evidenced through ecstatic experience (e.g., speaking in tongues). Would the Corinthian

---

6. I have reminded the reader elsewhere that the chapter divisions we find in our printed Bibles are not original, nor are they inspired. 12:31 is an example of a place in the text where a chapter break is particularly inappropriate. Chapters 12–14 are one coherent unit of thought. In some quarters, it is fashionable for scholars to hypothesize that chapter 13 was composed independently of the Corinthian situation and inserted into the letter from another source—a sort of cut-and-paste operation. Some are eager to argue that Paul did not write these words. See, for example, older commentaries by Johannes Weiss, Jean Hering, and Hans Conzelmann. Also Schmithals, *Gnosticism in Corinth* (90–96) and Titus, "Did Paul Write 1 Cor 13?," 299–302. But I am convinced that a careful analysis of the vocabulary and themes discloses that it is entirely relevant to the concerns which are on Paul's heart throughout the pastoral letter (e.g., being puffed up, self-seeking, patience, kindness, rejoicing in truth, not shameful, etc.). Chapter 13 completely fits into 1 Corinthians and its issues. It's not a poetic interlude.

population who came into contact with the members of this *ekklēsia* have described them as a loving family committed to laying down their lives for others as imitators of the community's Lord, Jesus? The evidence suggests the answer is "no." So Paul sets out to resocialize these relatively new Christ-followers and to guide them into a new narrative which will result in a new value system.

Let me present my working definition of love. I think it is obvious to most that the English language's semantic sign "love" is so thoroughly devalued that it is pretty much useless today since it can refer to such a dramatic range of behaviors, experiences, and feelings. In Scripture, love refers to *passionate, unrelenting, courageous pursuit of what is best for the beloved other. This creative, persistent engagement proceeds without regard for the cost or amount of sacrifice required of me. Love is a consuming determination to do good for you.* John Piper reminds us of the true source of this powerful love. He defines *agapē* thusly: "Love is the overflow and expansion of joy in God, which gladly meets the needs of others"[7]

Any form of religious expression is totally worthless if *agapē* is missing (13:1–3).

> If I speak in the tongues of men or of angels, but do not have love, I am only a resounding gong or a clanging cymbal.
> If I have the gift of prophecy and can fathom all mysteries and all knowledge, and if I have a faith that can move mountains, but do not have love, I am nothing.
> If I give all I possess to the poor and give over my body to hardship that I may boast,[8] but do not have love, I gain nothing.

Paul makes reference to three prominent modes of religious expression or experience and he declares that all are worthless without love. He mentions: ecstatic experience (beloved in the Pentecostal tradition); deep insight into revealed truth and bold faith (treasured among evangelicals); and radical service and sacrifice (nonnegotiable in the social justice movement, e.g., Mother Teresa). Professor James Dunn summarizes this provocative point:

---

7. Piper, *Dangerous Duty of Delight*, 44; see 1 John 4:19.

8. There is uncertainty over the best way to render this Greek phrase into English. This is the result of the fact that a few early Greek manuscripts have a slightly different word at this point. The best manuscripts indicate we should translate verse 3, "give my body so I can boast."

Without love, even the most soaring experiences of worship and devotion are meaningless jangle (see 13:1). Without love, even prophecy and the most profound insights into God's mysteries, even faith to do what seems impossible, makes the charismatic no better (13:2). Without love, even the most self-sacrificing service to others improves him in no way (13:3). In short, even man at his religious best, at the limit of charismatic possibility, if in all that he lacks love, does neither himself any good (nor presumably his community).[9]

Should we take this literally? We are inclined to dismiss these words of Paul as a bit of homiletical hyperbole. Is it all worthless? In fact Paul is quite serious. Over and over through the voices of the Old Testament prophets, we hear Yahweh saying to his people that no matter how lush and fervent their religious practices might be (praying, fasting, sacrificing, singing, etc.), if such overt expressions of what seems to be worship are not accompanied by mercy and justice (agapē!) especially for the poor and oppressed in their community, then all their reverential exclamations and sacrificial performances are utterly worthless (see Isa 58). In fact the prophets[10] often will say that Yahweh is absolutely disgusted and he has stopped paying any attention to them. Jesus affirms the same in his disturbing parable about the sheep and the goats found in Matt 25. He said that when we fail to do agapē among the poor and outcast persons whom we encounter (e.g., feeding the hungry, welcoming the stranger, clothing the naked, visiting the prisoner), we are ignoring the Lord himself.

Paul's opening words in chapter 13 are completely consistent with the biblical prophetic tradition. Elsewhere, Paul will write to the Galatians and say, "the only thing that counts is faith working through love" (5:6).

Anatomy of love (13:4–7)

Philosopher Peter Kreeft observes that the Spirit has not provided us with a definition of agapē, but instead a description (of Jesus): "Paul does not give us a philosophical definition, an abstract and logical setting-out of genius and specific difference. Instead of thus defining agapē, he describes it by giving us fifteen concrete and identifiable attributes of it. They tell us what it is by telling us what it does."[11]

---

9. Dunn, Jesus and the Spirit, 294.

10. Isa 58; 1:11–17; Amos 5:21–24; Hos 6:6.

11. Kreeft, God Who Loves You, 64 (italics original).

This mosaic of fourteen[12] qualities which Paul has given us through the inspiration of the Spirit in verses 4–7 is such a wonder. So I have struggled with how to approach this most profound and preeminent of all themes.[13] The wisdom in these words needs to be digested slowly. While each quality or attitude on the list is worthy of careful consideration in and of itself, there is also a benefit to trying to make some sense of the items grouped together as a whole—like a mosaic. Let's look at them not as specific stones or tiles of the mosaic, but let's step back and see what picture they make when seen together.

Here is the list of attitudes Paul mentions in verse 4–7:

NIV	MSG[14]
Love is patient,	Love never gives up.
love is kind.	Love cares more for others than for self.
It does not envy,	Love doesn't want what it doesn't have.
it does not boast,	Love doesn't strut,
it is not proud.	Doesn't have a swelled head,
It does not dishonor others,	Doesn't force itself on others,
it is not self-seeking,	Isn't always "me first,"
it is not easily angered,	Doesn't fly off the handle,
it keeps no record of wrongs.	Doesn't keep score of the sins of others,
Love does not delight in evil	Doesn't revel when others grovel,
but rejoices with the truth.	Takes pleasure in the flowering of truth,
It always protects,	Puts up with anything,
always trusts,	Trusts God always,
always hopes,	Always looks for the best,
always perseveres.	Never looks back, but keeps going to the end

When taken together, what do we see? What is the unifying focus? The heart of Paul's provocative list is that all attitudes or qualities are centered in doing what is best for others. Love is focused on the other. Love seeks God's best for the other person. This leads me to reaffirm our definition of *agapē*: In

12. Whether you see the list of qualities as containing fourteen or fifteen items depends on how you treat verse 6. "Love does not delight in evil but rejoices with the truth." Some read this as two distinct items.

13. I will not provide a technical historical-cultural analysis of the vocabulary, since such treatments already exist and many are masterful analyses, for example, that of Thiselton, *First Epistle to the Corinthians*. There is also a now-classic study of the fourteen qualities that Paul mentions in his description of *agapē*. I hope you will carefully digest the little book by evangelical ethics professor Lewis Smedes, *Love within Limits*.

14. Peterson, *Message*.

Scripture, "love" refers to passionate, unrelenting, courageous pursuit of what is best for the beloved other. This creative, persistent engagement proceeds without regard for the cost or amount of sacrifice required of me. Love is a consuming determination to do good for the other person.

This is the identical emphasis that Paul urges Christ-followers to embrace in Philippians. There he refers to this other-centered focus as "the same mindset as Christ Jesus," (2:5). If we think like Jesus thinks, then we eagerly seek to become "like-minded, having the same love, being one in spirit and of one mind; doing nothing out of selfish ambition or vain conceit. Rather, in humility value others above yourselves, not looking to your own interests but each of you to the interests of the others" (2:2b–4). For Paul, this is the necessary behavioral expression of sound Christology. If our doctrine of Christ is orthodox, certain attitudes and behaviors are inevitable. What do we believe about Jesus?

For Paul the cross is the center of Jesus' identity. Our perception of Jesus must be reimagined in light of God's act in Christ's death. Now we see Christ and his execution as the power of God and the wisdom of God. The community of Christ-followers has a totally new paradigm which shapes their actions—the example and mind of Christ. This is cross power.

So we must grasp that 1 Cor 13 is not an aesthetic interlude where Paul rhapsodizes on ethereal themes of romantic beauty. The penetrating analysis of 1 Cor 13 is rooted in Jesus and his cross. Other-centered *agapē* is the heart of new-creation living because it is the quality which defines the life of God. Thus Paul exhorts the Ephesians, "Therefore be imitators of God, as beloved children, and live in love, as Christ loved us and gave himself up for us, a fragrant offering and sacrifice to God" (Eph 5:1–2).

Final unit: Agapē never fails—it alone is eternal (13:8–13).

> Love never fails. But where there are prophecies, they will cease; where there are tongues, they will be stilled; where there is knowledge, it will pass away. For we know in part and we prophesy in part, but when completeness comes, what is in part disappears. When I was a child, I talked like a child, I thought like a child, I reasoned like a child. When I became a man, I put the ways of childhood behind me. For now we see only a reflection as in a mirror; then we shall see face to face. Now I know in part; then I shall know fully, even as I am fully known. And now these three remain: faith, hope and love. But the greatest of these is love.

Paul completes his profound description by declaring that of all the excellent virtues, only one, *agapē*, is eternal. He says love will never fail or die out or cease to be the main thing. He argues that all other modes of highly prized spiritual knowledge and experience (ecstasy) have value in this present interim age only. This statement does not denigrate these charismata. They are in fact gifts from God, graciously given, as Paul has been teaching in chapter 12. But they are time-sensitive, have an expiration date, and are limited and incomplete. Paul is clear that at the point of the future consummation when Jesus returns to comprehensively make all things new,[15] only then will our experience of God and our knowledge of him be total and complete.

Paul offers a wonderful analogy to capture his argument. Our current spiritual experience can be compared to the way of knowing I experienced as a child. (This might have been a bit of a shock to some Corinthians.) Our current experiences of ecstasy are analogous to the kind of knowing that is appropriate for an infant. It is not wrong or useless, but quite partial by adult standards. Notice that Paul speaks here in the first person, using "I" and "we." Paul is not criticizing the ecstatic Corinthians and placing his own apostolic knowledge on a higher level. Paul's own humility is evident because Paul sees it all in the eschatological framework. Our present limitation is not ascribed to evil or failure. But it is characteristic of this preconsummation era. We are limited in everything we do. Our obedience and our love and our forgiveness are limited. The longed-for future *teleion* can be described as a face-to-face encounter. We will see Jesus the risen Lord. Our relationship with Jesus then will no longer be distant or clouded. Rather the believer's future is promised to be a time of direct engagement with the Trinity. This is the future glory Paul refers to. We will know the Trinity without the limitations which our current physical capacities impose on us all.

So in his final poetic stanza (8–13), Paul affirms that three virtues are fundamental and "remain." Faith, hope, and love are the core of our existence. Faith remains, but will no longer be required in the moment of direct encounter and fulfillment of all promises. The oft-quoted definition of "faith" in the Letter to the Hebrews explains why faith, which is so central in this present era, is not as fundamental as love. The author of Hebrews says, "Now faith is confidence in what we hope for and assurance about

---

15. Paul uses the Greek word *teleion*. In Koine Greek this word has a wide semantic range. Thiselton says that it, "includes the double meaning *the complete* (NRSV) and *wholeness* (REB). Depending on the specific force required by the context, the word may also mean *perfection* (NIV, NJB) . . . here there is also a further hint of *teleios* as denoting a goal. . . . No English word alone can fully convey the meaning in this context" Thiselton, *First Epistle to the Corinthians*, 1065.

what we do not see" (Heb 11:1). So when we "see face to face," the role of faith will cease.

Hope remains as well. But once we experience the *teleion,* no longer is our full salvation a future hope. As Paul writes: "For in this hope we were saved. But hope that is seen is no hope at all. Who hopes for what they already have?" (Rom 8:24).

But love will never become unnecessary. Why does Paul believe it to be the center and that which is greater than even faith and hope? Because love is the never-ending, essential dynamic which characterizes and energizes the Trinity. *God is love.* It is therefore, the greatest.

Croatian evangelical theologian Miroslav Volf is a careful guide as we seek to probe the mystery of the Trinity:

> When we say that God is the Holy Trinity, we mean that the divine persons are mysteriously one and three. The oneness of the Three and the threeness of the One make up the divine communion of love. But how is that communion achieved? Divine persons give themselves to each other, and they do so in a special and exclusively divine way. Each dwells in others and is indwelled by others. . . . By such mutual indwelling, the Holy Three are the Holy One. Because the Godhead is a perfect communion of divine love, divine persons exchange gifts—the gift of themselves and the gift of the other's glory. . . . God is the utterly loving giver. God doesn't just love; God is love. . . . Luther offered a very vivid "definition" of God: God is "nothing but burning love and a glowing oven full of love." That's the character of God's being, not just some of his actions.[16]

Paul's way of understanding the reality of God was totally turned inside-out once Paul encountered the crucified Jesus.[17] Jesus' cross is now the definitive revelation of God's being. Paul's deep-rooted Jewish monotheism was transformed by the death of Jesus: "For God was pleased to have all his fullness dwell in him, and through him to reconcile to himself all things, whether things on earth or things in heaven, by making peace through his

---

16. Volf, *Free of Charge,* 62, 69, 85.

17. Michael Gorman writes: "The initial and ongoing encounter with Jesus . . . reformulated his [Paul's] understanding of who God is and how God is most fully experienced. That the Messiah, God's Son was sent by God to be crucified, and then raised by God, meant that somehow *God and the cross were inextricably interrelated.* That connection led Paul to see not only Jesus, but also God the 'Father of our Lord Jesus Christ' as defined by the cross . . . *The cross is the interpretive, or hermeneutical, lens through which God is seen; it is the means of grace by which God is known*" (Gorman, *Cruciformity,* 9, 17; italics ours).

blood, shed on the cross" (Col 1:19). In Paul we find an "unyielding affirmation that in the cross we see the character of God; the crucifixion of Jesus is the gauge of God's immeasurable love just as it is the ultimate object lesson for God's unorthodox notion of the exercise of power."[18]

HARVESTING THE SPIRIT'S REVEALED WISDOM REGARDING *AGAPE* IN 1 COR 13

Today, in both the West and in parts of Africa, the Christian movement has a credibility problem. Our voice is increasingly devalued. There are many reasons contributing to this. Some are gleeful at the demise of what they regard as a bastion of institutional oppression. Concerned Christ-followers are increasingly troubled and seeking fresh ways to fulfill God's mission. *Christianity Today* published an urgent appeal to the American church, saying:

> The church has a serious image problem. A recent book titled, *unchristian,* reveals much about how Millennials, the emerging generation—both those inside and around the church— view Christianity. The results weren't good. An overwhelming majority of young people view Christians as hypocritical, too judgmental, too focused on the afterlife, and too political in the worst sense of the word. And that image is often particularly true of evangelicals. . . . But other studies show that when you ask people what they think about Jesus, you get answers like: compassionate, loving, caring, hung out with sinners and poor people, for peace. We have a serious image problem. People think that we should stand for the same things as Jesus did. So it's time to change the image.[19]

The great idea discovered in 1 Cor 13 is the Spirit-given breath which can bring dry bones back to life again. *Other-centered agapē is the heart of new-creation living because it is the quality which defines the life of God.* A global movement of Jesus' disciples, among whom love is actually lived out as the main thing, can have great impact in our word-resistant era. Mahatma Gandhi once said, "The difference between what we do and what we are capable of doing would suffice to solve most of the world's problems."[20]

18. Carol and Green, *Death of Jesus in Early Christianity,* 128.

19. Wallis, "Evangelical Manifesto," paras. 1–2.

20. Quoted in McLaren, *Great Spiritual Migration,* 146. This quote is widely attributed to Gandhi, though there is some debate in wikiquote.org as to whether there is any evidence that he actually said it. See https://en.wikiquote.org/wiki/Talk:Mahatma_Gandhi.

He did not have the church in mind when he said this, but this provocative comment is, in fact, true of the movement of Jesus' followers—and true only of this movement. We must believe the good news.

It happened before! It can happen today.

Sociologist Rodney Stark studied the reasons for the success of the early Christian movement. His book, *The Rise of Christianity: How the Obscure, Marginal Jesus Movement Became the Dominant Religious Force in the Western World in a Few Centuries,*[21] presents empirical evidence which supports his thesis that "Christian values of love and charity, from the beginning, had been translated into norms of social service and community solidarity. When disasters struck, the Christians were better able to cope."[22] Stark underlines the fact that Christianity brought a new *agapē*-based culture capable of making life in Greco-Roman cities more tolerable:

> To cities filled with homeless and the impoverished, Christianity offered charity as well as hope. To cities filled with newcomers and strangers, Christianity offered an immediate basis for attachments. To cities filled with orphans and widows, Christianity provided a new and expanded sense of family. To cities torn by violent ethnic strife, Christianity offered a new basis for social solidarity. And to cities faced with epidemics, fires, and earthquakes, Christianity offered effective nursing services. . . . The chief doctrine, of course, which was radically new to a pagan world groaning under a host of miseries and saturated with capricious cruelty . . . was that "because God loves humanity, Christians may not please God unless they love one another."[23]

Agapē is the one thing which must define our brand and shape our identity.

The implications of *agapē* are pervasive. Michael Gorman has given us an expanded rendering of chapter 13 which guides us into the far-reaching actions which are the way of love. We can see in this why Paul can write: "The entire law is summed up in a single command: 'Love your neighbor as yourself'" (Gal 5:14), and elsewhere, "love is the fulfillment of the law" (Rom 13:8).

21. Stark, *Rise of Christianity*.
22. Stark, *Rise of Christianity*, 74.
23. Stark, *Rise of Christianity*, 86, 161, 212.

Cruciform love is faith in action. It does not seek its own good but the good of others. Indeed, for the good of others it renounces the use of certain rights. Cruciform love edifies others and never harms them, not even enemies. It never retaliates or uses violence. Cruciform love welcomes diversity. It is not judgmental, but neither is it tolerant of values antithetical to the cross, and at times it can be tough.

Cruciform love is hospitable and generous, especially to the poor and weak—those marginalized or rejected by others. If it has worldly status, it becomes downwardly mobile in order to lift others up. It gives of itself and its material possessions. Cruciform love, in a word, continues the story of the cross in new times and places. Cruciform love is imaginative.[24]

In the United States today, we have so many opportunities to demonstrate the "more excellent way" of Jesus. We can express *agapē* in response to the epidemic of gun violence in the USA which is fueled by a loneliness epidemic. The evidence of the insanity of our obsession with firearms is ubiquitous.[25] What if 65 million Christians united to say, "Jesus does not carry a concealed weapon?" What if we stood together and confronted the fear-mongering of the weapons lobbyists and the greed of weapons manufacturers? What if we went after the root causes of the frequent mass shootings? What if we lived out an alternative value system which offers a "more excellent way" and rejected racism, bullying, domestic violence, and the celebration of violence in entertainment? What if we say "no" to our culture's obsession with killing in gaming and recreation, which shapes a violence-based value system and renders us desensitized to the slaughter of persons who are loved by God? As Barbara Glasson wrote: "We are not people who protect our own safety: we are people who protect our neighbors' safety."[26]

24. Gorman, *Cruciformity*, 267.

25. See "America's Gun Culture in Charts" for the disturbing statistics. Additional data can be found in Yablon, "U.S. Gun Death Rate Hit 20-Year High in 2017."

Charlie Warzel argues in *The New York Times* that we have become desensitized to gun deaths. He writes: "As a country, we seem resigned to preventable firearm deaths. Each year, 36,000 Americans are killed by guns—roughly 100 per day, most from suicide, according to data from the Giffords Law Center. Similarly, the Everytown for Gun Safety Support Fund calculates that there have been 583 'incidents of gunfire' on school grounds since 2013. In the first eight months of 2019, there were at least 38 mass shootings, *The New York Times* reported. Last August, 53 Americans died in mass shootings—at work, at bars, while shopping with their children. Some of these tragedies make national headlines; many don't. The bigger school shootings and hate-crime massacres can ignite genuine moral outrage" ("Open States, Lots of Guns," paras. 6–7).

26. Glasson, "Prayer," 23.

Agapē respects and celebrates the God-given dignity of every person and delights in experiencing Spirit-enabled unity amidst diversity.

During the summer of 2020, peaceful protests took place in hundreds of American cities (and in cities around the world.) The catalyst to this new civil rights movement was the death of an African-American man while he was being restrained by police officers in Minneapolis. One police officer, who was white, kept his knee on George Floyd's neck for eight minutes and forty-six seconds, while Floyd struggled to breathe and repeatedly cried out, "I can't breathe." Then he died. The death of George Floyd alone did not cause the outrage. Floyd's death fit into what evidence suggests is a pattern of racial injustice and of the use of lethal force by some white police officers. Millions of people of all races took to the streets in protest in the weeks that followed the incident. They were demanding that we as a society recognize that the disproportionate number of extrajudicial killings of African-American men is an insufferable violation of basic justice and an assault on human dignity. The lives of African-Americans matter, have dignity and value, just as non-black lives certainly matter, have dignity, and value.

This tragic season of crisis in American life can actually represent a *kairos*[27] moment for Christ-followers. This could represent an opportunity for the church to be a living demonstration that Jesus is not a white supremacist and that his followers are committed to obeying his teachings, which declare, "You shall love your neighbor as yourself" (Matt 22:39); "Do to others what you would have them do to you" (Luke 6:31); "Love your enemies" (Luke 6:27); and "Be merciful just as your Father in heaven is merciful" (Luke 6:36).

Imagine the impact of a global movement of Jesus' disciples, among whom *agapē* is passionately expressed through serving others and seeking justice (at a minimum) for those in our communities who are victims of discrimination and systemic injustice. Sacrificing our security and privileged status as white American Christians in order to secure respect, equality, economic opportunity, and justice for black- and brown-skinned persons is *what agapē does*. Jesus' reputation (glory) would be honored if his followers were to do this.

---

27. The concept of a *kairos* moment draws on the Greek word *kairos*, which is translated as "time," but it has a richer sense of a particularly significant moment in time in which God's purposes are disclosed and implemented in fresh ways.

There is systemic racism

As we struggle to address America's systemic racism, it is increasingly clear to me that because I was born with white skin, I received and continue to receive massive (undeserved) privilege as a result of some prejudices and patterns that are pervasive in my homeland. The fact of skin color has been assumed to imply an entire profile of personal qualities and intellectual capacities. In my case, all these assumptions brought me undeserved positive benefit because my skin is white and not black. As a follower of Jesus (who became incarnate as a brown-skinned, Middle-Eastern minority) the racial prejudice that penetrates everything in my culture, like the air I breathe, must be rejected and repented of. Jesus does not see people the way America sees people. I got a powerful theology lesson from my kindergarten Sunday school teacher. She taught me a song: "Jesus loves the little children; all the children of the world; red and yellow, black and white, they are precious in *his* sight. Jesus loves the little children of the world." The society I inhabit does *not* agree with that little song.

America's original sin

Robert P. Jones wrote *White Too Long: The Legacy of White Supremacy in American Christianity*[28] from the perspective of his deep roots in Southern Baptist churches. Jones contends that "white Christian churches have not just been complacent; they have not only been complicit . . . as the dominant cultural power in America, they have been responsible for constructing and sustaining a project to protect white supremacy and resist black equality. . . . This project has framed the entire American story."[29]

Jones laments that white Christian theology's "'free will individualism' insists that Christianity has little to do with social justice." He discerns that such a theological shift involves "the reorientation of religious faithfulness, with its radical contraction of human social responsibility." This theological syncretism has strongly influenced white evangelical thought not just on race, but also on most other social issues. Jones confesses that we "white Christians have been conditioned to move through our lives preoccupied with personal sin but unburdened by social injustice," and that "the [theological] system protects white Christian interests on the one hand and white consciences on the other."[30] Clearly, it's pretty comfortable for our white

28. Jones, *White Too Long*.
29. Jones, *White Too Long*, 6.
30. Jones, *White Too Long*, 94, 105, 227.

Christian churches to proclaim that our theology is about personal salvation and personal holiness. Everything outside of salvation has been labeled "politics."

If we take the Bible seriously as the word of God, we cannot accept such compartmentalizing of personal piety from seeking social justice. The determination to pursue justice, which is an ineliminable dimension of *agapē,* is grounded in the character of the God revealed in the Bible. "For the Lord your God is God of gods and Lord of lords, the great God, mighty and awesome, who shows no partiality and accepts no bribes. He defends the cause of the fatherless and the widow, and loves the foreigner residing among you, giving them food and clothing. And you are to love those who are foreigners, for you yourselves were foreigners in Egypt" (Deut 10:17–19).

Biblical basis for our applied agapē

Our response to the cry for justice and racial equality that we as Americans are hearing once again must be guided by the Bible. Baptist Bible scholar Jarvis J. Williams has given the evangelical church a brief but cogent overview of the central themes of God's word.[31] The scriptural teachings summarized in Professor Williams's article should become the subject matter for a mandatory sermon series in our white evangelical churches. Williams grounds our rejection of discrimination based on race in the biblical doctrine of creation:

> Genesis 1:26–27 clearly states God created all humans in his image and bestows upon us God-given dignity, and that he promises to redeem us, to reconcile us, and to restore the entire creation through Christ. When black lives are dehumanized and treated as though they don't matter simply because they're black, Christians everywhere should be able to stand up and assert without hesitation and with their Bibles open that black lives certainly matter, have dignity, worth, and value, just as non-black lives certainly matter, have worth, dignity, and value.

Professor Williams builds on this foundation by showing that the biblical doctrines of the work of Christ and eschatology require us to oppose racism:

> Racism is opposed to the gospel of Jesus Christ and against God's vision to redeem and unify creation through Christ. God recreates through Christ a diversity of different tongues, tribes, peoples, and nations into one new (but diverse) people. God

31. Williams, "Black Lives Matter in the Bible."

commands us to live in pursuit of reconciled community with one another and with our neighbors in anticipation of the age to come (Isa 65:17–25; Rom. 8:19–22). God's kingdom is an already-and-not-yet kingdom, whose king is a brown-skinned Jewish Messiah.[32]

Similarly, a grasp of Christian ethics will move us to pursue equality for all persons. "As Christians, we must intentionally oppose racism because God through Christ both empowers us and commands us to walk in love with the power of the Spirit. One way Christians walk in the Spirit is when we love our neighbors as ourselves (Gal 5:13–14)."[33]

Williams's concise conclusion must be a central focus of all Christ-followers in America in response to this *kairos* moment in our society. "God created black people in his image. God redeems black lives in Christ. Black lives matter to God because the Bible teaches they matter."[34]

Let us do Jesus' Great Commandment: A new agenda for doing agapē in the face of racism

If we repent of our complicity and renew our commitment to obey Jesus as Lord, the Jesus movement can be the change we want to see in the world. Paul writes: "Watch what God does, and then you do it, like children who learn proper behavior from their parents. Mostly what God does is love you. Keep company with him and learn a life of love. Observe how Christ loved us. His love was not cautious but extravagant. He didn't love in order to get something from us but to give everything of himself to us. Love like that" (Eph 5: 1–2 MSG). Since we are persons being transformed by cross power, let us determine to be imitators of God. In choosing to follow Jesus, we will be determined to respect the dignity of every human being and to strive for justice and peace. This is how we love our neighbors as ourselves. Let us pray for the strength of heart and mind to look beyond ourselves and address the needs of our brothers and sisters throughout the world.

As ambassadors of the crucified Jesus, let our churches actively practice *agapē* by embracing the new-creation vision. Let our mission focus include: praying and acting so that racism, sexism, and all other forms of discrimination will be forever banished from our hearts, our society, and our laws. Let us unite in prayer for an end to prejudice throughout our country and the

32. Williams, "Black Lives Matter in the Bible," para. 8.

33. Williams, "Black Lives Matter in the Bible," para. 9.

34. Williams, "Black Lives Matter in the Bible," para. 11.

world, and back up our praying by the way we respect all people as precious children of God. In Jesus' name, let us pray also for an end to the growing disparity between the rich and poor and for the grace and courage to strive for economic justice. This is what we plead for when we pray, "Thy Kingdom come; thy will be done on earth, as it is in heaven" (Matt 6:10).

The powerful example of unity amidst diversity.

Ugandan Christian leader and former Anglican bishop Zac Niringiye has written a book on the church in which he expresses hope and explains how a church in which Christians from diverse backgrounds and cultures live together in love can have a huge impact in Africa. Zac says,

> The unity in diversity which love engenders in the Christian community is at the heart of Christian witness. . . . Firstly, it provides a more complete, though always provisional, portrait of Jesus . . . by love and in love, the Christian community is to be a display of what community truly is, as God intended: unity and communion in diversity. In today's world, in spite of much talk of and hype about globalization we are faced with an unprecedented rate of breakdown of community in all its forms. In Africa the breaking down of community is simply on a spiral course. . . . The witness of the gospel is the presence of authentic Christian community in a world characterized by breakdown of community: a community in which unity thrives in diversity and diversity in unity.[35]

In our teaching and discipleship, let us make *agapē* the main thing.

In most of our churches, we make a serious effort to give solid basic instruction to new believers. Reflect on the topics which are addressed in our "essentials of the faith" classes for new members. How much attention is given to *agapē*? What topics do we deal with in this new believers' discipleship curriculum? What is the main thing?

I propose that we make *agapē* a central focus in our discipleship (along with typical topics like answered prayer, financial stewardship, sharing your faith, having quiet time, etc.). We have been describing discipleship as resocialization through these chapters. We are recognizing that when a person comes into Christ that there is a need for a comprehensive reorientation to

35. Niringiye, *Church*, 189.

life and its most essential values and ideas. Every new convert who comes to Jesus by faith comes in broken and messed up by the person's culture of origin. Isn't it reasonable to argue that lesson number one in the resocialization journey should be this most foundational of all concerns? Let's begin with *agapē*, and let us create learning environments which are holistic and which address every dimension of the person. Our thinking must definitely be transformed. At the same time, our emotions and bodily habits and social connections must also be transformed by the Spirit of Jesus. Pastor and author Brian McLaren writes,

> The Christian religion has been around for two thousand years, and as far as I know we have no well-conceived pedagogy of love, no love curriculum. All we have are scattershot sermons, songs, readings. . . . We test people's beliefs before we'll ordain them, but we don't assess whether they embody the skills and practices of love. . . . Thankfully, a growing number of churches are not only announcing their intention to put love first but also actually developing a curriculum of love to back up that intention.[36]

His book, *The Great Spiritual Migration*, offers some thoughtful and possibly transformational proposals on what such a love curriculum might look like.

It can be argued that Jesus' discipleship curriculum started here. As the gospel writer Luke lays out his portrait of Jesus' life, he shows us that the first time Jesus gathers his followers and gives them an extensive body of teaching is on the plain (Luke 6). And guess where Jesus begins his explanation of life in God's kingdom? After his introductory declaration that the most unexpected persons are indeed blessed by the arrival of God's new era of salvation, Jesus starts the lesson with a counterintuitive directive on *agapē*:

> Love your enemies, do good to those who hate you, bless those who curse you, pray for those who mistreat you. If someone slaps you on one cheek, turn to them the other also. If someone takes your coat, do not withhold your shirt from them. Give to everyone who asks you, and if anyone takes what belongs to you, do not demand it back. Do to others as you would have them do to you. . . .Be merciful, just as your Father is merciful. (Luke 6:27–31, 36)

That's Discipleship 101 according to Jesus. We must all continuously be growing in our ability to do love. When Paul prays for his good friends

36. McLaren, *Great Spiritual Migration*, 55. The presiding bishop of the Episcopal Church, Michael Curry, has recently produced such a curriculum, titled, "The Way of Love." Available at https://episcopalchurch.org/way-of-love.

in Philippi, he prays that they will grow in love: "So this is my prayer: that your love will flourish and that you will not only love much but well. Learn to love appropriately. You need to use your head and test your feelings so that your love is sincere and intelligent, not sentimental gush. Live a lover's life, circumspect and exemplary, a life Jesus will be proud of" (Phil 1:9 MSG). Jesus' own credibility, as well as our own as Christ-followers, depends on this.

POWER TO LOVE

First Cor 13 describes authentic *agapē*. The elegant language of this "hymn to love" inspires many of us and stimulates a strong desire to live the beauty of *agapē*. But if we summon up our willpower and vow to behave in more consistently loving ways, we soon crash head-on into a humiliating realization: we can't generate *agapē* ourselves. How does Paul expect us to behave in such other-centered and sacrificial ways? Does he really think we are all Mother Teresas? The current Dalai Lama recognizes our dilemma: "We are too self-centered; we place too much stress on our own interests with not enough consideration for the needs of others."[37] Well and good. But how do we control our innate selfishness? Is this teaching just more moralism that blandly urges us to try to play nice? No, Paul is brutally honest about our broken human natures in most of his writing. Recall the depth-assessment of each one of us found in his Letter to the Romans, chapter 3.

This lengthy exhortation to lay down our lives for others in 1 Cor 13 is rooted in our experience of God's first love. Paul knows these Corinthians and he knows them to be a community made up of persons who have genuinely tasted the grace given in and through Jesus (see 6:11). The apostle John says, simply, "We love because he first loved us" (1 John 4:19). Here is the source! Paul is empowered in every way by his realization that in Christ, God has loved and reconciled him. In his second letter to these friends in Corinth, he will write: "For the love of Christ controls us, because we have concluded this: that one has died for all, therefore all have died; and he died for all, that those who live might no longer live for themselves but for him who for their sake died and was raised" (5:14–15).

The cross is the means by which we gain access to the grace of forgiveness. In the exultant doxology that begins the Letter to the Ephesians, Paul celebrates, "In Him we have redemption through his blood, the forgiveness of sins, in accordance with the riches of God's grace." (Eph 1:7). Gorman explains: "In the cross, according to Paul, we learn that God is *pro nobis*—for us; in some unfathomable way, Christ's death for us both *demonstrates* and

37. Quoted in Williams, *Leadership for a Fractured World*. ix.

defines divine love. This divine love is the love of the Father who sends in love, the Son who dies in love, and the Spirit who produces the fruit of love in those he inhabits."[38]

We Christ-followers are those into whom, "the love of Christ has been poured . . . by the Spirit" (Rom 5:5). For Paul then, "the love of God that was revealed in history through Christ's one-time act is experienced in human lives through the Spirit's ongoing action."[39] Paul knows that getting saved is not merely mental assent to some ideas and doctrines; it is an experiential encounter with the *love of God*.

Paul assumes that the journey to union with Christ (regeneration) passes through the death of each believer. The cross gives us life. Here is his own testimony: "I have been crucified with Christ. It is no longer I who live, but Christ who lives in me. And the life I now live in the flesh, I live by faith in the Son of God, who loved me and gave himself for me" (Gal 2:20). The pathway to life must be through death—death to demanding self-centeredness and autonomous self-rule. Paul teaches that the initiation ritual, by means of which believers publicly declare their saving faith, is a drama which starts by dying with Christ: "Do you not know that all of us who have been baptized into Christ Jesus were baptized into his death? We were buried therefore with him by baptism into death, in order that, just as Christ was raised from the dead by the glory of the Father, we too might walk in newness of life" (Rom 6:3–8).

So in Paul's experience, the normal Christian "getting saved" experience involves repentance and death—becoming united with Jesus and his cross as we die to the old self that is 100 percent self-absorbed. That me that demanded its own way has died. Death is the only pathway to real life.

So does Paul think just anybody can decide that tomorrow I will be less selfish and start doing *agapē*? No. But in Christ, real change has taken place and Paul is convinced that Jesus' own presence and power is unleashed within us and that Jesus is the change agent. "Now the Lord is the Spirit, and where the Spirit of the Lord is, there is freedom. And we all, with unveiled face, beholding the glory of the Lord, are being transformed into the same image from one degree of glory to another. For this comes from the Lord who is the Spirit" (2 Cor 3:17–18 ESV).

Of course, full disclosure demands that we acknowledge that this transformation is not an obstacle-free fast track to perfection. This is why Christ-followers return to the cross daily—or perhaps hourly. This is why we must preach the gospel to ourselves and return again and again to the

38. Gorman, *Cruciformity*, 73 (italics original).

39. Gorman, *Cruciformity*, 73.

Lord's Table. I continually fail in my attempts to love. As the Confession of Sin in the *Book of Common Prayer* correctly states, "We confess that we have sinned against you in thought, word and deed, by what we have done, and by what we have left undone. We have not loved you with our whole heart; we have not loved our neighbors as ourselves."[40] Aware of my failures, I run to Jesus and discover again that his grace is greater than all my sin. This fresh encounter with God's grace and forgiveness offered to us on the basis of Jesus' cross is profoundly humbling—but also powerfully motivational. In fact, restoring and maintaining spiritual vitality involves discovering again and again the power of Jesus and his cross to free us from sin and guilt, and learning to live as persons who are clean and completely forgiven because of God's unconditional covenant love.

This is not a one-off encounter. Explaining to us the dynamics of bold love, Dan Allender writes: "Given the reality of sin, love and forgiveness are inextricably bound together. God is continually, literally, second-by-second covering our sin under His Son's blood and forgiving us our sins. God cannot love us unless He forgives us and cannot forgive us without a commitment to love us."[41] But in discovering again and again the power of Jesus and his cross to free us from sin and guilt, we experience refreshment from the Holy Spirit who empowers us with the courage to love by filling us with the life of the risen Lord. "Love is dependent on forgiveness. . . . The extent to which someone truly loves will be positively correlated to the degree to which the person is stunned and silenced by the wonder that his huge debt has been cancelled . . . gratitude for forgiveness is the foundation for other-centered love."[42]

Four decades ago, Francis Schaeffer told us that *agapē* is the main thing. He wrote, "We must not forget the final apologetic. . . . Our love must have a form that the world may observe; it must be seeable. . . . Love—and the unity it attests to—is the mark Christ gave Christians to wear before the world. Only with this mark may the world know that Christians are indeed Christians and that Jesus was sent by the Father."[43]

As Paul wraps up the entire Corinthian letter, he returns again to the main thing. He gives us a concluding, comprehensive exhortation in 16:14:

"Let all you do be done in love."
Panta humōn en agapēginesthō

---

40. The Episcopal Church, *Book of Common Prayer,* 320.

41. Allender and Longman, *Bold Love,* 42.

42. Allender and Longman, *Bold Love,* 43.

43. Schaeffer, *Mark of the Christian,* 34–35.

Chapter 12

An Open Letter to the Leaders of Christ's Church Everywhere

Dear Leaders of the Church of the Christ,

Thank you for taking this journey through 1 Corinthians with us. We have seen and heard much. The main thing we have seen is this: *cross power produces resurrection living*. That is true in the pulpit, the pew, and the public square. Now is the time to act. We want to speak from our heart about what the apostle would have us do based on the word of God to the house churches of Corinth. If God speaks to you about a new engagement with the ten truths from this letter, as he has spoken to us, then what must we do?

We begin by warning against what we should not do. These ten great ideas from 1 Corinthians for the renewal of our churches are not mean to be a new program. We do not envision starting a "Ten Great Ideas" ministry complete with t-shirts and branded coffee mugs. We are not suggesting a "Forty days of the Ten Great Ideas." And we do not recommend that for you either.

We must also caution that these ten ideas are not all the ideas that we need. While these ten great ideas represent a Corintheology (crucial truths about the church), they are not an entire biblical ecclesiology. They are not comprehensive. They are apostolic teaching for a group of house churches in Corinth. Because they are part of God's word they have eternal relevance and authority. But Paul's thirteen letters to the churches cover a wide variety of needs and issues that should all be explored. The whole counsel of God is ultimately needed to get the full picture of what God is doing for and in his beautiful bride and what role he wants us to play.

Those cautions aside, what, then, are these ten ideas, and what should we do with them? These ideas are but starting points for renewal. They are ten conversations leaders should have in their churches. Out of such Spirit-guided conversations could emerge new hope and new action to get your church moving again.

What kinds of conversations do we have in mind? We summarize the ten ideas one last time. According to God's word in 1 Corinthians, to renew the church, then and now, leaders and congregations need to wrestle, together, with the following truths.

First, we need to talk about the fact that the unity and solidarity of the church must come from the gospel of cross power (1 Cor 1 and 15). This gospel we need is one in which God, in apparent weakness and foolishness, has done what no human power could do—destroy the power of sin and death, and thereby make foolish the wisdom of this world. The gospel changes everything when we learn to see our world as full of his active presence. Spiritual maturity and unity is not boasting in our lofty thoughts of God, but rather being humbled by the death of Christ that alone has unleashed all of the Father, all of the Son, and all of the Spirit into all of our world, for all of time, to make all things new. This includes the resurrection of our bodies, ultimately, and resurrection living through the Spirit now.

Second, we need to talk about our need for the Holy Spirit to apply cross power to all of life (1 Cor 2). Cross power equals living in the power of the Spirit. The cross creates a new epistemology that transcends human wisdom and rationalism by sending the Spirit to indwell and enlighten. Only the Spirit of God can make sense of the message of the cross and the new creation it is creating.

Third, we need to talk about leadership (1 Cor 3 and 4). The church is renewed when leaders build to last rather than focusing on short-term goals. Leaders who will make a difference in the church are those who are building for eternity and not just time. This means leaders cannot make decisions just on what is popular or trendy; they must carefully select the building materials that are used in building up God's people.

Fourth, we need to talk about how to change lifestyles in the church (1 Cor 5). We are going nowhere as a people of God if we live like the world. The church is renewed when we let the Spirit resocialize us to act like kingdom citizens, not just world citizens. The gospel of the cross accepts us where we are but calls us on a journey of change and growth. If we are to flourish as persons, each of us must unlearn the values and worldview of our before-Christ culture and be formed by the new-creation community vision.

Fifth, we need to talk about sex (1 Cor 6). The church is renewed when we work with the Spirit to change our sexual behavior. Because we are resurrection people, longing for the day in which our bodies are transformed like the risen Christ was transformed, we are people that have a special love for bodies and for how we should use them. We must love our bodies because God made them, owns them, redeemed them, and will transform them. Only God has a comprehensive knowledge of sexuality and the path to sexual flourishing. We should follow his design.

Sixth, we need to talk in new ways about freedom and personal rights (1 Cor 9 and 10). The church is renewed when we let the Spirit change the way we use freedom. The power of the cross gives us a new model for how we use freedom and rights. Followers of Jesus can express their freedom by choosing to restrict their God-given rights in order to do what is best for the other person—especially the pre-Christian whom we wish to see encounter Jesus through the community's witness.

Seventh, we need a new conversation about women in the church (1 Cor 11). The church is renewed when women are treated with honor and find their place in serving the body of Christ and living for the coming new creation. We need to find a way to unleash the power of women in the church that avoids the excesses of the liberation model ("it's all about me and my rights") and the patriarchy model ("it's all about us men and preserving our privilege").

Eighth, we need a new conversation about communion (1 Cor 11). A focal point of worship is communion. The church is renewed when we work with the Spirit to use communion to remind ourselves of the gospel of a crucified Savior and release new surges of cross power into our common life. Celebrating the community's common meal with Jesus and his friends can be a profound and formative experience which the Spirit can use to shape and revive the community's identity, values, and vitality.

Ninth, we need a new conversation about empowering the whole church for the work of God (1 Cor 12–14). The church is renewed when we use our spiritual gifts for the health and flourishing of the body of Christ, not our own self-aggrandizement. All ministry, work, and service that results in transformation of persons and societies is the activity of the risen Lord through the Holy Spirit. In every believer (no exceptions), God manifests his indwelling presence in some way for the good of the whole body. Reliance on grace given through the Spirit is the dynamic of the new-creation community.

Finally, we need a new conversation about the power of love (1 Cor 13). The church is renewed when the Spirit fills us with agapic love and overcomes our fallen loves. Other-centered *agapē* is the heart of new-cre-ation living because it is the quality which defines the life of God. The Spirit has poured *agapē* into our lives through cross power. *Agapē* love is the one thing which must define our brand and shape our identity. No renewal is complete that does not end with the unleashing of radical love.

What happens after the conversations? Here we must ask our final question of you, the leaders of the churches of Christ in many places: What will you do with these words? To help answer that final question, we ask you to leave Corinth and travel back with us to a different city, in a different land, in an earlier decade. The new scene before us is described in John 5. We are now in Jerusalem. We are just inside a city, at the gate popularly called the Sheep Gate. The first thing that our eyes see are not the buildings around us but the large double pool in front of us.

The pool's name is Bethesda. The pools were a short walk from the Temple Mount. The meaning of Bethesda in Aramaic, the common language for Jesus and his Palestinian contemporaries, is "double-edged." It means "house of grace or mercy." But it can also mean "house of disgrace." The reality of the man lying under the cover of one of the five pillared porches reflected more of the latter than the former. He was a man in ruins. He lay among the blind, the lame, and the paralyzed. The text gives a generic diag-nosis of his condition as "disabled." Tradition has called him the paralytic, and that is a useful shorthand for his condition.

His backstory is blunt. Paralyzed for thirty-eight years, he had lived by the pool in hopes that the angel of the springs would stir the waters. The sick believed they would be healed if they could but come to the waters at that moment. After nearly four decades of futility, Jesus walks into his life.

Jesus begins the conversation with an unexpected question. "Do you want to be healed?" (John 5:6). We would expect the man to respond with a quick, "of course!" What he actually said was a functional "no." To para-phrase the paralytic's words: "Every time the pools rumble, I am left behind in the dust with no one to bring me to the healing waters. And everyone rushes ahead of me and leaves no room for me." His answer seems to be one of self-pity, bitterness and perhaps, envy. It is an answer without hope.

Jesus's question is one that we, as leaders of his church, need to be asking. Many of us have been stuck in no-growth situations in Europe and America for over a generation. Our brothers and sisters in the majority world have seen numbers surge, but have also been overwhelmed by the challenge of disci-pling the newly converted. Leaders in both situations may feel stuck and may have felt that way for a generation. When it comes time for explanations of the paralysis, the temptation to blame-shift may be strong. Like the paralytic, we may respond to Jesus's question with excuses: "This new generation has no interest in the gospel. The culture has made the church and its message irrelevant. The sheer number of converts in the Global South has overwhelmed the discipleship resources available." And on and on we answer our Lord with statements that are not wrong, but tend to sound like self-pity and bitterness. Such explanations do little to renew the church and get it unstuck.

In Corinth, leaders may have responded to Christ's question less with self-pity than with arrogance. They may have raised their eyebrow in protest to the idea that anything needed to be healed. What about the divisions in the church? The superior ones could dismiss that problem by blaming the spiritual immaturity of the masses and their inability to keep up with the super spiritual elite.

Despite the broken man's hopeless response, Jesus issued a command of immense spiritual power: "Get up, take up your bed, and walk" (John 5:8).

We see the man stir. He feels new sensations in his once-dead limbs. He staggers to his feet. He feels power returning to his entire legs. He leans low and gathers up his bedroll with its four decades' worth of disease and dirt. And then he walks. He takes the first baby steps into a new future with Jesus. No cartwheels. No leaping of tall buildings in a single bound. But on the road to the future again. Unstuck. Moving forward.

There were always critics of change. They freely shared their thoughts about rules that were being broken, about traditions being violated, about things being done that had never been done before. To these critics Jesus had only one answer: "The Father is working now and so am I" (John 5:17). The almighty God and his incarnate Son and our Savior are at work all around us, making things new. The electricity of resurrection power is in the air. Change is possible. Faith and hope, however, are needed.

The American church lives in a moment in which many evangelicals, who for over a century have been a leading voice for the gospel in America, have lost confidence in cross power, the power of the gospel to change people and this world. Many have exchanged cross power for political power. Even the secular world has been shocked at this turn. Thomas Edsall, writing in *The New York Times* about the support by evangelicals for the insurrection on Capitol Hill in Washington DC, on January 6, 2021, quotes sociologist Gerardo Marti:

> Today's evangelical conservatives have given up on spiritual revival as a means of change. Even in the recent past, conversion—a change of heart and mind that is the fruit of repentance and spiritual regeneration—was thought to be the means by which America would become a morally upright nation: change enough individuals, and the change on a personal level would

result in broad change on a collective level. . . . [Revivalism] has been abandoned as a solution to changing society.[1]

Some may say good riddance to the political naïveté of past evangelical belief that conversion and revival can change the world. Ironically, the power of conversion to change not only individuals but systems is exactly what we are seeing in the majority world in the early decades of the twenty-first century. New converts and local revivals have created influential new nonstate actors that are changing the social, political, and economic face of the Global South.[2]

Christ still speaks the words of healing that can lift a paralyzed church from its cultural captivity and make it stand on its two legs again as a bold witness to a world being made new. Cross power, not Caesar power, will ultimately transform the world.

We must get used to this pattern of healing and transformation. Allowing a man to suffer for years and then raise him to new life at an unexpected time and in an unexpected way is what cross power is all about. He brings us low only to lift us high. Paul has called it the foolishness and the weakness of God in 1 Cor 1, but it is the way healing, renewal, and transformation happens to his people now as he gets them ready for the coming new creation. Paul summarized the new politics of the cross practiced by an almighty God "who gives life to the dead and calls into existence the things that do not exist" (Rom 4:17). May we each answer our Lord's question about wanting to be healed with a strong affirmative and may we hear the words of power to rise up, baggage and all, and walk with him into the new world so close at hand.

In Christ,
Mark and George

---

1. Edsall, "Capitol Insurrection," para. 16.

2. See Ranger, *Evangelical Christianity and Democracy in Africa*; Freston, *Evangelical Christianity and Democracy in Latin America*; Lumsdaine, *Evangelical Christianity and Democracy in Asia*.

Bibliography

Aaron, Charlene. "After Deadly Church Shooting, Rodney Howard-Browne's Church Warns 'We Are Heavily Armed.'" *CBN News*, November 20, 2017. https://www1. cbn.com/cbnnews/us/2017/november/after-deadly-church-shooting-rodney-howard-brownes-church-warns-we-are-are-heavily-armed.

Alexander, John. "Stop Going to Church." *The Other Side* 25.3 (May-June 1989) 43–44.

Allender, Dan B., and Tremper Longman, III. *Bold Love*. Colorado Springs, CO: NAVPRESS, 1992.

"America's Gun Culture in Charts." BBC, April 8, 2021. https://www.bbc.com/news/world-us-canada-41488081.

Aune, David E. *Prophecy in Early Christianity and the Ancient Mediterranean World*. Grand Rapids: Eerdmans, 1983.

Banister, Doug. *The Word and Power Church: What Happens When a Church Seeks All God Has to Offer*. Grand Rapids: Zondervan, 1999.

Banks, Robert. *Going to Church in the First Century*. Beaumont, TX: Christian, 1980.

———. *Paul's Idea of Community: The Early House Churches in Their Cultural Setting*. Revised Edition. Peabody, MA: Hendrickson, 1994.

Beasley-Murray, George R. *Baptism in the New Testament*. Grand Rapids: Eerdmans, 1962.

Bellah, Robert N., et al. *Habits of the Heart: Individualism and Commitment in American Life.*Oakland: University of California Press, 2007.

Berger, Peter L., and Thomas Luckmann. *The Social Construction of Reality: A Treatise in the Sociology of Knowledge*. Garden City, NY: Doubleday, 1966.

Bilezikian, Gilbert. *Beyond Sex Roles: A Guide for the Study of Female Roles in the Bible*. Grand Rapids: Baker, 1985.

Bindra, Sunny. "Who Taught You to Hate?" *Sunday Nation*, Oct 22, 2017. https://sunwords.com/2017/10/22/6532/.

Blass, F. and A. Debrunner. *A Greek Grammar of the New Testament and Other Early Christian Literature*. Translated by Robert Funk. Chicago: University of Chicago Press, 1961.

Blomberg, Craig. *First Corinthians*. NIV Application Commentary 7. Grand Rapids: Zondervan, 1995.

Bonhoeffer, Dietrich. *Life Together*. Translated by John Doberstein. New York: Harper and Row, 1954.

Bruce, F. F. *Paul: Apostle of the Heart Set Free*. Grand Rapids: Eerdmans, 1994.

———. *Tradition: Old and New*. Grand Rapids: Zondervan, 1970.

Brueggemann, Walter. *Prophetic Imagination*. Revised Edition. Minneapolis: Fortress, 2001.

Bruner, Frederick Dale. *The Gospel of John: A Commentary*. Grand Rapids: Eerdmans, 2012.

Burrows, William R., and Mark R. Gornik. *Understanding World Christianity: The Vision and Work of Andrew F. Walls*. Maryknoll, NY: Orbis, 2011.

Carol, John T., and Joel B. Green. *The Death of Jesus in Early Christianity*. Peabody, MA: Hendrickson, 1995.

Chesterton, G. K. *What's Wrong with the World*. Monee, IL: Pantianos Classics, 1910.

Choung, James, and Ryan Pfeiffer. *Longing for Revival: From Holy Discontent to Breakthrough Faith*. Downers Grove, IL: InterVarsity, 2020.

Clapp, Rodney. "Tacit Holiness." In *Embodied Holiness: Toward a Corporate Theology of Spiritual Growth*, edited by Samuel M. Powell and Michael E. Lodahl, 62–78. Downers Grove, IL: InterVarsity, 1999.

Cohick, Lynn H. *Women in the World of the Earliest Christians: Illuminating Ancient Ways of Life*. Grand Rapids: Baker, 2009.

Collins, Jim. *Good to Great: Why Some Companies Make the Leap . . . And Other's Don't*. New York: Harperbusiness, 2001.

Covey, Stephen R., et al. *First Things First: To Live, to Love, to Learn, to Leave a Legacy*. New York: Simon & Schuster, 1994.

Craven, Jackie. "Biography of William Le Baron Jenney: Father of the American Skyscraper." *Thought Co.*, November 17, 2019. thoughtco.com/william-le-baron-jenney-american-skyscraper-177855.

Crowe, Jerome. *From Jerusalem to Antioch: The Gospel across Cultures*. Collegeville, MN: Liturgical, 1997.

Cullman, Oscar. *Immortality and Resurrection*. Edited by Krister Stendahl. New York: Macmillan, 1965.

Dawn, Marva J. *Sexual Character: Beyond Technique to Intimacy*. Grand Rapids: Eerdmans, 1993.

deSilva, David. *Honor, Patronage, Kinship, and Purity: Unlocking New Testament Culture*. Downers Grove, IL: InterVarsity, 2000.

Donovan, Vincent. *Christianity Rediscovered*. Maryknoll, NY: Orbis, 1978.

Dunn, James D. G. *Jesus and the Spirit: A Study of the Religious and Charismatic Experience of Jesus and the first Christians as Reflected in the New Testament*. Philadelphia: Westminster, 1975.

Dupont-Sommer, Andre. *The Essene Writings from Qumran*. Gloucester, MA: Peter Smith, 1973.

Dupree, Max. *Leadership Is an Art*. New York: Currency, 2004.

Earls, Aaron. "Evangelical Vote Once Again Split on Ethnic Lines." *Christianity Today*, September 29, 2020. https://www.christianitytoday.com/news/2020/september/evangelical-white-black-ethnic-vote-trump-biden-lifeway-sur.html.

Edsall, Thomas B. "The Capitol Insurrection Was as Christian Nationalist as It Gets." *The New York Times*, January 28, 2021. https://www.nytimes.com/2021/01/28/opinion/christian-nationalists-capitol-attack.html.

Edwards, Jonathan. *The Sermons of Jonathan Edwards: A Reader.* New Haven: Yale University Press, 1999.

The Episcopal Church. *The Book of Common Prayer.* New York: Seabury, 1979.

Erickson, Millard. *God in Three Persons: A Contemporary Interpretation of the Trinity.* Grand Rapids: Baker, 1995.

Farhadian, Charles E., ed. *Introducing World Christianity.* London: Wiley-Blackwell, 2012.

Fee, Gordon D. *The First Epistle to the Corinthians.* The New International Commentary on the New Testament. Grand Rapids: Eerdmans, 1987.

———. *Gospel and Spirit: Issues in New Testament Hermeneutics.* Peabody, MA: Hendrickson, 1991.

———. "The Great Watershed—Intentionality and Particularity/Eternality: 1 Timothy 2:8–15 as a Test Case." In *Gospel and Spirit: Issues in New Testament Hermeneutics,* 52–65. Peabody, MA: Hendrickson, 1991.

———. *Listening to the Spirit in the Text.* Grand Rapids: Eerdmans, 2000.

———. *Paul, the Spirit, and the People of God.* Peabody, MA: Hendrickson, 1996.

Foster, Richard J. *Freedom of Simplicity.* San Francisco: Harper and Row, 1981.

———. *Money, Sex, and Power: The Challenge of the Disciplined Life.* San Francisco: Harper and Row, 1985.

———. *Streams of Living Water: Celebrating the Great Traditions of the Christian Faith.* San Francisco: HarperSanFrancisco, 1998.

Francis, Pope. "*Evangelii Gaudium.*" https://www.vatican.va/content/francesco/en/apost_exhortations/documents/papa-francesco_esortazione-ap_20131124_evangelii-gaudium.html.

Freston, Paul, ed. *Evangelical Christianity and Democracy in Latin America.* New York: Oxford University Press, 2008.

Garland, David. *1 Corinthians.* Grand Rapids: Baker Academic, 2013. Kindle.

George, Carl F. *Prepare Your Church for the Future.* Grand Rapids: Baker, 1984.

Gerson, Michael. "The Last Temptation: How Evangelicals Lost Their Way." *The Atlantic* 322.3 (April 2018). https://www.theatlantic.com/magazine/archive/2018/04/the-last-temptation/554066/.

Getz, Gene A. *Building Up One Another.* Elgin, IL: Cook, 2002.

Giles, Kevin. "The Doctrine of the Trinity and Subordination." *Priscilla Papers,* July 31, 2004. See https://www.cbeinternational.org/resource/article/priscilla-papers-academic-journal/doctrine-trinity-and-subordination.

———. *The Trinity and Subordinationism: The Doctrine of God and the Contemporary Gender Debate.* Downers Grove, IL: InterVarsity, 2002.

Gladwell, Malcolm. *The Tipping Point: How Little Things Can Make a Big Difference.* New York: Little, Brown, 2000.

Glasson, Barbara. "Prayer." *Sojourners* 49 (June 2020) 23.

Gorman, Michael J. *Cruciformity: Paul's Narrative Spirituality of the Cross.* Grand Rapids: Eerdmans, 2001.

Guinness, Os. *The Gravedigger File: Papers on the Subversion of the Modern Church.* Downers Grove, IL: InterVarsity, 1983.

Guy, Laurie. *Introducing Early Christianity: A Topical Survey of Its Life, Beliefs, and Practices.* Downers Grove, IL: InterVarsity, 2004.

Hadaway, C. Kirk, et al. *Home Cell Groups and House Churches.* Nashville: Broadman, 1987.

Hauerwas, Stanley. "The Sanctified Body: Why Perfection Does Not Require a Self." In *Embodied Holiness: Toward a Corporate Theology of Spiritual Growth*, edited by Samuel M. Powell and Michael E. Lodahl, 19–38. Downers Grove, IL: InterVarsity, 1999.

Hays, Richard B. *First Corinthians: Interpretation: A Bible Commentary for Teaching and Preaching*. Louisville: John Knox, 1997.

Heschel, Abraham Joshua. *The Sabbath*. New York: Farrar, Strauss and Giroux, 1951.

Hindmarsh, Bruce. "What Is Evangelicalism?" *Christianity Today*, March 14, 2018. https://www.christianitytoday.com/ct/2018/march-web-only/what-is-evangelicalism.html.

Hummel, Charles E. *Fire in the Fireplace: Charismatic Renewal in the Nineties*. Downers Grove, IL: InterVarsity, 1978.

"Inspirational Quotes about Life, Love, Faith, and Hope." https://www.guideposts.org/system/files/booklet/guideposts_inspirationalquotes.pdf.

Irvin, Dale T. and Scott Sunquist. *History of the World Christian Movement: Vol. 1: Earliest Christianity to 1453*. 2 vols. Maryknoll, NY: Orbis, 2001.

Jacobs, Alan. *The Narnian: The Life and Imagination of C. S. Lewis*. San Francisco: HarperSanFrancisco, 2005.

James, Carolyn. *Half the Church, Recapturing God's Global Vision for Women*. Grand Rapids: Zondervan, 2011.

Jenkins, Philip. *The Next Christendom: The Coming of Global Christianity*. Third edition. New York: Oxford University Press, 2011.

Jeremias, Joachim. *The Eucharistic Words of Jesus*. London: SCM, 1966.

Jones, L. Gregory. *Embodying Forgiveness: A Theological Analysis*. Grand Rapids: Eerdmans, 1995.

Jones, Peyton. "In His Absence: When We Feel on Our Own, Can We Recover the Power and Presence of God?" *Christianity Today*, September 2015. https://www.christianitytoday.com/pastors/2015/september-web-exclusive/in-his-absence.html.

Jones, Robert P. *White Too Long: The Legacy of White Supremacy in American Christianity*. New York: Simon & Schuster, 2020.

Justin Martyr. "First Apology." In *The Ante-Nicene: Translations of The Writings of the Fathers down to AD 325. Vol 1: The Apostolic Fathers with Justin Martyr and Irenaeus* (American Edition) edited by A. Cleveland Coxe, translated by Alexander Roberts and James Donaldson, 163–87. 10 vols. Grand Rapids: Eerdmans, 1950.

Katho, Negura Feli V. "Rethinking Women's Dignity: A Case Study of Irumu County, in Ituri Province, DRC." DMin diss., Africa International University, 2018.

Keener, Craig S. *The IVP Bible Background Commentary: New Testament*. Second Edition. Downers Grove, IL: InterVarsity, 2014.

Kim, Sebastian C. H., and Kirsteen Kim. *Christianity as a World Religion: An Introduction*. Second edition. Oxford: Bloomsbury Academic, 2016.

King, Martin Luther, Jr. "MLK at Western." https://wmich.edu/sites/default/files/attachments/MLK.pdf.

———. *Stride Toward Freedom: The Montgomery Story*. New York: Harper and Brothers, 1984.

Knox, Ronald A. *Enthusiasm: A Chapter in the History of Religion*. Oxford: Clarendon, 1950.

Kouzes, James M., and Barry Z. Posner. *The Five Principles of Exemplary Leadership*. San Francisco: Pfeiffer, 2003.

Kraft, Charles. *Christianity with Power*. Ann Arbor, MI: Servant, 1989.

Kreeft, Peter. *The God Who Loves You: Knowing the Height, Depth, and Breadth of God's Love for You*. Ann Arbor, MI: Servant, 1988.

Kristoff, William, and Sheryl WuDunn. *Half the Sky: Turning Oppression into Opportunity for Women Worldwide*. New York: Knopf, 2009.

Kuruvilla, Carol. "Televangelist Creflo Dollar Defends His Plans For $65 Million Private Jet: 'I Dare You To Tell Me I Can't Dream.'" *Huffpost*, April 23, 2015. https://www.huffpost.com/entry/creflo-dollar-jet_n_7129548.

Lederach, John Paul. *Reconcile: Conflict Transformation for Ordinary Christians*. Scottdale, PA: Herald, 2014.

Lewis, C. S. *The Four Loves*. New York: Harcourt, Brace, 1960.

———. *The Screwtape Letters*. New York: McMillian, 1962.

———. *The Weight of Glory and Other Addresses*. Grand Rapids: Eerdmans, 1949.

Longenecker, Richard. *Paul: Apostle of Liberty*. Second Edition. Grand Rapids: Eerdmans, 2015.

Longman, Tremper, III. *How to Read Genesis*. Downers Grove, IL: InterVarsity, 2005.

Lumsdaine, David, ed. *Evangelical Christianity and Democracy in Asia*. New York: Oxford University Press, 2009.

Luther, Martin. *Luther's Commentary on the First Twenty-Two Psalms*. Edited by John Nicholas Lenker. Sunbury, PA: Lutherans in All Lands, 1903. https://babel.hathitrust.org/cgi/pt?id=nyp.33433082263843&view=1up&seq=7&q1=%22the%20cross%20alone%22.

———. "A Treatise on Christian Liberty." In *Three Treatises*, by Martin Luther, 251–90. Philadelphia: Muhlenberg, 1943

Malina, Bruce. *The New Testament World: Insights from Cultural Anthropology. Louisville:* John Knox Press, 1981.

Mallone, George. *Furnace of Renewal: A Vision for the Church*. Downers Grove, IL: InterVarsity, 1981.

Marshall, I. Howard. *Last Supper and Lord's Supper*. Grand Rapids: Eerdmans, 1980.

Martin, Ralph P. *Worship in the Early Church*. Grand Rapids: Eerdmans, 1974.

Marty, Martin. *The Lord's Supper*. Minneapolis: Augsburg Fortress, 1997.

Mathews, Alice. *Gender Roles and the People of God: Rethinking What We Were Taught about Men and Women in the Church*. Grand Rapids: Zondervan, 2017.

McGrath, Alister. *Christian Theology Reader*. Grand Rapids: Baker, 1995.

McKnight, Scot. *A Fellowship of Differents*. Grand Rapids: Zondervan, 2014.

McLaren, Brian D. *The Great Spiritual Migration*. New York: Convergent, 2016.

Meeks, Wayne. *The First Urban Christians: The Social World of the Apostle Paul*. New Haven: Yale University Press, 1983.

Mother Teresa. *A Simple Path*. New York: Ballantine, 1995.

Mouw, Richard J. *Uncommon Decency: Christian Civility in an Uncivil World*. Downers Grove, IL: InterVarsity, 1992.

Neill, Stephen Charles. *Jesus through Many Eyes: Introduction to the Theology of the New Testament*. Philadelphia: Fortress, 1979.

Niringiye, David Zac. *The Church: God's Pilgrim People*. Carlisle, UK: Langham, 2014.

Njeru, Lilys. "JTM: Church Where Prayers, Miracles Cost an Arm and a Leg." *Daily Nation*, December 2, 2019. https://www.nation.co.ke/counties/nairobi/City-church-where-prayers-cost-an-arm-and-a-leg/1954174-5370040-20259d/index.html.

Noll, Mark. *The New Shape of World Christianity*. Downers Grove, IL: InterVarsity, 2009.

Nouwen, Henri J. M. *Making All Things New: An Invitation to the Spiritual Life*. San Francisco: Harper and Row, 1981.

O'Donovan, Oliver. *Resurrection and Moral Order: An Outline of Evangelical Ethics*. Second edition. Grand Rapids: Eerdmans, 1994.

Oh, Michael. "The Gospel Strategy of Christ-Like Leadership." *Lausanne Movement (blog)*, July 16, 2018. https://lausanne.org/about/blog/the-gospel-strategy-of-christ-like-leadership.

Otto, Rudolf. *The Idea of the Holy: An Inquiry into the Non-rational Factor in the Idea of the Divine and Its Relation to the Rational*. Translated by John Harvey Oxford: Oxford University Press, 1923.

Pelikan, Jaroslav. *The Christian Tradition: A History of the Development of Doctrine. Vol 1: The Emergence of the Catholic Tradition (100–600)*. 5 vols. Chicago: University of Chicago Press, 1971.

Peterson, Eugene H. *Living the Resurrection: The Risen Christ in Everyday Life*. Colorado Springs, CO: NAVPRESS, 2006.

———.*The Message: The Bible in Contemporary Language*. Colorado Springs, CO: NAVPRESS, 2002.

Piper, John. *The Dangerous Duty of Delight: Daring to Make God Your Greatest Desire*. Colorado Springs, CO: LifeChange, 2001.

Posner, Sarah. *Unholy: Why White Evangelicals Worship at the Altar of Donald Trump*. New York: Random House, 2020.

Purves, Andrew. *The Resurrection of Ministry: Serving in the Hope of the Risen Lord*. Downers Grove, IL: InterVarsity, 2010.

Ranger, T. O., ed. *Evangelical Christianity and Democracy in Africa*. New York: Oxford University Press, 2008.

Richards, E. Randolph, and Brandon J. O'Brian. *Misreading Scripture with Western Eyes: Removing Cultural Blinders to Better Understand the Gospel*. Downers Grove, IL: InterVarsity, 2012. Kindle.

Riesman, David. *The Lonely Crowd: A Study of the Changing American Character*. New Haven: Yale University Press, 2020.

Robinson, Anthony, and Robert Wall. *Called to Lead: Paul's Letters to Timothy for a New Day*. Grand Rapids: Eerdmans, 2012.

Rostovtzeff, Michael. *The Social and Economic History of the Roman Empire*. Oxford: Clarendon, 1957.

Rutledge, Fleming. *The Crucifixion: Understanding the Death of Jesus Christ*. Grand Rapids: Eerdmans, 2015.

Sande, Ken. *The Peacemaker: A Biblical Guide to Resolving Personal Conflict*. Grand Rapids: Baker, 2004.

Sanders, Fred. *Deep Things of God: How the Trinity Changes Everything*. Wheaton, IL: Crossway, 2010.

Sanneh, Lamin. *Disciples of All Nations: Pillars of World Christianity*. New York: Oxford University Press, 2008.

———. *Whose Religion Is Christianity? The Gospel Beyond the West*. Grand Rapids: Eerdmans, 2003.

Schaeffer, Francis. *The Church before the Watching World: A Practical Ecclesiology*. Downers Grove, IL: InterVarsity, 1971.

————. *The Mark of the Christian*. Downers Grove, IL: InterVarsity, 1970.

Schmithals, Walter. *Gnosticism in Corinth: An Investigation of the Letters to the Corinthians*. Nashville: Abingdon, 1971.

Scott, J. Duvall, and J. Daniel Hayes. *Grasping God's Word*. Grand Rapids: Zondervan 2001.

Sempangi, F. Kefa. *A Distant Grief*. Glendale, CA: Regal, 1979.

Shellnutt, Kate. "Packing in the Pews: The Connection Between God and Guns." *Christianity Today*, November 8, 2017. https://www.christianitytoday.com/news/2017/november/god-gun-control-white-evangelicals-texas-church-shooting.html.

————. "White Evangelicals Are Actually for Trump in 2020, Not Just against His Opponent." *Christianity Today*, October 14, 2020. https://www.christianitytoday.com/news/2020/october/white-evangelical-voters-for-trump-pew-lifeway-survey.html.

Sittser, Gerald L. *Love One Another: Becoming the Church Jesus Longs For*. Downers Grove, IL: InterVarsity, 2008.

Smedes, Lewis. *Love within Limits: Realizing Selfless Love in a Selfish World*. Grand Rapids: Eerdmans, 1978.

Smith, Gordon T. *Transforming Conversion: Rethinking the Language and Contours of Christian Initiation*. Grand Rapids: Baker Academic, 2010.

Smith, James K. A. *You Are What You Love: The Spiritual Power of Habit*. Grand Rapids: Baker, 2016.

Snyder, Howard. *The Radical Wesley and Patterns for Church Renewal*. Downers Grove, IL: InterVarsity, 1980.

Stark, Rodney. *The Rise of Christianity: How the Obscure, Marginal Jesus Movement Became the Dominant Religious Force in the Western World in a Few Centuries*. San Francisco: HarperSanFrancisco, 1996.

Stott, John R. W. *Baptism and Fullness: The Work of the Holy Spirit Today*. Downers Grove, IL: Intervarsity, 1964.

————. *Evangelical Truth: A Personal Plea for Unity*. Downers Grove, IL: InterVarsity,1999.

Thiselton, Anthony C. *The First Epistle to the Corinthians: A Commentary on the Greek Text*. NIGTC. Grand Rapids: Eerdmans, 2000.

Thune, Robert, and Will Walker. *The Gospel-Centered Life*. Greensboro, NC: New Growth, 2009.

Titus, E. L. "Did Paul Write I Corinthians 13?" *Journal of the Bible and Religion* 27 (1959) 299–302.

Tournier, Paul. *To Understand Each Other*. Richmond, VA: John Knox, 1973.

Tozer, A. W. *The Knowledge of the Holy*. San Francisco: Harper & Row, 1961.

————. *The Root of the Righteous*. Harrisburg, PA: Christian, 1955.

————. *That Incredible Christian*. Harrisburg, PA: Christian, 1964.

Vanier, Jean. *Man and Woman, He Made Them*. Mahwah, NJ: Paulist, 1984.

Van Leuween, Mary Stewart. *After Eden: Facing the Challenge of Gender Reconciliation*. Grand Rapids: Eerdmans, 1993.

————. *Gender and Grace: Love, Work, and Parenting in a Changing World*. Downers Grove, IL: Intervarsity, 1990.

Volf, Miroslav. *After Our Likeness: The Church as the Image of the Trinity*. Grand Rapids: Eerdmans, 1998.

————. *Free of Charge: Giving and Forgiving in a Culture Stripped of Grace.* Grand Rapids: Zondervan, 2005.

Vonnegut, Kurt. *Palm Sunday: An Autobiographical Collage.* New York: Delacorte, 1981.

Wallis, Jim. "An Evangelical Manifesto." *Sojourners,* May 7, 2008. https://sojo.net/articles/evangelical-manifesto.

Waltke, Bruce. *Genesis: A Commentary. Grand Rapids:* Zondervan, 2001.

Warzel, Charlie. "Open States, Lots of Guns. America Is Paying a Heavy Price for Freedom." The New York Times, May 5, 2020. https://www.nytimes.com /2020/05/05/opinion/coronavirus-deaths.html

Washington National Cathedral. "December 2, 2020: A Service of Morning Prayer and Reflection at Washington National Cathedral." https://www.youtube.com/watch?v=FjL5sR4UJdM&list=PL1nLVw6M_fPisN8Gfk_tRsjTXqSexemlK &index=148&t=17s.

Watson, David. *I Believe in Evangelism.* Grand Rapids: Eerdmans, 1976 .

Wax, Emily. "New Generation of Men in India Shaving Off Mustaches." *Washington Post,* February 16, 2010. http://www.washingtonpost.com/wp-dyn/content/article /2010/02/15/AR2010021503409.html.

Weil, Simone. *Gravity and Grace.* Translated by Emma Craufurd. London: Routledge, 1952.

"Who Do People Say We Are?: It Doesn't Hurt to Listen to What Non-Christians Think of Us." *Christianity Today,* December 12, 2007. https://www.christianitytoday. com/ct/2007/december/23.21.html.

Willard, Dallas. *The Divine Conspiracy: Rediscovering Our Hidden Life in God.* New York: HarperCollins, 1998.

————. *Renovation of the Heart: Putting on the Character of Christ.* Colorado Springs, CO: NAVPRESS, 2002.

Williams, Dean. *Leadership for a Fractured World: How to Cross Boundaries, Build Bridges, and Lead Change.* Oakland: Berrett-Koehler, 2015.

Williams, Jarvis. "Black Lives Matter in the Bible." *Christianity Today,* June 26, 2020. https://www.christianitytoday.com/ct/2020/june-web-only/black-lives-matter-in-bible.html.

Willimon, William. *Sunday Dinner: The Lord's Supper and the Christian Life.* Nashville: Upper Room, 1981.

Winter, Bruce. *After Paul Left Corinth: The Influence of Secular Ethics and Social Change.* Grand Rapids: Eerdmans, 2001. Kindle.

Wise, Justin. *The Social Church: A Theology of Digital Communication.* Chicago: Moody, 2014.

Witherington, Ben, III. *Conflict and Community in Corinth: A Socio-Rhetorical Commentary on 1 and 2 Corinthians.* Grand Rapids: Eerdmans, 1995.

————. *Making a Meal of It: Rethinking the Theology of the Lord's Supper.* Waco, TX. Baylor University Press, 2007

————. "Not so Idle Thoughts about *Eidōlothuton,*" *TynB* 44 (1993) 237–54.

————. *A Week in the Life of Corinth.* Downers Grove, IL: InterVarsity, 2012.

Wittgenstein, Ludwig. "Ludwig Wittgenstein on the Resurrection." https://externalword. blog/2013/10/22/ludwig-wittgenstein-on-the-resurrection/.

Wright, N. T. *The Day the Revolution Began: Reconsidering the Meaning of Jesus' Crucifixion.* New York: Harper Collins, 2016.

———. "Loving to Know." *First Things*, February 2020. firstthings.com/article/2020/02/loving-to-know.

———. *Paul for Everyone: 1 Corinthians*. London: SPCK, 2014. Kindle.

———. *Simply Christian: Why Christianity Makes Sense*. San Francisco: HarperOne, 2006.

———. *Simply Good News: Why the Gospel Is News and What Makes It Good*. San Francisco: HarperOne, 2015.

———. *Surprised by Hope: Rethinking Heaven, the Resurrection, and the Mission of the Church*. New York: HarperOne, 2008.

———. *Surprised by Scripture: Engaging Contemporary Issues*. New York: HarperOne, 2014.

Yablon, Alex. "U.S. Gun Death Rate Hit 20-Year High in 2017, CDC Data Shows." *The Trace*, December 10, 2018. https://www.thetrace.org/newsletter/gun-death-rate-2017-increase-cdc-suicide/.

Yamauchi, Edwin M. *Pre-Christian Gnosticism: A Survey of the Proposed Evidences*. Grand Rapids: Eerdmans, 1973.